SIMPLE GESTURES

ALSO BY ANDREA B. RUGH

Family in Contemporary Egypt

Within the Circle: Parents and Children in an Arab Village

The Political Culture of Leadership in the United Arab Emirates

RELATED TITLES FROM POTOMAC BOOKS, INC.

Fragments of Grace: My Search for Meaning in the Strife of South Asia
—Pamela Constable

SIMPLE GESTURES

A Cultural Journey into the Middle East

ANDREA B. RUGH

Potomac Books, Inc.
Washington, D.C.

Library of Congress Cataloging-in-Publication Data
Rugh, Andrea B.
　Simple gestures : a cultural journey into the Middle East / Andrea B. Rugh. — 1st ed.
　　p. cm.
　Includes index.
　ISBN 978-1-59797-434-9 (hardcover : alk. paper)
　1. Rugh, Andrea B.—Travel—Middle East. 2. Middle East—Description and travel. 3. Middle East—Social life and customs. I. Title.
　DS49.7.R84 2009
　956.04—dc22

2009030025

Printed in the United States of America on acid-free paper that meets the American National Standards Institute Z39-48 Standard.

Potomac Books, Inc.
22841 Quicksilver Drive
Dulles, Virginia 20166

First Edition

10 9 8 7 6 5 4 3 2 1

To Thomas, Meena, Katie, Tae, Livia, and Anais,
who have promised to save the world,
each in his or her own way,

and to William,
who has already made a major contribution

To this day in the simplest of ways I enjoy life there. I am drawn by the civilized propriety of the Middle East. Call the tradition hospitality or respect, generosity or decency, but the small easy-to-ignore gestures add texture and create familiarity. No one enters any room, anywhere in the Arab World, without being greeted. It never happens.

ANTHONY SHADID IN NIGHT DRAWS NEAR

Contents

Map of the Middle East and Southwest Asia viii
Preface ix

1 Foreshadowings (1945–1964) 1
2 Slow Beginnings: Beirut, Lebanon (1964–1965, 1970),
    and Cairo, Egypt (1965–1966) 9
3 Moving Ahead: Jidda, Saudi Arabia (1966–1967) 27
4 Into the Interior: Riyadh, Saudi Arabia (1967–1969) 45
5 Rima: Riyadh, Saudi Arabia (1967–1969) 63
6 Familiar Territory: Jidda Again (1969–1971) 79
7 Retooling: Home Leave (1971–1976) 93
8 Second Chance: Cairo Again (1976–1978) 103
9 Immersion: Bulaq, Egypt (1976–1978) 121
10 A New Direction: Cairo After Graduate School (1978–1981) 137
11 Change: Abdul Wahhab and the Religious Shaikhs 153
12 Finding a Niche: Syria (1981–1984) 169
13 Roadblocks: Sana, Yemen (1984–1987) 187
14 BRIDGES: Yemen (1987) and Pakistan (1987–1994) 207
15 On the Road to Reform: Pakistan (1990–1994) 225
16 New Worlds: Abu Dhabi, United Arab Emirates (1992–1995) 245
17 Ultimate Destination: Afghanistan Under the Taliban
    (1998, 2000) 263
18 Finish Line: Afghanistan After the Invasion (2001–2002) 281
19 Reflections 297

About the Author 311

THE MIDDLE EAST AND SOUTHWEST ASIA

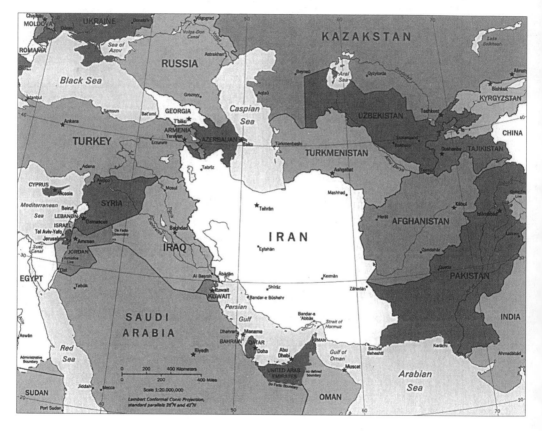

Preface

Starting out on a cultural journey is unlike any other journey. The traveler barely knows where the journey will lead, how long it will take, or how far she must go. How does she prepare for such a journey, or know what paths to take, or what stops to make along the way? How should she engage those she meets? How does she know when she has reached her destination? It reminds me of the comment in *Alice in Wonderland*: "When you don't know where you're going, any path will take you there." Nothing could be truer in a pursuit of culture.

My journey into Middle Eastern culture encompassed all these unknowns. I didn't know exactly where I was headed or how it might come out. Often I wasn't even sure I was moving forward. The journey had its ups and downs, its frustrations and setbacks, its moments of insight and its times of despair. How could I overcome the obstacles facing me or remove the blinders that clouded my own perceptions? How could I surmount the walls that separated me from those I wanted to know or work around my official and personal responsibilities that interfered with knowing them?

This book chronicles my forty-year cultural journey into a society that in many respects was very different from my own. The story is unavoidably one of time, place, people, and everyday events, but it is also one of reflection, insight, and growing awareness. Culture is not a static array of artifacts viewed behind glass in a museum. It is the conceptual framework that shapes human behaviors and shows up best in situations where people interact with one another and with outsiders.

When people hear I've spent decades in the Middle East, they invariably ask two questions: "Which country did you like best?" and "What was it like being a woman there?" Neither question deserves a short answer, no matter how well chosen the words. The first question is hard because the countries differ so much. If you want the sights and smells of nature, there is nothing like early mornings in a Lebanese village as the mist parts and reveals the shining Mediterranean below, while the smells of hot *manushi* (an herbed flat bread) drift out from the bakery. Or perhaps you prefer the scent of white roses rambling along stone walls in spring along the roads of Dir in the North-West Frontier Province of Pakistan or the sight of jagged peaks in Yemen with their well-tended terraces cascading into deep gorges. If you want to lift your spirits, you can watch the brightly colored kites soaring against the cold gray skies of a Kabul winter. If you enjoy lively, engaging people, you will find them in popular quarters of Cairo where, day and night, music, commotion, and laughter fill the air. If you want your senses assailed with pleasant smells, tastes, and surroundings, you will do no better than the courtyards of the older Damascene houses. If you prefer dignified, well-mannered company, you'll find relaxation and comfort in the generous hospitality of the Gulf people in the United Arab Emirates and Saudi Arabia. I have no idea how to choose the best of these—each has its flavor and appeal, and each offers insights into the culture of the Middle East.

The second question reflects genuine concerns about women that are not always accurate. A reply like: "Well, my husband can only meet half the population while I can know them all" shortchanges at least three countries—Lebanon, Syria, and Egypt—where he probably knows as many women as I do. Short answers don't satisfy such emotion-laden questions. This book lets me describe my life as an American woman living in the Middle East and talk about the local women I came to know there. Neither narrative is complete without the everyday activities that affected us both.

There are three aspects of my life in the Middle East that give my account a depth that would not have been possible otherwise. The first is my role as mother of three boys who spent much of their childhoods in the Middle East. I only write briefly about them because I plan a personal family memoir some day. The second role is as wife of an American diplomat—or "Foreign Service dependent," as we were once called. This role changes over the course of this journey, not only because the State Department's expectations for spouses changed, but also because as my husband rose in the ranks to become ambassador in two countries, my activities became more visible. My final role as professional anthropologist—writer and consultant—has brought me into contact with local people in ways not possible for the usual diplomatic spouse. Perhaps the most important part of the story is how my thinking about Middle Eastern culture evolved over the years I lived there and how more than anything else the insights I gained gave me a new way of looking at my own culture.

I've taken liberties in calling the region the "Middle East." This is because I don't want to call the countries either "Muslim" or "Arab." The first suggests a monolithic influence of Islam when in many cases it is not so much religion as cultural tradition that has the greatest influence on daily life. Although Islam is the religion of the majority in most of these countries, many also have minorities, including Christians, Jews, and others. I don't call them "Arab" countries either—a meaning that for me denotes countries where Arabic is the language of the majority. I have left out some obvious Arab countries that I don't know well enough and include others that are distinctly not Arab. To the truly Arab countries of Lebanon, Syria, Egypt, Saudi Arabia, Yemen, and the United Arab Emirates, where I lived, I have added non-Arab Pakistan and Afghanistan in South Asia, where I worked sufficiently long to feel at home. I have not written about the countries of Africa, Nepal, or India, where I also worked, since my experiences there were too limited to feel I know them well.

During the years we spent in the Middle East, we felt the storm clouds gathering. We never completely imagined their ominous potential, even though we could see local society becoming more conservative. It started with the humiliating defeat of the Arabs in the 1967 June War, where many blamed their loss on people not being as religiously observant as they should have been. That same year the writer-activist Sayyid Qutb was executed for his criticisms of the Egyptian government and became a ready-made martyr for a movement that was gaining momentum. We had no idea his writings would become the foundation for the radicalization of the Arab world. As the people became more devout, they saw encouraging signs that Allah might again be favoring their actions: Egyptian president Anwar El Sadat's battle against Israel in October 1973 in the Sinai was a limited success, then Iran was taken over by Ayatollah Ruhollah Khomeini in 1979, the Soviets were expelled from Afghanistan in the late 1980s, and by 1996 a band of religious students called the "Taliban" took over a large section of Afghanistan. All these events seemed to argue for the power of coalescing under the banner of Islam. Women started dressing more conservatively, and people began seeking authoritative pronouncements on the details of proper Islamic observance from religious shaikhs in mosques and in newspaper columns. Ultimately these actions created a more conservative atmosphere across the Muslim world, with people seeking solutions in religion rather than in nationalism, socialism, or communism as before.

In Peshawar it is possible I unknowingly witnessed a meeting of the "Afghan Arabs" where Usama Bin Laden may have been present. I know he was in Peshawar in the early 1990s when I worked there on education projects. Did the Taliban know of my secret visits to girls' schools in Kabul in the late 1990s, and did they temporarily close the home schools as a consequence of my visits? How could the U.S. government so cynically undermine Pakistani and Afghan education before and after the 2001 occupation, and did that lead to further upheavals in the years to follow? The effects of these incidents took time to emerge, and although I was an observer at the margins, it was apparent throughout this period that tensions were rising.

Several people suggested I write this book after 9/11 and our invasions of Afghanistan (2001) and Iraq (2003), when Americans became acutely aware of how little they knew about Middle Eastern societies. I had earlier written books on Arab culture for academic audiences, but what was needed, people told me, was a personal, everyday account of the peoples of the region. The version I tell is the one I experienced myself. Every outsider who knows the area even slightly draws his or her own conclusions—there are, as an Arabic saying goes, as many points of view as there are people to voice them. This book is the personal story of an outsider who lived many years in the Middle East.

I want to acknowledge the help I received along the way. First, I want to thank my son Doug for the sensitive and beautiful cover he created that exactly fits the theme of the book. Special thanks go to my friends—my "salon," I call them. The ones who put up with me the longest are Nayra Atiya, Ansaf Aziz, Mona Habib, Mouna Hashem, and Mary Megalli. They visit me on Cape Cod and welcome me as a sister in whatever part of the world they currently occupy.

Then there are my sisters-in-interest who form the core of our "anthropology group" that meets weekly from June to September in Woods Hole, Massachusetts: Anna Lawson, Lynn Lees, Zella Luria, Jane Parpart, Linda-Anne Rebhun, Brooke Grundfest Schoepf, the late Lillian Trager, Sylvia Vatuk, Ruth Hubbard Wald, and others who joined us for shorter periods. The most important reader of the manuscript as it was taking shape was my long time friend and supporter, Ellen Weiss, who reviewed the draft of every chapter and sent it back within hours with useful comments. Betty and Jerry Downs similarly supported my efforts and gave me good advice. June Rugh read a draft to her 100-year-old mother, Belle, who figures in the early pages of the book. Others like Ken Ingham encouraged me to continue; Robert Le Mar helped with the pictures; Simon Braune, the librarian at the Middle East Institute, found a map of the region for me; and John Gillies gave permission to use several pictures of Afghanistan from our trip there. At Potomac, Hilary Claggett and Claire Noble were helpful in moving the process of publication along. Last but not least are the sisters-in-writing, members of the Garrett Park Writers' Workshop led by Elizabeth Henley: Susan Ingenham, Elaine Kennedy, Ulla Lustig, Pam Morgan, and Barbara Shidler. These women helped me with the task of transforming myself from a writer of academic works to an author of books aimed at a general audience. I feel grateful for their patience.

1

FORESHADOWINGS
(1945–1964)

Unlikely as it might seem, my journey started during the long, languid days of summer on my grandparents' farm when I was ten years old. Grandmother would have been appalled to think she had anything to do with it, for she never looked favorably on my desire to travel or engage with people so different from the people she knew. One time when I showed her pictures of a ragtag Bedouin group setting up camp, she asked with alarm what on earth made me find such people interesting. Who knows, Grandmother, what causes someone like me to find faraway places and people so compelling? Who knows also which steps were crucial in starting me on my journey?

Grandmother was a frail, elegant lady who went about her tasks with a slow deliberation that bespoke her limited endurance. Brought up a Quaker, she used "Thee" and "Thou" with me in a tone, I distinctly remember, that signified her approval or disapproval of my behavior. Grandfather was superintendent of schools and a gentleman farmer. In the late afternoons after he finished mending fences or calling in the sheep, we would sprawl on the front lawn and compete to see who knew the most poems by heart. It was an unfair contest because he knew all the poems in the *McGuffy Readers* by heart, and I had only begun collecting inspirational ditties that would be ready-made to express my feelings on momentous occasions. Grandfather was wise enough not to question such choices as "I want my boy to have a dog, or maybe two or three . . . ," or "I want to go down to the sea again, to the lonely sea and the sky."

Grandmother's limited energy had two consequences for me. The first was that she could only cope with one of us at a time—my sister or me—and therefore the long summer days stretched out endlessly with no playmates and only the pastimes I devised for myself: making hollyhock dolls in her flower garden, copying Audubon bird pictures from a heavy book she propped up in front of me, searching out eggs in the hen house, or swinging in the corn crib over the backs of the sheep seeking shade there. My favorite pastime was a miniature golf course I fashioned in the rough grass of the barnyard. Grandmother's sense of duty only allowed one round of golf a day after dinner when her chores were done, and although I looked forward to that game all day, she played with so little enthusiasm I invariably won. "Please," I begged her, wishing for a more satisfying victory, "try harder."

The second consequence of her frail health was the nap she took religiously after lunch each day to restore her energy. Before she went upstairs, she settled me on a sofa in her cool, dark parlor with a pile of *National Geographics*. And there, to the whirring of the fans and the crescendos of the cicadas, I lost myself in exotic places beyond anything my ten-year-old mind could imagine. I pondered what people who looked and dressed so differently from me could be thinking and took my time absorbing every detail of each picture before moving on to the next. It was during Grandmother's naps that my craving to visit these strange places began. I wanted to know what these people with the painted faces and exotic dresses thought. I wanted to see mountains and tropical jungles and villages—even the word "village" struck a romantic chord in my heart. There were no villages in America, only towns and cities and suburbs. I returned again and again to my favorites—the pictures of Afghanistan with its high mountains, desolate landscapes, flowering valleys, and colorful herders and tribesmen. The faces of the people seemed to shine with an inner contentment that to my childish mind had something to do with their way of life—the freedom to move from one thrilling landscape to another, beyond the control of any authority.

~

Two years later I went to live with Aunt Margie in Vancouver, British Columbia. I was there because my stepmother and I didn't get along, and I was becoming a handful. Daddy was a professor at MIT and didn't have the patience to keep the peace between us. Grandmother disapproved of the way my step-mother treated me and prevailed on her daughter to take me away for a year. Margie agreed, feeling her own fifteen-year-old daughter could use the company of a younger sister. But in truth we never bonded. My cousin, a beauty, was into boys and clothes and I into dogs and sports. I was delighted, though, to be in a foreign country for the first time, and every novelty took on a special aura to my adoring eyes. I loved the misty weather, the constantly falling rain, the lush greenery around me, and the gigantic fruits and vegetables Aunt Margie produced in her garden. I reveled in the snakes that stretched themselves across the warm pavement on my way to school. I sang "God Save the King" with gusto and mentally collected the odd English spellings I had to memorize in school. I encountered subtle anti-American undercurrents in people's conversations, but felt that since I had none of the stereotypic traits, I couldn't be held responsible for their deficits. Until one day . . . I went on an outing with a friend and forgot to thank her mother for taking me along. "So American," I overheard her exclaiming to another mother, and I realized for the first time what it meant to be held responsible for a whole category of people. But it didn't dampen my enthusiasm. At Christmas my father wrote asking what gift I wanted with the money he was sending. Without hesitation I answered, "An atlas with all the places in the world."

Jump ahead to August 1958 and Bill and I have been married for a month. We had met several years before as college students with summer jobs at the Marine Biological Lab in Woods Hole—he as tennis groundsman and I as kitchen helper. We were preparing to embark on a boat for Bremerhaven and a full year of his graduate work in Germany. The savings from my year working as a Duke University counselor bought a car, a Lloyd, with *liegesitze* (lying down seats) for camping across Europe. The tiny car sounded like a sewing machine but ran well and took us as far as Yugoslavia. At long last I experienced real foreign countries, where we had to negotiate our way in new languages.

During the year, we lived with two German families in an apartment in Hamburg, and since none of them knew English, I expanded my limited knowledge of written German into reasonable spoken fluency in six months. Moreover,

I learned for the first time that hot water doesn't simply flow through faucets, what it's like to heat with a coal stove, and that we could survive the winter despite only washing our bedsheets once. Our landlady, Tanta Ella, insisted that boiling such large items and hanging them out to dry were far too difficult in cold weather where they would only freeze. I learned that foods purchased fresh from the market were delicious when prepared the way Tanta Ella instructed me in the kitchen we shared. The daily sights, sounds, and smells kept their novelty during the nine months we were there, even though the winter sun barely rose before it set again in that far northern city.

The next year we prolonged our stay in Europe when Bill entered the first year of a master's program at the Johns Hopkins Bologna Center in Italy. Our finances were so limited—the proceeds of the Lloyd we sold for $900—that although some people considered Bologna one of the gastronomic centers of the world, we were too poor to find out if it was true. We lived in a small cold-water flat over a butcher shop, where my newfound knowledge of coal-burning stoves came in handy. My learning continued as I coped with bathing in a galvanized washtub filled with lukewarm water I laboriously heated over a butagas burner. I washed sheets one at a time so when they took a week to dry in the cold, dank apartment, we still had one left (Tanta Ella was right). I learned "shopping Italian" and enough words to know when I was being reprimanded by the butcher's wife for throwing out ("wasting") the legs and head that came with the chicken I bought for dinner. She taught me how to make chicken foot soup. I felt like a fool "teaching" English in a Montessori preschool to supplement our finances when the tiny children giggled as they tried to imitate the gibberish I spoke. This was their first experience with an adult who didn't know Italian. That, of course, was the point of my being there, but the children learned so little from me and I was so often the butt of their four-year-old jokes that I melted in embarrassment.

In the summer of 1960 we headed reluctantly back to the United States for the second year of the Johns Hopkins program in Washington—this time with the advantage of an all-expense paid fellowship. The extreme seasickness I experienced on the boat turned out to be the early signs of David. In Washington we found an apartment that like many others at the time refused to take children. I was clearly pregnant, but the house manager took pity on us when we promised to move out three months after David was born. David arrived in February, just in time to give me the excuse of long walks pushing his carriage through the splendors of a Washington spring. Meanwhile, Bill was taking the Foreign Service exam and applying for a Ph.D. in case he failed the State Department exam, which this time he did.

Bill chose Columbia for the full $2,000 fellowship plus free tuition that made it possible to rent a spacious, rent-controlled apartment for $100 a month in the same building where Bill's parents lived. I set to work furnishing the place for another $100, mostly from the street castoffs of graduating students. Bill completed the course work for his Ph.D. in international law and diplomacy in a year while I became involved in the politics of our local block association.

The next year, 1963, Bill received a year's fellowship to do his Ph.D. dissertation research in Germany, and we were off again on a boat to Europe. This time we had David with us, and Doug was already filling out the front of my dress. In Berlin, it was easier this time to talk to neighbors and storekeepers with my reasonably fluent German. David and I took daily excursions to the park, where I made friends with the mothers, and David learned how to play without getting too dirty. His first German word was *schmutzig* (dirty) from the frowning mothers commenting on the state of his clothing. Doug came late, after we spent a restless New Year's Eve walking along the Berlin Wall to encourage him to appear. He arrived on New Year's Day 1964 in the *Frauenklinik* of the University of Berlin, where I shared a room with three other mothers and babies and ticked off the differences between my American and German birthing experiences. In Germany no one mentioned weight gain, but I still tried to keep within reasonable limits. Midwives attended me until the last crucial minutes of delivery. They brokered no foolishness, informing me sternly as they grabbed my magazine away that I was there to have a baby, not to read. The nursery was filled with wailing babies who were only allowed to feed on a three-hour schedule. I was to drink tea to bring on my milk but was forbidden the "unhealthy" practice of drinking cow's milk.

A few months later we started searching for a place to live near Bonn, where Bill planned to take his second semester. We could only afford $50 a month rent, and after placing ads in newspapers, found only one possibility that fit our budget. It turned out to be in the idyllic village of Lommersdorf in the Eifel

Mountains, an hour's drive from the university. The "apartment" consisted of two rooms over the kitchen of a German farm family of three generations. The bathroom was an outhouse downstairs on the other side of the cow and pig shed, and the washing room where I boiled diapers everyday was in the back of the barn. War veterans dropped by in the evenings to tell us the "true" story of the war and the Nazi regime "that we Americans might not have understood fully."

People were curious but friendly even though we were the only foreigners in the village and probably the only Americans they had ever met in a peaceful capacity. With Doug in his stroller, David and I walked every day to the village center to mail letters and buy food for dinner. David became known as the little "Amerikaner" who wore different hats everyday—cowboy, Indian, baseball, Tyrolean—and returned "guten Morgen" across every garden gate.

David played with little Alvin downstairs and took rides with him on his father's tractor. I sat with Doug in the *hühnerpiech* (chicken yard), enjoying the sun and listening to old Opa, with his war-injured leg stuck stiffly out in front of him, describing how the waves of troops came "over that ridge" and pointing with his pipe to the not-very-distant hills. Certain of my position, I argued with Alvin's mother, who insisted my nursing was making "a skeleton" out of Doug, as she pointed to her blimp-like bottle-fed second son to show me how Doug should look. We joined the celebrations in town—waltzing somewhat unsteadily to militaristic "oompah" music in the local high school gym, watching blindfolded young men with swords swiping at the head of a rooster suspended over the town square, and stringing our front gate on May Day with garlands of wildflowers from the fields in back of our house. Probably best of all we "helped" with the gathering in of the winter wheat, with David and Alvin up in front on the tractor and Doug nestled with me in the fragrant straw of the hay wagon.

Too soon we were on our way back to the United States. By then Bill had passed the Foreign Service exam and would be starting a training program in Washington in the late summer of 1964. We found a furnished apartment in Virginia that was to be our home for at least a year. The apartment was adequate but undistinguished after the other places we'd lived, and I was happy that the boys kept me occupied.

An immediate decision faced us. Bill's status in the Foreign Service was provisional on his passing an exam in a "hard" language. The languages we knew—German, French, and some Italian—were world languages that didn't fit the hard definition. Bill brought home a map of the world that we spread out on the dining table. We had to decide by the next day where we wanted to focus our career and, more immediately, which of the hard languages he should study. We eliminated parts of the world that didn't interest us. Spanish was not a hard language, and neither of us knew even a smattering of it. South America and a few countries were crossed off. We decided Bill should downplay his limited knowledge of French (not hard anyway) when we noticed that many French-speaking countries lay within the red belt of hot, humid places and also because French speakers at the time were being sent to Vietnam. We rejected single-country languages like Japanese or Korean, feeling they would limit us if we stayed any length of time in the Foreign Service. We planned to continue in the service for three or four postings for "foreign experience," and then Bill would spend the rest of his career teaching. The plans for me were to be a full-time mother and wife.

We decided the only language with the flexibility we wanted was Arabic. It qualified as a hard language and was spoken in twenty countries on two continents. While several Arab countries dipped into the red zone, others had fairly nice Mediterranean climates. An additional incentive—maybe the main one—was the glowing reports from Bill's uncle Doug and aunt Belle who had lived a considerable time in Lebanon. Their reports may already have inclined us unconsciously toward the Arab world.

Still we held back. Bill hadn't finished his dissertation on a German topic, and it might be better to be closer to his adviser, who visited Europe frequently. We prudently listed Austria or Switzerland for a first choice and Germany for second choice, although I longed for something more like the images in *National Geographic*. Our third choice became Lebanon, Syria, or Greece. We made these choices casually, not realizing how momentous that one hour of pouring over maps might be for the rest of our lives. More immediately they set in motion events that caused us to move much sooner than we expected. Two weeks later we received our assignment: Morocco for language training and Tunis for junior officer training. No sooner had we informed our friends and relatives than the orders changed. Morocco and Tunisia were out, and we had a few weeks before we would go to Beirut for a year of language study and then Cairo for a year of training. We canceled our car order, changed the electric current for our washing machine, and regretted the shots we didn't need to prevent the various diseases we now wouldn't be exposed to. Bill brought home new post reports, and Aunt Belle and Uncle Doug sent ecstatic letters from Beirut filled with lists of what not to bring. I was stunned that my wish to move into new territory had so suddenly come true.

I packed up with no regrets at leaving the drab apartment behind. This time we had the magnificent salary of $7,000 a year, a housing allowance, and professional packers to take care of our few possessions. It was a move that by comparison was "a piece of cake." We spent the last few days in New York with Bill's parents, who drove us to the airport for the flight to Paris and then on to Rome and finally Beirut. In the terminal, David suddenly realized he wouldn't see his grandparents for a while. "Mommy, I'm so sad about Grandma and Grandpa!" And torrents of tears rushed down his face. Each time they subsided, he said, "Oh, oh, I'm getting sad again," and a fresh torrent started. We were all sad to be leaving such devoted grandparents. Beginnings and endings we were discovering were the hardest part of our moves, especially when they happened so often. This was our tenth move in only six years of marriage, but this time I felt I was finally about to realize my dreams.

2

SLOW BEGINNINGS: BEIRUT, LEBANON (1964–1965, 1970), AND CAIRO, EGYPT (1965–1966)

Beirut

The trip was smooth out of Paris and continued that way as we touched down in Rome and took off again for Beirut. Panoramic views of the Matterhorn, Mt. Etna, and the Aegean islands spread out like pages in my atlas but with each landscape seamlessly joining the next.

Behind the embassy officials helping us with customs were the familiar faces of Aunt Belle, Uncle Doug, and June. They had thoughtfully arranged for us to stay in the American University of Beirut (AUB) guest quarters. The combination of private space to retire to each evening and help with the tasks each morning made those early days more comfortable than we ever expected.

Our immediate need was to find a furnished apartment, so the next morning Aunt Belle and I, following up leads from her Lebanese friends, climbed long stairways and knocked on doors. The women opening them, taken aback at the sight of two foreign women standing on their doorsteps, were soon inviting us to tea when Aunt Belle, in her courteous Arabic, explained what we wanted. The conversations turned immediately to where Aunt Belle learned her fluent Arabic and then to exclamations of approval when they learned she was the granddaughter of Daniel Bliss, the founder of the much-respected AUB. She couldn't have a nobler lineage.

In Aunt Belle's eyes there was always something wrong with the apartments. The location was bad, the space too small, the stairs too long! Although she politely covered up her strongest objections until we were outside, her piercing

9

questions indicated what she was thinking. Each hostess followed us down the stairs, with warm entreaties to come back. I was learning my first lessons—the importance of unhurried greetings before getting down to business, the necessity of taking tea no matter how inconvenient it might be, and the certainty that even complete strangers would be ready to help. It was my first experience with "the cocoon effect"—the feeling of sinking into a warm and comforting world where someone would always provide encouragement and sustenance. The one proviso was that there be a mutual language in which to offer explanations. I resolved to learn Arabic as quickly as possible and in the meantime memorized the litany of greeting phrases I knew would take me a long way.

I was also learning that my "one image fits all" of Arab women was rapidly fading and being replaced with the images I saw on the street—a miniskirted, heavily made-up coquette; the classically attired, aloof, just-stepped-out-of-a-salon beauty; a European fashion-clad sophisticate; an unpretentious, double-knit-suited middle-class woman with a stiff hairdo; a plump matron in a flowered, knee-length housedress; and the long-skirted, head-covered, traditional woman—all with degrees of mobility and choice not possible to orchestrate from a single mind-set. I felt their dress should be telling me more, but as yet I was too ignorant to read the messages they conveyed.

We settled on a furnished apartment, the kind Gulf Arabs rented when they came to Beirut and where Lebanese told us disdainfully they built wood fires on the floor to make their tea. When I first saw the apartments, they seemed too expensive at $200 a month; it had only been eight months since we had scoured Germany for a $50 apartment. The apartment had few rooms, but the high ceilings gave a feeling of spaciousness. I planned to do the housework, shopping, and cooking myself, but I soon realized the mopping of the marble floors alone would leave little time for anything else.

The next concern, therefore, was to find someone to clean and take care of the boys for the hour or two I might have to be out. Again with the help of Aunt Belle's friends, I interviewed potential helpers until I settled on Um Tanyos. She spoke no English, but seemed mature, even slightly wizened; looked alert and energetic; and was quiet. She could have passed for a stereotypic Native American, with two long braids, darkish skin, and slightly Asian eyes. Perhaps her only drawback was that she didn't look as if she would know what to do in an emergency. She feared the telephone, shouting into it when her daughter called, and I couldn't imagine she'd ever been to a regular doctor's office. Still, she proved reliable as a cleaner, walking down from her village every other day, slipping off her shoes at the door, and starting her work. The boys and I retreated to dry areas as she sloshed water through the house, until by lunchtime we were backed onto the kitchen balcony. She focused on floors but ignored toilets and anything above floor level. Not used to having house help, I filled in where she left off.

With cleaning in competent hands, I had time to begin noticing the world around us. We started with the compelling views from the balconies lining three sides of our apartment. From the back balcony we looked into a vast world of compounds that were concealed from anyone at street level. Aunt Belle said Beiruti houses were traditionally surrounded by unadorned compound walls to hide any wealth that might be inside. Whether they believed in it or not, the owners saw no point in showy displays that might attract the evil eye. To the right, we looked down into the courtyards of a cluster of mud and brick houses, a virtual village in the midst of the city, where all day long people ate, drank tea, washed clothes, and hung them out to dry. Voices and music drifted up to us, and every now and then a banging on a metal gate announced a visitor. We gave the actors in this daily drama names to describe their personalities—"jolly mother," "lounging father," and "talkative friend." Beyond the village, a dirt path sloped upward to a cluster of houses on a hilltop. From morning until night, a trail of ant-sized people and donkeys laden with supplies trudged to the top and returned with empty baskets and pots. Beyond the village a small sliver of the Mediterranean Ocean sparkled in the sun.

Directly below our balcony was a fortress-like prison where sentries stood in pillboxes at the corners of its massive walls, and lights illuminated its courtyard at night. Watching prisoners in the yard gave David material for shows organized with his puppets from Germany, among them a grizzly criminal called "Tue-nichts-gut" (Do-no-good) and a policeman "Haltefest" (Hold tightly). Once, a polite officer knocked at the door and asked us not to go out on our balcony since there was an uprising and he feared stray bullets.

We began exploring the neighborhood. A favorite spot was the cliffs next to Beirut's famous Pigeon Rock, a large stone arch just offshore, where we found fully formed snail fossils as big as our fists. Mornings we stopped by the grocery store downstairs. One day I noticed plastic jerry cans covering the floor. After initial pleasantries, which by then I could do in Arabic, I asked the shopkeeper about the jerry cans. He replied that he was filling them to send to Saudi Arabia. He then asked casually, "Do you know if you could taste the difference if water were added to whiskey?" I replied that it depended on how much water was added. The next day the jerry cans were gone, but they reappeared several times during our stay in Beirut.

Before long we enrolled David in a small Lebanese preschool a few blocks from our house. He took easily to the uniforms and drills of the school and made friends whom we invited to play in the afternoons. I loved dropping him off at school in the mornings. Early mornings in Beirut are a heavenly time. The air is fresh and cool, and the smell of roasting coffee permeates the air, intermingled with the smells of freshly baked bread, hot *manushi*, and garlic and *foul* (fava) beans. Boys careened down streets on bicycles with bamboo racks piled high with fresh loaves, occasionally dropping the load in the street and casually picking them up again. Shopkeepers swept the sidewalks in front of their stores and sprinkled them with water to quiet the dust, releasing the pungent, less pleasant aromas of yesterday's debris.

Beirut had no parks near us, but a welcome substitute was the campus of AUB. The boys tumbled on the grass between buildings and played hide-and-seek in the massive banyan tree that stands at the center of campus. Its trailing roots formed an endless labyrinth of tunnels and "rooms" that have entertained generations of children. From my bench I watched students from every corner of the world moving from class to class. On weekends Bill played tennis with Uncle Doug, and both of us played squash on nearby courts. Uncle Doug was dean of bursary students and was especially popular with the Chinese students because of his years growing up in China. Arabs, he told us, particularly revered the Chinese because of Koranic verses that said Muslims should seek education wherever it leads, even if they have to go to China.

While Aunt Belle was introducing me to local manners, Uncle Doug was teaching Bill the "survival skill" of getting around by *service* taxi. The *services* made regular runs along the main streets of Beirut, picking up the passengers that flagged them down. For a few cents you could go almost anywhere in the city. These rides were a good way to practice Arabic and to witness the civility that marked most interactions between people.

Uncle Doug also took us on rambles along Bliss Street to visit his store-owner friends. Naturally they were delighted to meet his relatives and insisted we stop for tea. They were so generous with sweets for the boys that after the first time we left them with Belle and June. We were impressed that the goodwill felt for Uncle Doug transferred so easily to us, his relatives, and very soon we had good friends up and down Bliss Street. But we were too American to slow down and cultivate these friendships, even though we could have rationalized them in terms of improving our Arabic. We had a long way to go before we greeted people properly or exchanged small talk when we entered a shop, as all Arabs do. We were learning, though, to accept generosity more graciously and realizing we didn't have to thank people so profusely for acts that to them were no more than their "duty." In our fast-paced, impersonal world, these kindnesses seemed extraordinarily thoughtful. Later I wondered if always looking to do favors for others didn't instill a sensitivity in Arabs that eludes Westerners. Eventually we reconciled ourselves to taking more time for everything.

It took a while to get used to the subtle humor of Uncle Doug. He would tell stories that kept us hanging on his words with amazement until at the punch line it became clear he had concocted them. He published a collection of aphorisms and wise sayings in a small book with the title *Sayings of Omar*. Examples included "Fish never see water," "A thief always locks his door," and "Old age is welcome when you have friends." The preface said that Omar was a shoemaker who came to Beirut from Persia and became famous for his sayings. It was not until after his death that we learned Uncle Doug was Omar and many of the sayings were told to him by his shopkeeper friends.

Uncle Doug made sure we saw the sights of Lebanon, and traveling with him was always a chance to see his wit at work. In the ruins of Byblos he offered to exchange old license plates for the "antique" coins two urchins were selling. Doug explained that they could make so many more coins out of his license plates and therefore would gain in the end. They looked abashed for a moment before laughing and moving on to their next victim. He made up for his joke by giving them some real coins.

One day Uncle Doug took us in a taxi over the snowy passes and down into Damascus, where in the old souk we bought a warm sheepskin to cover our knees on the way back. The smell of the uncured skin forced us to roll down the windows, so it wasn't clear we gained any warmth from our purchase. We of course stopped in Zahle, the mountain town famous for its good food and especially for its *lebani* (yoghurt cheese) sandwiches of flatbread sprinkled with mint, thyme, and olive oil. Uncle Doug always asked the same driver to take us on trips because of his calm, reasonable driving. The Lebanese say, "You know a Lebanese driver when you see him passing a car passing another car on a curve with no visibility."

Other memorable trips were to the Crusader castles of Marjayoun in the south and Krak des Chevaliers in the north, as well as the monuments of Baalbek in the Bakka Valley and the pottery village at Jisr al Qadi. Perhaps our favorite trip was on donkey-back up to the Cedars of Lebanon, with Uncle Doug wearing a *kafiya*—a man's head scarf—made from little Doug's diaper.

We loved it most when Aunt Belle or Uncle Doug engaged people in conversation. We would stop to rest in an olive grove and see a group of workers eating their noonday meals. "Tfaddalu (come help yourselves)" was the phrase that always greeted us. I could imagine their horror at Americans casually munching food in public and not once stopping to share it. We loved the countless teas and conversations along the way that reinforced for us how important it was to learn Arabic. Arabic was more than just a language—it was a passport into the culture and a new way of thinking.

Bill was making good progress with his Arabic in the embassy's language school in Beirut, but I was learning it less quickly with the boys. I dutifully memorized dialogues from Bill's textbook with help from him on pronunciation. I tried out my few words everywhere. One day I prepared a dialogue and set off for the shoemaker to have some shoes repaired. "Good morning," I said. He saw I was a foreigner and nodded. "I wonder if you could fix this hole." He nodded in the affirmative. "Can it be ready tomorrow?" He jerked his head back and clicked to indicate "no." "When can it be ready?" I was determined to make him say something. He looped his finger in the air, to indicate the day after tomorrow. "How much?" I asked, and he held up his fingers to show me. I was discouraged. Was my Arabic so bad? After similar experiences I realized people were so sure foreigners didn't speak Arabic that they automatically reverted to sign language. Once in Egypt, after a conversation with two schoolgirls, I heard one say to the other as they walked away, "I didn't know I spoke English so well," assuming the whole discussion had been in English.

In Beirut the main foreign language was French, and when people found I couldn't speak French, they were disdainful. Every cultured person spoke French—how was it possible I couldn't speak French! Educated Lebanese even used French in their homes instead of Arabic, seeing Arabic as a language for servants and illiterates. Some simply couldn't bring themselves to speak Arabic with a foreigner, as though they might appear uneducated. Mostly though, people were patient with my struggles with the language.

Bill was allowed to stay in Lebanon for an additional few months to continue studying Arabic. Rather than renew our rental contract in the Boutagy building, we decided to move to the mountain village of Chemlan, where Aunt Belle spent summers as a girl. We rented the first floor of a house with a large veranda. Nearby were trails with views of the Mediterranean, where as we walked we crushed wild thyme with its heady aroma.

Bill commuted down the mountain each day, ironically since the British had a language school for its diplomats in Chemlan, known to everyone as the British "spy school" where Kim Philby learned Arabic. On Fridays, friends from Beirut often joined us for ratatouille and fresh bread from the bakery. Or we would visit Uncle Doug and Aunt Belle in the small stone cottage they rented in a Druze village nearby. Looking out through the arches of their porch, we could see distant peaks beyond a deep gorge that dropped precipitously at the edge of their property. Their landlord Shaikh Abu Shekib told us an orchard from Baysour once slipped in an avalanche and landed upright in another village down the mountain. The shaikhs of the two villages had to decide whether the orchard still belonged to Baysour or to the farmer where it landed. The shaikh would ride his donkey out to his orchards in the morning, and when Belle and Doug awoke they found a pile of fresh vegetables and fruit on their back wall. Several years later when we visited the shaikh he sent the boys out after tea to pick walnuts from his trees. We returned to Saudi Arabia with indelibly brown hands that took weeks to fade.

When we visited Aunt Belle, she always insisted we stay for *mejdra* (the biblical pottage of Esau), a rice and lentil dish that, according to her, had to have the right proportion of one-quarter rice to a full portion of lentils and topped with crisp fried onions. The side dish was a vinegary tomato and cucumber salad, followed by fruit. At teatime, there would be Aunt Belle's signature gingersnaps, a recipe from Abby Bliss, the wife of the founder of AUB. A member of the family said these cookies would keep forever, if you kept them in a securely locked container. After lunch the boys happily followed ant trails and, as Belle taught them, looked for wild geranium seeds that corkscrewed around each other "in battle" as they dried.

Another Baysour story told of a young woman who ran away with a slave into the mountains. Her family followed and captured them. Belle in her delicate way didn't say what happened to the man, but the girl was brought back and imprisoned in a small stone tower. Food was pushed through a hole, and in Aunt Belle's words, "She never came out again." We walked down to the crumbling room one day with its small hole for the food. I thought of stories like this as mythical cautionary tales against flaunting social mores, but with the evidence still there, perhaps this story was true.

Uncle Doug had a small *khaime* (hut) built of oak branches on the precipice, where cool breezes rustling through the leaves made a kind of air-conditioning. Uncle Doug's friends loved to come on Fridays to take long naps in the khaime after lunch. In his spare time Uncle Doug fashioned a rough bench to extend the seating capacity for guests. Abu Shakhib found it astonishing that an educated man would do manual labor, so when they left Beirut Uncle Doug presented the bench to him. He was still telling the story of the educated man who built the bench when we next saw him.

〜〜〜

In the summer of 1970, we returned to Chemlan from Saudi Arabia and rented a smaller house. Bill had another three months to work on Arabic. This second summer the boys were nine, six, and four (with Nick born in the meantime), and they loved climbing the gnarled olive trees and finding caves in the hills near us. One day sitting with guests, we heard explosions down the mountain. Not seeing the older boys, I headed for the noise and a few hundred yards away found them sitting on the stone wall of a neighbor—a member of the Executive Committee of the Palestine Liberation Organization. His teenage son, dressed in camouflage, was throwing petrol bombs at an old tree. My boys watched with admiration as each explosion ricocheted off the surrounding rocks. The boys were about to take their turn when their irate mother swept them away.

Lebanon was our first taste of Arab life. In most ways it was a good introduction, but in one way I was disappointed. Before our arrival, I imagined there must be a simple formula for fitting into local society. We had lived comfortably with people in Germany, so why was it more difficult here? The Lebanese were invariably friendly, but we were a long way from breaking through their formality and their sense of privacy. I could see it meant making important changes in our thinking. We would have to develop a profound sensitivity for others so we could read the deeper meanings in what they were saying. We could not take anything at face value and had to learn how to respond correctly to what was being offered. We couldn't continue American schedules and hope to relate to people with a different sense of time. We had to savor life, to enjoy leisurely meals and conversation, and to live in the moment. We had to think of food as a means of facilitating contact instead of as a hurried way to refuel our bodies. We had to learn to appreciate the richness of everyday encounters, to truly take an interest in people, and to spare the time to show it. We had to find pleasant places like Baysour or Chemlan to share with others. In indescribably subtle ways, we were finding these adjustments would be necessary if we wanted to participate in a deeper way.

Beirut prepared us in a gentle way for what we would experience with more intensity in future decades, but it also obscured many things. We were leaving Beirut barely aware of the crises that afflicted other countries in the region. The mid-1960s in Lebanon were relatively quiet between the civil wars of 1958 and 1975–1990, and so we were not prepared for the conflicts that would affect our relationships later on. In Cairo we would no longer have Uncle Doug and Aunt Belle as intermediaries, and much as we knew we would miss them, we looked forward to trying to make our own way. We wondered if a ten-month assignment was long enough to make good friends. The answer came all too quickly in the Cairo of the mid-1960s.

Cairo

The bright skies and noisy activity of Beirut changed into grim, slow motion in Cairo. We felt the heaviness but had not yet sprouted the antennae that tell Middle Easterners something is amiss. We had not thought the gathering storm in the Middle East would cast so gloomy a shadow over a city known for its gaiety and humor. Gamal Abdul Nasser was president, and he and the Israelis were exchanging threats that ultimately ended in the June 1967 War. Nasser's relations with the United States had begun deteriorating as early as July 1956 when the United States and Britain refused to support World Bank funding for the centerpiece of Nasser's economic plans, the Aswan Dam. In retaliation he nationalized the Suez Canal. Then in October, Israel invaded the Sinai with support from Britain and France but eventually withdrew as a result of pressure from the United States. In 1964, just before we arrived in Cairo, the first stage of the Aswan Dam had been completed with Russian support. Nasser told the Americans they could "go drink the water of the sea." Some claimed he built the Cairo Tower like an insulting finger poking into the air with American assistance money.

Although we knew of these events, we naively believed our personal lives wouldn't be affected. The Embassy Post Report blandly described the living arrangements we could expect. Typical of post reports, the details were positive enough to encourage newcomers but not so positive as to raise their expectations. It didn't report the sandbagged entrances of buildings or the painted windows giving off their bluish light at night. It didn't explain that *boabs* (doormen) were informants, watching the comings and goings of people, or that most Egyptians didn't dare be seen with Americans.

Years later when we returned to Egypt in the late 1970s, people asked whether life hadn't been much better under Nasser. They felt President Sadat's subsequent "opening to the West" was a disaster—an invitation for crass material- ism to enter Egypt and erode its traditional values. We answered truthfully that we remembered poverty everywhere in the mid-1960s with the poor begging on every corner and the average person looking underfed and poorly dressed. A few old-model cars comprised the totality of traffic in those days. The Sadat era brought its own problems, but people looked well fed and well clothed and traffic picked up considerably.

~~~

Our first impressions of Nasser's Egypt were from the comfort of the Hilton Hotel while we waited for the embassy to prepare our apartment. I busied myself with the protocol tasks that couldn't wait. A whole section of Bill's "Efficiency

Report" asked how well I contributed to embassy activities, and since this report would decide his future, I needed to be a model wife for him to qualify for a permanent position. Cynicism had not yet clouded my thinking, and to be honest it pleased me to play such an important role.

In those years Foreign Service spouses took protocol courses in Washington and brush-up meetings at post. We learned the right way to set a table, how to address dignitaries, and how to write invitations. We learned that the American ambassador should be called "Mr. Ambassador" to show American egalitarianism while all other ambassadors were addressed "Your Excellency." We learned about calling cards and the proper initials to write on them when a person wasn't home. We learned the correct protocol arrangements for seating guests at dinner, on sofas, or in cars. We learned that embassy officers must arrive fifteen minutes early to an official party to help with guests. At all other parties we arrived before our ambassador but couldn't leave before he did. When we arrived at post, we had to call on the wives of our husbands' superiors, and when we left, the top officers' wives. This seemed an inordinate amount of time spent with Americans, but I supposed it was meant to make us a close community.

In Cairo we put our protocol training into practice. We listened carefully as the ambassador's wife explained her system for "working receptions." We were to "pick" guests off the end of the ambassador's receiving line and offer them "appropriate" drinks. We were to ask discreetly if they would like "juice, a soft drink, or anything else." The "anything else" was either at the back of the waiter's tray or on a table hidden behind palm trees in a darkened part of the garden. With drinks in hand, we guided the guests to persons of like interest where, when the conversation was under way, we could leave and pick up another guest. It took an intense focus on others to make it work, but mostly it took self-control to get through such tedious evenings. I went home exhausted—the sign of an introvert, I learned, as opposed to an extrovert like Bill who went home energized.

One rule engraved on our minds was that we must *never* be seen talking with our spouses or sitting next to them at dinner. One ambassador sent a couple home as "unpromising Foreign-Service material" when they were always together at official functions instead of circulating separately. We didn't question the rules. We had entered the Foreign Service to serve our country and assumed our superiors with more experience knew what to do.

Privately I hated the demands on spouses but felt I couldn't complain. The worst duties were American "morale boosters." A U.S. Navy ship, for example, might come into port, and we wives would put on a social event for the officers. We spent hours planning community events and were supposed to join women's organizations. Their get-togethers consisted of dull business meetings followed by lectures on the art of home decorating, flower arrangements, and other topics thought to interest spouses.

As I knew from my protocol training, my first duty in Cairo was to call on spouses. We were still in the hotel when I started the calls on wives of officers above Bill in rank—virtually every spouse in the embassy. We had been warned to wear a hat and white gloves and to bring calling cards. I was prepared with a hat and cards but had inadvertently packed my gloves in baggage that had not yet arrived. I searched Cairo for gloves, but in those lean Nasser years, the only gloves available were elbow-length satin ones meant for brides. Fortunately another low-status wife arrived in Cairo, and we made our calls together. She clutched one white glove and I the other of her pair, and we got through the ordeal without our lapses in protocol becoming known. I returned to the hotel each time with a sense of guilt that my children had been left with unknown hotel staff. But I felt so strongly that I would ruin Bill's career if I didn't do the calling that I never seriously questioned the sanity of calls.

From the hotel I regularly visited our apartment to see how the preparations were coming. The apartment was on the fifth floor of a dismal building overlooking the embassy compound that had been rented for reasons of security. As the most junior officer, we were assigned to this least desirable living arrangement. Little sunlight penetrated the cavernous walls of surrounding buildings so, in an effort to make it more cheerful, workers were painting the walls a light cream. One day I visited when the painters were on their lunch break. The apartment reeked of a smell similar to cat urine. On further inspection I came across a bathtub filled with the cat urine paint. When the painters returned, I watched them dip out smaller buckets of paint, fill their mouths with the paint, and spit-spray it over the walls in a fine mist. I went from outrage to concern over the potential health risks to the workers. In broken Arabic, I told them they shouldn't put the stuff in their mouths—it might harm them. They snickered at my Arabic and kept repeating, "Ba'id isshar" (meaning "may that bad thing be distant from us"). For them the mere mention of a dire consequence might bring it down on them. They filled their mouths and went on spraying. I felt helpless to do anything about it.

Eventually we moved in and set up housekeeping. We hired two Nubians—Abdu to shop and cook one main meal a day and Zeinab to clean and help with the children since I was pregnant and expecting our third child in February. We found David a local private kindergarten, St. Joseph's in Zamalak. Zeinab walked him to the bus each morning in his blue-checked smock and carrying his "snack" box like other Egyptian children. When she returned she got Douglas ready for the playground, disdaining the haphazard collection of clothes I felt appropriate. Then while Zeinab cleaned, I would push him in his stroller past the lovely, old decaying mansions in Garden City to the small children's park a half mile away. There I sat on a park bench with the nannies, until they moved respectfully out of range. As I became more cumbersome, Zeinab happily took on the park duties. Before they set off each morning, she scrubbed Doug until his chubby cheeks shone a bright pink and plastered his hair into a neat part. When he met her standards, they would be off. Two hours later she would be back happily reporting (with all exclamations of protection to ward off the evil eye) that no other child came anywhere near the perfection of Douglas. Both boys were home by two, and after lunch the rest of the day was mine with them. This pattern I hoped would carry on when the baby arrived.

One thing we had to get used to in Cairo was the constant scrutiny by Egyptian intelligence. Knowing our servants submitted regular reports about us, I consciously monitored my behavior for actions that might inadvertently be misinterpreted. Soon I was explaining anything suspicious and adding details so the servants wouldn't have to look any further for information. I became ultra sensitive to the impression I was creating—if a male friend dropped by and Bill wasn't home, I made sure servants were coming and going to observe our behavior. Or if I dropped something off at a hotel for a guest, I left it at the desk and explained what it was, rather than taking it directly to his or her room. Transparency was the name of the game in the Nasser era.

Curiously, when we returned to Egypt in the 1970s the same surveillance existed but was focused more on "moral" issues. Once, dropping off a report in a male colleague's hotel room, I ordered a lemonade to drink while he read the report. The waiter informed us we would have to go to the lobby and could not be in the room alone! We meekly retired to the lobby. When I told my friend Nayra about the incident, she said I should have rebuked the staff member and said we would do no such thing.

The Egyptians were not the only ones interested in us. In "sweeping" our quarters during our second posting in Cairo, the embassy found a Russian-style listening device in the bookshelf of the cozy study where I entertained my friends. In retrospect, I realize the Russian diplomat who befriended us must have planted it. He "so much" enjoyed borrowing books from our "wonderful collection." Leaving him to browse in the study alone was a mistake, but we found it hard to distrust "nice people." It was unlikely the Russians discovered much of interest since Bill and I knew we had to find an open area outside if we wanted to discuss anything political or private.

The phones were another story. It was clear from the regular clicks of the antiquated recording devices the Egyptians used that they were tapped. When foreign spouses spoke in unusual languages, they were told to switch to a language the listeners understood or the telephones would go dead. Or if we challenged the billing—we were regularly overcharged to pay for calls of the telephone company's staff and friends—they would play our call back as proof. The telephone service was like any other service in Egypt—the people who controlled the "choke points" used their positions to make money. If you didn't pay the "tip," you returned many times before you got what you needed. This was true for anything from gaining access to medical lab results, to buying tickets in a railway station, or paying your utility bill. We foreigners could feign ignorance of the *baksheesh* (bribes) system or resign ourselves to paying the "foreigners' tax."

~~~

Meanwhile, Bill and I were trying to get to know people in the foreign and Egyptian communities but with discouraging results. As trainees we could work at parties of our superiors but couldn't invite them to our parties or entertain others "above our level." Egyptians were forbidden from associating with us if they were officials and afraid to do so if they were not. We tried to engage Egyptians in conversation at other embassy parties but knew we wouldn't be able to meet again outside. Once we met a charming Egyptian who seemed less reticent than most, but when we invited him to come to dinner he refused. Then several days later he called to say he could meet us for tea in the dining room of Shepherd's Hotel. We felt he'd been given permission to meet us in a public place, and when he questioned us about U.S. policy, we believed our fears were confirmed.

Meanwhile, we spent weekends visiting the pyramids and exploring Cairo's many charming old bazaars and neighborhoods. Everything in those days was run down and in a state of disrepair, but nonetheless, it had the distinct air of a once elegant city. One of the most egregious despoilers of buildings was plumbing pipes trailing down outside walls that emitted sewage from every faulty connection. Adding to the decrepitude was the soot from kerosene cooking fires that covered the city with a coat of black, oily grime. A white shirt worn for two blocks would be marked with a black ring around the neckline. One day I was caught in a quick rain shower and found my clothes covered with large dirty spots as the rain "washed the air." My father, an amateur gardener, visited Cairo and admired the fine black dirt that produces fruits and vegetables of incomparable size. He called it "the human excrement of the ages." This dirt sifted into our home and left smudges everywhere, including on our newly painted cream walls and the white carpets installed to lighten the gloom. It presented a challenge to Abdu, Zeinab, and me to keep a reasonable level of cleanliness. Soon, though, I lost my finicky fear of microbes when I saw how the children thrived in this incredibly dirty environment.

One oppressively hot evening we invited some Americans to dinner. After the meal, we sat on our balcony overlooking a major street in Garden City. We were deep in conversation when a loud crash sounded below and the ripping and scraping of metal. Rushing to the rail we saw one of Cairo's vintage cars hung up on a concrete divider that had been erected a few hours before to change the direction of traffic from two to one way. Several nearby workers lifted the car off the concrete divider and pushed it to the side of the road. At this point, a police officer arrived and demanded to know why the driver hadn't paid attention to the median strip. The driver shouted verbal abuse back at him for not setting up signs to indicate the change. Eventually the driver handed out money to the laborers, hailed a cab, and left. As soon as the cab rounded the corner, the policeman collected his share of the tip. A half hour later, another crash and the same scene unrolled with the smashed car stopping, the workers helping the driver and being given money, and the same policeman taking his share. Another quiet descended, and then the same scene, again and again, all night long. The crashes continued for the rest of the week.

I was outraged at the willful destruction of what in Cairo were lovingly tended vintage cars, but who should I tell? Who was responsible? When I asked Egyptian staff in the embassy what I should do, they only shrugged and talked sympathetically about the poorly paid police and workers who "were only trying to make a living." They warned that if I reported the incident the workers' families would lose their breadwinners while the men were held in jail. What hadn't registered with me was how much money the crashing cars were generating for mechanics, lower-ranking policemen, and poor laborers at the expense of the comparatively "wealthy" car owners. Still, this didn't seem the best way to redistribute Egyptian wealth. By the end of the week, the drivers got used to the new traffic pattern, and with no more crashes, my anger subsided.

We brought a secondhand car to Cairo for weekend trips into the country-side. During the week, we parked it in the garage beneath our building and, as was customary, paid a car-*boab* to keep a watchful eye over it. One day we found the tire flat. The boab helped us change it and offered to have the old tire patched. Bill, of course, gave him an additional sum for this service. Next month the same problem occurred and the following month the same, each time the boab sympathetically commiserated about our bad luck with tires. It took us a while to see what was happening, and when we threatened to have him removed from his job if it happened again, the flat tires stopped. We became less trusting over time, realizing Egyptians operated at a level of ingenuity and need we would never fully appreciate.

Watching Egyptians interacting with one another, I was surprised to see how easily they resolved their differences even after shouting matches that seemed irreconcilable. Rarely did they leave a scene without a reconciliation mediated by a bystander. And they seemed much better than I at sympathizing with the factors that initiated the conflict, whether poverty, the frustrations of everyday living, or casual insults. The labels I applied as an American to people's actions—such as "lying" or "stealing"—framed the behavior as immoral and therefore left me little room to back down or heal a disrupted relationship. After several experiences, I realized how unproductive my approach had been and tried to sympathize—not always happily—with the underlying causes Egyptians saw more clearly. Instead of condemning the man who destroyed our tires, I took the hint that more money was needed and saw to it that he got it before any more tires went flat. At the same time I made it clear to him that I knew what was going on. No one likes to be taken advantage of, and we "rich" foreigners were too easy a mark. His sheepish look reminded me it was a game to test our limits. But I was pleased that my moderate approach was producing better results than my moralistic one.

Meanwhile, February was drawing near and the baby was about to arrive. The embassy doctor recommended I deliver the baby at Dar el Shifa Hospital in Cairo under the care of an Egyptian doctor trained in the United States. This was my third delivery in a third country (the United States, Germany, and now Egypt), and there had been no complications. The doctor's discussion of the delivery felt familiar, undoubtedly because of his training in the United States. He watched my weight, and his instructions were ones I remembered from David's birth. He took more time with me and his bedside manner was definitely warmer and more caring than that of either American or German doctors.

Having a child born overseas involves extra hassles to make sure he is correctly registered. The embassy automatically gives citizenship to children of Foreign Service personnel born overseas, but before a passport is issued it's necessary to complete the Egyptian registration process. A hospital official appeared in my room the day after Nick's birth to ask what we planned to name the baby. Fortunately the name was recognizable as a Christian saint's name since not every name is allowed in Egypt. "Nicholas," we said, and the official left the room only to reappear with a paper in Arabic saying that our new son was named "Nicholas William Roberts." "No, no," we said. "His name is Nicholas Alexander Rugh." "But you told me his father was William and his paternal grandfather was Roberts, so Nicholas William Roberts." Although we couldn't change his Egyptian papers, the embassy gave us papers with the correct name.

After luxuriating for a week in the hospital, the day came to go home. As we drove up to our building I saw boabs from our building and surrounding buildings lined up to greet us. By then I was suspicious enough to wonder if they were expecting a token of the happy occasion or genuinely admiring of a woman who only produced boys. I felt like a queen when they congratulated us on the birth of our son. Abdu prepared a wonderful dinner and a large cake with lettering on the top that spelled out "God Lak Boy." I wasn't sure whether the cake said "Good Luck Boy" or "God Likes Boys"—it could have been either.

I barely had time to think how my dreams of knowing Egyptians had been frustrated in the tense atmosphere of the Nasser period. In ten months I had learned a great deal about Egyptians but from a distance where it was easier to see the negative side. The lesson was perhaps that, without the warmth of close personal contact, people become objectified and their differences magnify. Does that explain the racism of colonialism? I know that my perceptions of Egypt were not very positive this time around—that I was unable to distinguish between Egyptians I could trust and those who sought me out with ulterior motives. Moreover, I felt uneasy about the way my values were being challenged—was corruption warranted in the face of need, for example? And it didn't feel personally good to be portrayed by the Egyptian government as the embodiment of evil. Whether I could more effectively have gotten to know Egyptians, given the difficulties between our countries and my preoccupations with the children, is hard to know. Ten years later our experiences in Egypt were entirely different. So although I was disappointed at the time, from the vantage point of more than forty years later, I am glad I had a second chance to revise my view of Egypt and Egyptians.

Fortunately my luck was about to change as we headed off for our first full posting in Jidda. We had weathered the Efficiency Reports and training, and Bill was now a full-fledged member of the Foreign Service.

3

MOVING AHEAD:
JIDDA, SAUDI ARABIA (1966–1967)

The topaz sea glistened in the afternoon sun as we descended over a desert reaching as far as we could see. The plane followed an asphalted road along the Red Sea until in the blink of an eye a second road shot out perpendicularly and disappeared into the hazy distance. There was little to see other than scrub brush and a scattering of low buildings linked to the road by tracks. It struck me that we planned to spend two years in this desolate place, and I wondered whether we had thought the matter through enough before accepting this assignment. I looked at the boys and felt a twinge of guilt at removing them from the advantages of life in the United States. David was five, Doug two, and Nick only a few months old. Would there be a minimum of health care, schooling, and other necessities for them? Was it right to drag them on an adventure we sought eagerly for ourselves? I looked again at the landscape and knew this was going to be different from anything we had experienced before.

In 1966 Jidda was a frontier town, not the modern luxurious city it eventually became. Jidda is the Arabic name for "grandmother," referring to the belief that Eve and the Garden of Eden had been located here. Drivers would point out the walled compound downtown where she was said to be buried. But at that moment from the air, Jidda bore no resemblance to a paradise. Had I not had confidence in the embassy to prepare a decent place for us to live, I might have taken the next plane out.

We were met by embassy officials in four-wheel drive vehicles and set off in a whirl of dust over rutted tracks skirting construction sites and retreating

27

from open sewer lines. Nearing the outskirts of town, mud and brush dwellings huddled more closely together until blocks of concrete dwellings, two or more stories tall and surrounded by privacy walls, rose above them. The few men in sight wore white gown-like *thobes*.

Our house stood in an area of town just then being developed. Surrounding it were empty lots, and across the street was King Faisal's modest whitewashed palace on Medina Road—the road we had flown over coming in for a landing. The other perpendicular road was Mecca Road. Both headed for the main places of importance in this religiously conservative country. To our west where the sun sank each day into the Red Sea were extensive mud flats that ran the length of Jidda and gave off a rich, fetid smell when the tide was out. From my rooftop in the evenings, I watched King Faisal's limousine emerge from the palace with a two-motorcycle escort and head off toward the desert, where the king performed his evening prayers. Our nearest neighbor, in a compound across a dirt track, was a man with three wives in three identical villas. On 'Iid holidays they wore identical dresses in the same vibrant colors. It was my first view of what it meant to follow the Koranic injunction that a man could take up to four wives as long as he treated them equally. From my rooftop I watched the noisy comings and goings of the wives in the garden as their children scampered around in the cooler air of evening. When the women went out, they rode in cars with darkened windows.

We were welcomed the first day by Hamud, the Yemeni houseman we inherited from a departing staff member. He was unimpressive in appearance—little and wiry with a dark complexion that contrasted with his white teeth when he smiled. I screwed up my courage the next morning to tell him I was sorry but I needed a woman who could clean and take care of the children. I was certain no Arab man could do those tasks as well as a woman. Thankfully I waited long enough to find out that Hamud could do all these tasks superbly and with a cheerfulness it would be hard to match. He shopped and cooked delicious meals for us, cleaned, did the washing and ironing, and planted the garden. He proved to be a perfect nursemaid for Nick and was moved to tears when any of the boys suffered a minor scrape or disappointment. He loved the boys as if they were his own.

Hamud became the manager of our growing menagerie. It started with his rabbits and chickens that he begged us to let him keep, "so we could have meat and eggs," although he never actually killed any of them. He insisted we have a rooster or there could be no eggs. When the noisy creature died, he thought a miracle had occurred when the chickens continued to produce eggs. Soon, to Hamud's delight, we added a donkey. A Saudi heard us talking about how much the boys would enjoy a little donkey as a pet. We meant the good-natured little gray donkeys that patiently carried loads around town. The next day our friend opened the trunk of his car and lifted out a baby Hasawwi donkey. He had interpreted our saying "little" donkey as meaning we wanted a baby one—an alternate meaning of the word "little" in Arabic. Hasawwi donkeys grow to be as big as mules, with temperaments to match, and only while "Pinocchio" was young and manageable were the boys able to ride him. With Hamud in charge, life settled into a smooth routine.

Not long after we arrived in Jidda, I received an invitation to a wedding at the house of the wives next door. I was overjoyed at the thought of attending my first Saudi wedding and conjured up visions of neighborly visits between our two houses. I felt I was on the verge of a breakthrough in getting to know my neighbors. Unfortunately I was scheduled to attend an important embassy party at nine o'clock the same evening. But since the invitation said the wedding started at sunset, I believed there was plenty of time to attend both functions.

On the appointed evening, I knocked at the neighbor's gate just after sunset wearing my best finery—hopelessly drab by Saudi standards—and was ushered up the back stairs by the servants. I was becoming uneasy, for no cars were arriving and I was being taken to a modest sitting room with no sign of festivities. After a time the mother of the bride entered in a housedress, and soon the bride, looking annoyed at the interruption. She was dressed in a robe as though she had just bathed, her head covered with large pink curlers. They assured me this was indeed the right day and that I was "very, very welcome," but didn't explain the absence of wedding signs. I quickly said I could only stay a short time because I had to go to another party, and they shook their heads in disbelief that I would attend another party the same night. I wanted desperately to retreat since it was obvious I was keeping these women from important wedding preparations, but decided to stay for a polite interval.

At the time my Arabic was limited, and the women knew no English. Even if I had been more proficient, the Saudi accent and vocabulary would have been difficult. Furthermore, their contact with foreigners was nonexistent so they had no idea how to slow down or adjust their vocabulary to make it easier for me. To them I must have seemed a half-wit, unable to express myself well in Arabic and clearly knowing nothing about weddings. I realized I would only survive the conversation if I did all the talking myself and didn't have to decipher what they were saying to me. So I ran mentally down the list of Arabic dialogues I had memorized in Beirut: "ordering food in a restaurant," "buying food from the grocery store," "asking directions," and "talking about the weather." None seemed relevant except maybe the one about weather, even though Saudi weather was hardly worth discussing.

I started out, "What I nice sunny day it is." They looked confused . . . in reality it was hotter than Hades. "Has it rained lately?" "Not for a year," they replied. "I think I saw a cloud today," I remarked. By then, they were totally befuddled, and as I had exhausted my vocabulary I lapsed into silence. Eventually they brought tea and sweets and I escaped. Needless to say, they never invited me again, and I learned my first lesson—never arrive at Saudi weddings less than three hours after the invitation specifies.

It was just one lesson I learned painfully through mistakes. Other lessons also related to time. When we arrived in Saudi Arabia in the late 1960s, there were three ways to tell time, not to mention different ways of perceiving and using it. Local time was calculated by setting clocks to 12:00 just as the last lip of the sun disappeared into the Red Sea each evening. This also signaled the time for the obligatory Maghreb, or sunset, prayer. Since the sun set at different times, it meant a cumbersome resetting of the clocks each day. From a Western perspective this was uncomfortably imprecise, so we clung to Greenwich mean time (GMT) plus three (for the three hours Saudi Arabia was east of Greenwich). GMT plus three made it possible to arrange our days according to the normal schedules in our home countries and in effect coordinate with the rest of the world in such activities as airline schedules. Mainly Europeans used the third and final system—called "Arabic time." They felt it meshed better with Saudi time if they just added six hours to local time to make it feel more like European time. In this system, the sun went down not at the local time of 12:00 but at the more European time of 6:00 p.m. Like "Saudi time," it required resetting clocks every day. Whenever we received an invitation, we had to figure out which time was meant and then adjust to the time we felt most comfortable with, hoping our hosts had not already made the adjustment for us. With the town operating on three time systems, no one was ever precise about appointments.

Then there was the matter of how each group viewed time as a concept. Differences in clock time were only part of the confusion. We would receive invitations to visit local homes—usually stated vaguely to indicate that we were welcome at anytime. It was insulting to invite anyone for a specific time as though they were not welcome any other time or that the host was insisting the guest drop everything to come at that moment. When we asked anxiously for a more precise time, the best we would get was the answer that, for example, we should come "after Maghreb." Maghreb was a specific prayer time, not just sunset, so we knew we needed to wait at least a half hour after sunset so as not to interrupt anyone's prayer. And actually "after Maghreb" really meant any time before the next prayer two hours later. For Saudis, in the 1960s, and perhaps even now for some older Saudis, time was divided conceptually into chunks instead of precise moments, and the chunks were bounded by the five religiously determined prayer calls each day. My invitation to the neighbor's wedding essentially meant "the wedding starts in the time period between sunset and *asr* prayer," and guests knew that near the end of the time chunk or even later was a more appropriate time to appear. It was also important for a guest to know that some prayers were obligatory—that they should take place at a particular moment, like the sunset prayer, while others could be made up later. A visit during the non-obligatory prayers was not as inconvenient as during the obligatory ones, even though the hostess might excuse herself in both cases.

The saving grace of all these practices from my perspective was that, as the Saudis explained, it was the intention that counted, so if you meant to do it right you would be forgiven. Once years later when we were waiting in the airport for a people mover bus to take us to the plane, the time for prayer came. An elderly Saudi asked his fellow passengers to point out the direction of Mecca and then rolled out his prayer carpet and began to pray. Halfway through his prayers, the people mover backed up and turned 180 degrees to head for the plane. When the others saw the man was pointed in the opposite direction from Mecca, they exchanged smiles. But all murmured respectfully as he finished, "May God accept your prayers," meaning that even though the prayers were technically incorrect, the intention had been good and God would surely accept them.

There was other important information about time, especially where
women were concerned. I found if I arrived for a visit in the mornings I was likely
to find myself sitting much of the time alone as my hostess scurried around giving
orders for the noonday meal, tending to her children, buying from peddlers, or
otherwise organizing her household. Periodically she would lavish attention on
me with tea and snacks, but I would feel decidedly secondary to her housework.
My hostess wouldn't excuse herself perhaps because she felt as a woman I would
understand. It was far more convenient to drop by during the late afternoons
when women had completed their main work and had time for socializing—but
of course that was inconvenient for me because my children were home from
school. For foreigners, spending time with Saudis meant turning their schedules
upside down, and most as a result were discouraged from making the effort.

Time elements were also embedded in the Arabic language, adding a
whole new level of difficulty for foreigners trying to learn vocabulary. Saudis,
for example, had many words for "dates" and "camels" that indicated such time-
related factors as, for example, "age," "ripeness," and "fertility," as well as other
distinctive qualities. Separate words were used for a newborn camel, a foal, an
animal coming into its fertile stage or in its first or subsequent pregnancies, or
when it became too old to bear, as well as other age and color characteristics. The
same held true for dates, with words that indicated flowering, their propagation,
color, shape, when they were green, and when they were at their sweetest. It was
useless to say much about dates if you couldn't be specific. I also found Saudis
had no words to distinguish important concepts to us like "snow," "ice," "sleet,"
and "hail." The word *telj* sufficed to cover all these forms of precipitation.

We settled into our spacious house in Jidda with its high ceilings, numerous
bedrooms, and traditional men's and women's receiving rooms, which we turned
into living and dining rooms. Marble tiles covered the floors, making our voices
echo loudly until we found inexpensive carpets to dampen the noise. In those
days, construction in Jidda was a necessity rather than an art, and houses always
gave the impression of not being quite finished. Grout spilled messily from around
the tiles, slopping onto the walls and into the corners of rooms. Plumbing pipes
snaked their ways up the outside walls, leaking their contents until conspicuous
repairs formed another obvious layer of plaster. Everything about the house was
designed for maximum effort—the floors needed to be scrubbed every day, and

the plumbing only worked sporadically as chunks of plaster lodged in pipes already too small to do the job. The "garden" provided ample sand to track into the house, and frequent sandstorms blew dust through the cracks in the ill-fitting window frames until there seemed no difference between the drifts inside and out. Fortunately, the sloping floors meant buckets of water could be sloshed easily over the expanse of tile to wash the dirt down the drain. Once when the boys' three-cornered juice containers lodged in the drains of our flat roof, the water from a surprise storm built up and flowed unimpeded under the gap in the door and down the stairs to form a lake on the living room floor. The water eventually cleared through a downstairs drain; we dried the carpets and went on undisturbed in our sometimes quite practical house.

I had great plans to augment the meager plantings in our garden, but soon found that the number of plants that could withstand the intense heat of Jidda was limited—not much beyond oleander and some fast-growing eucalyptus and palm trees. Our most successful agricultural effort was a kudzu-like vine that grew so quickly we felt we could see it crawl up and over the compound walls until it reached the ground on the other side and started creeping across the desert. As long as we watered the roots, nothing seemed to stop it. That is, until one late afternoon the boys and I were sitting on our crabgrass lawn when I suddenly saw one kudzu vine after another disappearing over the walls, roots and all. I rushed to the roof to see what was happening and found a herd of camels consuming our vines. Every afternoon from then on, someone had to stand guard when we heard the camels moaning with pleasure from their mud baths as they scratched the fleas off their backs and finished with a kudzu dessert. Talking to their herder had no effect. Hamud as a Yemeni received only withering dismissal from the "noble" camel herders, and I, of course, was a woman to be dismissed out of hand.

At one point we decided we needed some repairs to the property. The most important was the unfinished servant's quarters in the backyard so Hamud would have a place of his own. And we also needed an iron gate to replace a rickety old wooden one that didn't afford any security. The landlord said he would take care of it, and one day we found a new metal gate replacing the wooden one. We were pleased until we found it had been firmly cemented shut. The landlord was in Riyadh, and we couldn't use the gate for weeks until he returned. Next he sent workers to roof and paint the servant's quarters. Coming back one day I found the house painted but with the same pile of sand heaped against an outside wall. I cleared the sand away and asked the painter to cover the large exposed area. "No paint left," he replied and wouldn't do it. The electrician then came to install a light and because it was closer to the house next door connected the line to their meter. When I suggested the neighbor might not want to pay our bills, he replied that we should tell Hamud not to turn on the light very much, and then it wouldn't cost much more. I never learned to anticipate all the things that could go wrong, but it became clear to me why Saudis who built new homes went daily to supervise even the minutest detail.

To fill my time I agreed to research and write a report on girls' education. The embassy had received a request for information on women, and I was the only one willing to write the report. In those days, I shared the condescending view of most Westerners that the lack of girls' education was a reason the country was so "backward." I took the excuse of the report to visit the first girls' school in the country that was established around 1956. The school was supported by King Faisal's wife, Queen Effat, and directed by the able Syrian headmistress Cecille Rouschdi. The latter showed me around and related the difficulties of setting up a school in a country where powerful religious elements felt there was no need for girls' education. Luckily the Queen had been educated outside the country in Turkey and was a strong believer in education. One of the fears of Saudi parents was that foreign Arab women who might introduce customs contrary to local culture would teach their daughters. Miss Rouschdi, a kindly but imposing figure, allayed their fears with her uncompromising standards for both education and deportment.

By the time I arrived in Jidda, the school had been open about ten years. In 1960 Queen Effat also convinced her husband to start public schools for girls despite protests by the religious *ulema* (a council of scholars). When the first public school opened, King Faisal noted that education could not be bad if it taught girls to read and recite the Koran, and then to allay the ulema's fears, he put the administration of girls' schools under the direction of a religious shaikh. Many Saudis had begun to see the advantage of educating girls when they saw increasing numbers of young Saudi men coming home from studying abroad with foreign wives. Parents realized education might enhance their daughters' chances of marrying well. The government also wanted local women to replace the foreign teachers, doctors, and female professionals who served Saudi women. By the end of the twentieth century, Saudi girls were attending school at all levels, and from the secondary level on constituted a larger proportion of the student body than boys.

While living in Jidda, we were often aware of just how young a country Saudi Arabia was—being only formally established in 1932. Our ambassador related amusing stories about his posting to the country when the United States only had a legation there. He told how he and another embassy official traveled the thousand miles across desert tracks to present their credentials to the king in his tent in Riyadh. As was the custom, they changed into Arab robes just outside Riyadh and proceeded to the meeting. There the protocol officer explained how they should enter the *majlis* (audience place) and move toward the king, bowing as they went. Most important, they should remember that when they left they should back out of the majlis, bowing the whole way so as not to turn their backs on the king. According to Ambassador Eilts, within minutes of presenting their credentials and backing out, one tripped over his gown and the other tripped over him until the "entire U.S. legation was flat on the ground."

Ambassador Eilts also told the story of a letter he received from a coin and stamp collecting company in Connecticut. Enclosed in the letter was a $20 bill. The letter said, "Dear Sir, as we see you are near Afghanistan we would kindly request that you change the enclosed bill into a variety of coins from that country." Although Ambassador Eilts did not travel the thousands of miles to acquire Afghan coins, he did wait until near Ramadan when the Saudi currency was cheaper against the dollar so he could send the company more Saudi coins for its money.

Presumably he also sent some Maria Theresa *talers*, European coins that were the approved form of oil concession payment in those days. Anyone visiting the bank at the end of the month would find bank employees counting sacks of these coins. I was told that a picture of a male (I forgot which king) on the coin was worth more than those with the image of Maria Theresa. In our day, the Maria Theresa coins were popular as ornaments on the face masks and silver jewelry Saudi women wore.

I was beginning to make friends in Jidda by regularly attending women's parties. One group I particularly enjoyed consisted of women of varying nationalities married to Saudis; the women met for coffee once a week. I found their parties interesting because of the discussion about local issues. These Western wives showed considerable variation in their ability to adapt to local culture. Some learned fluent Arabic, adopted local social practices, sent their children to Arabic schools, and made themselves available at all hours to receive unexpected visitors. At the other extreme were Western wives who refused to learn Arabic and rarely visited their Saudi in-laws. I found those who made the greatest effort on the whole living more satisfying lives than those who spent their time complaining about local customs. Even the adapters, however, could not entirely protect themselves against the potential consequences of being foreigners in a country where they had few rights. I knew of at least three instances when American wives were precipitously divorced while abroad and had to leave their children behind. In one case, the husband from the ruling family decided he had no future in the government if he remained married to an American although I felt he still loved her and knew it would be difficult for his children without their mother. Twenty years later when I visited Riyadh, their daughter visited me in my hotel because I had been a friend of her mother, and I felt the sadness she experienced.

Through these Western wives, I learned that making an effort to adapt was seen locally as a way of expressing respect and enhanced rather than detracted from the person making the effort. At first I resisted the local dress codes and behavior expected of women but eventually realized that by violating the codes I only reinforced the negative stereotypes people had of Westerners. No Saudi thought, "Oh isn't it wonderful that she feels free to wear what she wants!" They were more likely to think, "See, she is an example of the way Western women go around exposing themselves." When I talked with Saudi women, most seemed to think we should cover our arms and bodies completely and wear longish skirts and a scarf on our heads in public, but no one felt we needed to cover our faces. Nor did we foreigners in those days wear an *abaya*, the enveloping cloak, although in later years foreign women were required to wear them. The Western wives often wore them out of respect for their Saudi families. An Arabic proverb says, "Eat what you like, but dress to please others," meaning that your dress reflects your respect for others. Americans often misunderstand modesty coverings, which although worn for many reasons, do not make the women who wear them feel oppressed.

Once I spent a weekend at the seaside cottage of an American friend married to a Saudi. Susan and I were alone preparing the meal for our families who were off exploring the coast. The meal was the conventional *bryani* Saudi women prepare when they aren't sure how many will come to lunch. We browned onions and chunks of meat, added tomato paste, and then water and left the pan simmering on the stove. When the number of guests was certain, we threw in enough rice to accommodate everyone. Suddenly we looked out the window and saw an unknown man walking along the shore. Both of us dived for a space behind a bed where we couldn't be seen through the window and smothered our laughter until we were sure he was out of sight. If he had seen us accidentally it would have been all right, but letting ourselves be seen knowingly would not have been proper and might have reflected poorly on Susan's in-laws. By then my instincts were as good as hers, and it didn't feel at all demeaning to dive for cover to respect her Saudi husband's family who had been unfailingly kind to both of us.

In Jidda I took advantage of every local invitation I received and soon was known as a foreigner who accepted invitations to Saudi parties. There were few foreigners at that time so we were still a curiosity. I began attending *shilla* (friendship) groups of local women and their female friends and relatives who met several times a month. Most of the parties were fairly sedate affairs with the conversations revolving around events in town: marriages, births, deaths, and, sotto voce, divorces and marital problems. The women preferred to be bearers of good news, but when they trusted me enough, they would tell me the bad news too, sometimes directly and at other times by circumlocution. Then everyone would nod their comprehension, and no one would have to come out with the specifics of the news. Sometimes we knew by the special solicitousness for a certain woman, as happened at one party when a minister's wife was present and we learned by the way others treated her that the minister was threatening to divorce her. Her friends sent their husbands to urge him to reconsider. Sometimes it might be the absence of a regular guest that would start the sympathetic clucking of the women, along with vague excuses about why she wasn't present, such as "she's visiting her parents," which might mean she was having difficulties with her husband.

Sometimes parties were full of joking and laughter, but where this was most common was at the popular parties hosted by an Egyptian woman married to a Saudi. The guests at her parties included a mix of Saudi, other Arab, and occasionally foreign women like me. To fully appreciate the discussion, I needed a better vocabulary than I had, but when I prevailed on someone to explain the jokes in simpler Arabic, I found most of them very explicitly sexual. She liked to describe her own prowess with her husband, describing him as putty in her hands as she did this and that to him, meanwhile leaving her guests shrieking with laughter. No woman dared leave early at her parties or she would accuse her of an urgent need to get home to her husband. Not many of her guests were as open as she was about sexual matters, but most thoroughly enjoyed the jokes.

I attended these women's parties knowing I could never fully reciprocate. My house was too much of an unknown territory for Saudi women: men might be present, the proper separation of the sexes might not be observed, and I undoubtedly did not understand the subtle social distinctions enough to invite the right mix of women. They knew my servants were men and might make an appearance at any time. And in any case, there was not enough interest in my house to make them want to see how a foreigner lived. My interior décor was far plainer than theirs, and my knowledge of the fine points of Saudi hospitality—seating arrangements and degrees of deference to important women—was rudimentary. It was a relief in some ways not to have to compete with the elaborate food, perfumes, and other rituals performed in Saudi homes.

The one time I tried to entertain a group of Saudi women was a disaster. It happened after I volunteered at a local women's language institute to help the students practice English. I thought by inviting the group of twenty students to tea it would give them a chance to practice English in a new setting. Three days before the event I started cooking to make sure I would have a respectable variety of food. Unfortunately I mistook difficulty of effort for respectability. I made an especially complex Danish roll recipe that called for mixing the dough the day before, leaving it in the refrigerator overnight, and baking it the next day. That night I put the large wad of dough into the refrigerator. Hamud's pounding on the door wakened me next morning—"Madam, come quickly." I raced downstairs and found the dough filling the refrigerator and expanding out onto the floor. I worked frantically all day to rescue what I could of the flattened contents of the refrigerator and make "airy" Danish pastries. As the party approached, I dressed in my best clothes, made sure there were sufficient quantities of drinks, cold and hot; and then sat down to wait . . . and wait. Nobody came but the Sudanese wife of Bill's employee who volunteered to help at the party. Someone later explained that Saudi women are sensitive to social gradations, and while they can mix in a public women's-only space, it's difficult for them to socialize in a private home. They didn't want to insult me by refusing my invitation even though they knew they couldn't come. After that I reconciled myself to mostly attending but not giving parties, and only invited women who were familiar enough with Western ways to feel comfortable in my home.

Bill and I were regular members of a group made up mostly of Europeans who spent weekends camping in the desert. I would like to say we were invited solely for our congeniality, but in truth we had the advantage of a liquor allowance that many of them did not. The sale of alcohol was officially prohibited in the kingdom, but there were many ways to obtain it. A number of foreigners had their own stills, and it was rumored that Saudi Arabia was the largest importer of copper tubing in the world, a commodity important in the manufacture of the Westerners' *Saddiqi* (meaning in Arabic "my friend"), a local brew somewhat like gin that could be converted into all sorts of alcoholic drinks. Embassies were unofficially exempted from the ban on alcohol and could import it for their employees. As the largest embassy, we had access to the greatest variety of liquors. Once a staff member received a call from a customs official at the port urging him to come quickly because the U.S. Embassy's "office furniture crates were leaking." On the camping trips we always brought a case of beer.

Pork was another commodity in high demand among foreigners. One eccentric British English teacher was reputed to have returned from vacation with a pig on a leash. The customs men, having no idea what a pig looked like, accepted his explanation that it was his pet dog but dutifully took down his address. The next day men from the Ministry of Agriculture came to see his dog. "Sorry," he said, "my dog died last night." I am not sure the story is true although the man was living in the kingdom at the time.

We found that when our Pekinese—a gift from a Saudi—traveled with us, he attracted crowds of Saudis wherever we went, especially at filling stations. The conversation among the onlookers always started with the suggestion that Bingo was probably a baby lion, but after a while they invariably concluded that he was more likely a pig. The Bedouin always brought sheep along in their pickup trucks to slaughter on their journeys, and since Christians ate pigs, it was logical to think they carried pigs with them.

The weekend camping trips turned out to be one of our greatest pleasures as a family—not so much for the food and drink but for the good times we had and the lifelong friendships we formed with other campers. The Red Sea beaches north of Jidda were unspoiled and the coral reefs unparalleled. Our Dutch leader kept a jeep filled with the basics we needed: a large tent, cots, pots and pans, wash-up equipment, and coolers. Pieter had two large Saluki dogs that, once his jeep turned onto the desert, loped in leisurely fashion alongside the vehicles. These were the only dogs Arabs felt were clean and if touched by them didn't require that they wash again before praying, I was told, because the Prophet used them as hunting dogs. The children would tumble out of the car at our chosen spot and wander at will with their "best friends," Doug with Carolientje and the toddlers Nick and Didi hand in hand nearer camp. David would be off collecting shells and other treasures.

As time went on the innocence of our first camping trips fell away as we came to know the dangers of the Red Sea and could distinguish between the creatures that were relatively benign and those we had to steer away from. In the first category were the ugly sea cucumbers, the prickly sea urchins and anemones, and the stingrays that would suddenly flush up from underneath as we swam. In the second category were lethal stonefish camouflaged as rocks, the beautiful scorpion fish fluttering their striped quills in warning, and moray eels with their snag-toothed smiles emerging from holes in the reef. The children played in the shallow water while Leisje and I took turns with Pieter and Bill trekking out to the deep reef fifty yards offshore. We swam as soon as the water was deep enough to see the creatures surrounding us and avoid the dangerous ones. In the deeper water we would find ourselves swimming among thousands of colorful fish, from tiny iridescent blue ones to striped clown fish and larger yellow parrotfish. They skittered in schools, twisting and turning in unison and hightailing it out of sight if we came too close. We maneuvered around the large grooved brain corals or swam through corridors of delicate fern corals, trying all the time to avoid the stinging corals that left painful welts on our skin. Finally the floor of the ocean fell out from under us, and we hung over the precipice like flying birds looking down at larger creatures below.

During my first several trips to the reef, I was so mesmerized by this beauty I didn't notice that many of the larger fish were actually sharks bigger than I was. From then on I saw them each time and beat a hasty retreat to shallower water where I hoped they wouldn't follow. The most fearsome were the large hammerheads moving their heads like a vacuum cleaner from left to right to keep us in view. I became keenly aware of my disadvantage in this watery environment, realizing my skills at swimming were not as great as theirs. We were told that sharks in the Red Sea were not very dangerous because of the abundance of fish more easily eaten. But that was little consolation, and it wasn't long before Liesje and I were spending less and less time out by the reefs.

Sometimes when the weather was too cool to swim, we chose more sheltered spots to camp. One of my favorites was in the scrub desert among the foothills of the steep escarpment to Taif, the town where the royal family and other Jidda families stayed in summer. At that spot among the camel thorns, we heard the hooting of baboons eerily echoing among the canyon walls at night. Once, a herder passed through our camp with his flock of camels and stopped to ask Bill for a remedy for his inflamed eyes. Bill gave him a pair of sunglasses that he gratefully accepted.

In his job as director of the United States Information Service's (or the "United States Information Agency," as it was called in Washington) Cultural Center in Jidda, Bill met Saudis everyday who came in to read magazines or take out books. One was an older man who had written a book on the creatures of the Red Sea. From time to time he brought us peculiarly striped lobsters from the Red Sea. Most Saudis then didn't consume them because, like pigs, they were scavengers and therefore considered unclean. In later years even when most Saudis were still not eating pork, many thought nothing of eating lobster and other sea scavengers. He took us one evening to look for sea snakes that Saudi fishermen feared because of their poisonous bite. We held lanterns high to attract the snakes, and when they came close it was clear by the wariness of the fishermen that they were something to avoid.

Like me, Bill was taking every opportunity to meet a variety of Saudis. When U.S. astronauts landed on the moon, he presented bits of moon rock to local dignitaries and showed films of the landing. One disbelieving shaikh asked him, "How can Americans think we believe this story. Tell me what happens

when the moon disappears each month—what then do your astronauts do?"
I was pressed into showing the moon film to an audience of Saudi women.
The male technician set up the projector in the empty auditorium and told me
all I had to do was push the button, and then he left. The room filled with
hundreds of women, including a number of royal princesses. I pushed the button,
and the figures in the film started moving backward. Someone had rewound it
incorrectly! Not being technologically skilled, I had a moment of panic until I
realized I had to solve the problem myself—no man could enter a hall full of
Saudi women. So I calmed down, read the instructions, and rewound the thing
correctly. The audience, used to long delays in social events, sat patiently until I
got it right.

Bill made a visit to pay his respects to the famous blind shaikh of Mecca,
Shaikh bin Baz, who had decreed that the earth is flat. Every Saudi returning
from abroad paid his respects to this holy man. Several said they had to grow
beards before visiting him because when they kissed his hand he ran his little
finger along their chins to make sure they had a proper Islamic beard. Another
shaikh asked Bill why he wore his wedding ring on his "dirty hand" (used in the
toilet). Bill's Syrian assistant, knowing there was no real answer, quickly made
up an explanation. "Americans," he said, "use the finger of the left hand because
it connects directly to the heart," saving Bill from giving the impression that
Americans were disrespectful of their wives.

Jidda was buzzing one day with the news that a dead mermaid had washed
up on the Jidda beach. She had been turned over to the university and would
eventually be put on display. Someone from the university contacted Bill to ask
him to recommend a taxidermist. A month passed, and the excitement mounted
until the mermaid was finally put on display. Some Saudi women invited me
to go with them on the afternoon reserved for women. We stood in a long line
that snaked through the hall where the mermaid was encased. For nearly half
an hour we could see a picture of a mermaid suspended over the display case
but because of the crowds couldn't see the "real" mermaid until we were almost
next to the case. When our turn came we only had a moment to look at her
before those behind pushed us forward. I immediately recognized the creature
as a dugong or manatee with folds of flesh that might be mistaken for breasts
but with a distinct hairy mustache that should give anyone pause. Over coffee

later my friends described how she looked to those who hadn't seen her. Their descriptions exactly matched the picture suspended over the case rather than the animal we'd seen. I kept repeating the English name of the animal, but not knowing the word in Arabic, I didn't make much headway in explaining what it was. They seemed disinterested in any other explanation and wanted to believe that it was a mermaid, so I refrained from saying anything further. No one I spoke to felt in the least cheated by the experience; indeed, no one but I saw the creature as anything less than a true mermaid.

Looking back on our life in Jidda, I remember being elated by the opportunities opening up to know Saudi women either directly or indirectly through the foreign wives of Saudis. And it couldn't have been a better time for us as a family to travel along the unspoiled shoreline of the Red Sea. In hindsight, though, I see also that mine was a fairly timid encounter with the society. If I had to label it as a phase, I would say I was still focusing on "them-us" distinctions and feeling more comfortable in the presence of the Western wives who were closer to my own point of view than the Saudis. My memories as I recount them still show that sense of distance.

4

INTO THE INTERIOR:
RIYADH, SAUDI ARABIA (1967–1969)

We had been settled less than a year in Jidda when two events interrupted our lives. It was June 1967, and the region was erupting in a flurry of recriminations between Israelis and Arabs. We listened anxiously to the BBC and Voice of America as the crisis escalated. War eventually came, and although hostilities were over in six days, the region remained tense. Americans were evacuated from most embassies in the Middle East, and in Jidda we were told to prepare to leave. It seemed inevitable when a bomb went off in the embassy's electric room, but Ambassador Eilts went to King Faisal and he urged us to stay, saying he would be dishonored if he couldn't protect guests in his own country. The embassy ordered us to remain at home indefinitely until it could assess the situation. Eventually the bomber was caught—a quiet Palestinian gardener—and life returned to normal.

The second event was a request that we move to the capital Riyadh. At that time foreign embassies were located in Jidda, where Saudi officials believed the sophisticated coastal people could better withstand the cultural onslaught of foreigners. Inland Riyadh was home to conservative religious elements that resisted the contamination of "infidels." The Ministry of Education, however, wanted U.S. government help in setting up an English-language teaching center, and Bill's boss thought Bill was the perfect candidate to do it. We were thrilled to think of living in a remote part of Saudi Arabia, where we would be among only a handful of resident Westerners.

Riyadh in the late 1960s was a settlement of small houses surrounding the famous fortress where in 1902 Abdel Aziz ibn Saud with forty men overcame the al-Rasheed rulers and restored the country to al-Saud rule. What impressed me about Abdul Aziz, who by all accounts was a charismatic leader, was that he had more than 200 children by 17 known wives. His sons continued to rule Saudi Arabia into the twenty-first century although by then the last sons were in their seventies and eighties.

When we arrived in Riyadh, more than half the buildings were mud brick, including many of the beautiful royal palaces. In the modest souk surrounding the fort, one could buy basic items for housekeeping, while outside the old city, the town branched into satellite housing areas. Our house was several miles from town in a place called the "Officers Defense Area" where officers of the Saudi armed forces held land distributed by the king. Many lived elsewhere but built modest concrete villas to rent to Hejazi Saudis and the foreigners like us who worked in Riyadh.

From the beginning Riyadh felt different from Jidda. The first inkling came with a loud knock on our garden gate and an angry voice berating us. A herder was complaining that we were burning "Allah-given" goat food. He was referring to the packing straw that cushioned our household goods on the way to Riyadh. In a fit of conscientiousness, I had asked Hamud to burn the trash that we, like everyone else, threw into nearby vacant lots. The goat herder could not be placated and strode off, muttering Islamic injunctions. Needless to say, our garbage—including tin cans—rotted in the sun from then on and eventually disappeared into the stomachs of hungry goats.

Another indication of the austere Wahhabi environment was the strange pedestrian crosswalk signs that featured walking figures without heads to show they weren't real people and therefore didn't challenge God's capacity to create human beings. The prohibition extended to sculpture, I learned, when a friend went secretly to an underground sculptor to sit for a bust her husband commissioned. And in schools I saw charts, for example, of sheep production, where the images of the animals had red ribbons around their necks to show they too were inanimate. The mosques of Riyadh had raised platforms for prayer call, not the usual minarets that "protruded into God's space." Schools were forbidden from teaching music, but one private school showed me a secret cache of percussion instruments for its kindergarteners.

From my reading of Wahhabism, some of these examples seemed extreme even for the eighteenth-century founder of the movement, Mohammad ibn Abdul Wahab. Although he seems to have been against music, idolatry, and minarets, his main ire was directed at people who sought intervention to God through saints. He was for rational interpretation of Islamic law and opposed the rigid codification of Sharia laws. His aim was to return to a less complicated religious faith like that at the time of the Prophet. Whenever someone asked about my religious faith, I gained high approval by answering, "Unitarianism (*muwahidiin*)," the word used for Wahhabis' "belief in one God." Although Muslims believe in Jesus as a prophet, they reject Christianity's view of his divinity.

In Riyadh I was more careful about what I wore. The Saudis had not yet required foreigners to wear abayas and head scarves, so I had to decide what was appropriate. Most resident foreigners dressed modestly, and it was rare that anyone intentionally violated the codes. We could thank the tolerance of King Faisal and Ambassador Eilts's insistence that Americans shouldn't have to conform to local dress codes. In Riyadh I wore long dresses with long sleeves and a scarf when I went to the souk but in my own house and garden wore what I would in the United States.

One day my driver dropped me off at a store just as the call to prayer sounded. I had selected a light bulb when a *mutawwa* (religious policeman) burst in and scolded me for not covering my face and not leaving the shop so the shutter could be closed for prayer. I responded perhaps too aggressively by saying I was not a Muslim and therefore didn't need to cover my face. At that he would have hit me, had the shopkeeper not held his arm. He went looking for reinforcements. I paid for my purchase and quickly retreated to the car. As we drove off, I saw brown-gowned reinforcements with uplifted canes storming in our direction.

Ambassador Eilts immediately asked King Faisal to clarify the dress requirements for foreign women. The king announced that non-Muslim women didn't need to cover their faces. I was pleased at his stand but was careful to avoid further confrontations that might confirm the government's belief that Riyadh wasn't yet ready for foreigners.

Our house was new and therefore needed a lawn, a vegetable garden, and fast-growing trees. The first step was to order truckloads of soil from a nearby *wadi* (valley) to add a fertile layer over the sand. After several loads were delivered, I found the boys poking sticks at some interesting "bugs" only to discover that hundreds of scorpions had been delivered with the soil. Hamud smashed them with great ferocity until the last was destroyed, and the boys went back to safely building sand castles in the backyard.

The boys and I loved the long afternoons in Riyadh as the sun crept toward the horizon and the world became bearably cool again. Sometimes we rode our donkeys (we had two now) to a friend's house a mile away. Other times we climbed the hill behind our house for an unencumbered view across the desert as the light faded into pale violets, pinks, and blues. Bill's parents sent us a kite shaped like an eagle, and one evening we sent the kite soaring into the darkening sky. Suddenly a volley of gunshots rang out, and ten or so Bedouins came rushing toward us, trying to shoot down the larger-than-life bird. When they realized it was "tied" to me, they approached cautiously to examine it. One sheepishly offered to buy it, but I declined, explaining it was a gift from the boys' paternal grandparents, the only gracious way of refusing such a request. I felt ashamed, knowing in the same circumstance a Saudi would have given it to me without hesitation.

Bill, meanwhile, opened the new language center and almost immediately had problems. On the first day of classes, students came to Bill to say they couldn't use the bathrooms because the toilets had been installed incorrectly. It was unacceptable that they were forced to face Mecca when they urinated. The bathrooms had to be redone. Most students used footprint toilets at homes and therefore found the Western toilets in the center difficult to use. After many seats were broken, a sign was installed saying, "Please don't stand on the seats!" The next, more serious problem involved a magazine that appeared inadvertently in the center's library with a picture of the Prophet Muhammad. The picture was removed quietly before it became a major crisis.

A persistent problem was the late arrival of Western periodicals that languished in the censor's office until he had time to scribble over the images of women's cleavages, bare legs, exposed arms, and other forbidden content. Among the taboo subjects were negative mentions of Islam or the Saudi government and any use of profanity or sexual references. Often the blacked-out portions leaked onto other pages, obliterating them as well, or the censor simply ripped out pages.

The center's staff established a small newsletter for English-speaking officials. At first the post office merely grumbled at the extra load of work each month. Then they rebelled completely and told our staff to cancel the stamps before bringing them to the post office. This worked until the day the staff was informed there were no more stamps in Riyadh. The government had forgotten to order new ones. "When would they be available?" "Well maybe six months." From then on the newsletters went to Jidda, where the post office worked more efficiently.

In Riyadh the older boys attended an international school. We especially liked the international student body that included Saudis and other nationalities. The school became the focus of our activities as a family—the one public place where we could relax in austere Riyadh. Foreigners and Saudis alike celebrated American holidays there. One Halloween I dressed as a fortune-teller to forecast the future through my crystal ball. Little did I know that this act was anathema to local Wahhabis—if they had known—a challenge to God's prerogative of knowing the future. At home the boys and I dressed in homemade costumes— the boys as munchkins with burlap sacks giving them grotesquely large heads and small bodies. David rang the doorbell to surprise Hamud, but upon seeing him, Hamud chased David around the compound, smacking him repeatedly with a broom. When he found out it was David, he was mortified. "Oh, Madam, I once saw exactly the same devil in the mountains of Yemen. I would never have harmed David."

A few months into the academic year, the boys brought home a notice saying the school was closed. The Saudi authorities objected to boys and girls studying in the same classes and to Muslim students not receiving sufficient instruction in Arabic and religion. The boys studied at home for several months with books and assignments sent out from the school. The negotiations dragged on from October through January with several prominent Saudis trying to intervene. Our school unfortunately came under the department headed by the conservative shaikh who had been appointed to oversee girls' education. (Girls' education remained under this shaikh until 2002 when a fire killed fifteen schoolgirls who had been prevented from fleeing by guards with instructions not to let them leave school uncovered.)

The two sides finally compromised. Two separate sections were arranged— the larger one for girls plus young boys through grade two, and another for older boys from grade three on. The girls had to wear long sleeves and skirts below their knees. Saudi children were banned from the school (those with American passports stayed on) while non-Saudi Muslims had to prove their foreign origins. The school went back to normal but sadly without many Saudi children.

Living in Riyadh we were relieved of most of the tedious obligations imposed by diplomatic life. But as the only American diplomats there, we often provided accommodations for U.S. officials coming on business. One particularly enjoyable guest was the director of the National Zoo in Washington. He had come to advise the Saudis on their zoo that consisted of animals either captured locally or presented to the royal family as gifts. To see the zoo in its natural state, he made his first visit before the authorities knew he was in town. He found cages too small, poor sanitation, improper food, and more. Indeed, the flimsy cages barely separated the animals from the people, and a favorite sport was for the visitors to flip their headscarves at the animals to see what they would do. The director was appalled at the teasing but later became intrigued by the two-way game and went back several times to watch. Once he arrived before the zoo opened and was surprised to find the animals obviously anticipating the arrival of the people. He eventually concluded the animals were psychologically better off than in most American zoos where no interaction was possible. The director made his report, and although I don't know if the games continued, the Saudis soon had a state-of-the-art zoo.

The director volunteered to watch the boys one Friday so we could go shopping. The souk opened on Friday after the noonday sermon at the Grand Mosque. The word "Friday" in Arabic means "the gathering," and the word for "mosque" is another derivation of "to gather." One of the main aims of early Islam had been to establish a community of believers whose solidarity would eliminate the divisive loyalties of family and tribe. Most towns had a main "Friday mosque" where the physically able went to pray. That particular Friday we timed our arrival for the end of prayers. People were streaming from the mosque and congregating in Judicial Square. Something seemed about to happen, so when a friend suggested we join him in his apartment overlooking the square, we agreed. A truck drove up and deposited fist-sized rocks in the middle of the square. Another brought a man with his hands bound behind his back and left him near the courthouse wall. Then the enormous bodyguard of the mayor of

Riyadh appeared with ten or so judges of the court. The audience hushed as he read a proclamation stating that the bound man's crime was adultery and the punishment death. The judges arrayed themselves in front of the accused while the victim's relatives moved forward to witness the stoning. They had been given the choice of accepting financial compensation or his death, and had chosen death. The bodyguard gave the signal, a hood was placed over the adulterer's head, and he was forced to kneel facing the judges. At another signal the judges began tossing stones at his head. Soon he was lying on his side with stones surrounding him. The bodyguard bent down to listen to his chest and with clicks of his fingers indicated that his heart was still beating. The judges threw the stones more forcefully, and twenty minutes later the man was dead. They loaded the body onto the truck and drove away.

Stoning to death was and still is an infrequent occurrence in Riyadh, and news spread quickly about the details of the case. The two people involved were from separate tribes. He, a married man, chanced upon the young woman not yet married as she was drawing water from a well. He raped her, and she became pregnant. When her condition became known, the government imprisoned her as protection from her relatives who might kill her to restore their honor. Somehow there had been enough evidence to convict the rapist. According to Islamic law either four witnesses must see the act or he must confess his crime. At the time of the stoning, the tribes would normally be readying themselves for revenge killings. By stepping in and executing the man, the government satisfied the honor of the wronged tribe and thereby prevented the deaths of many more on both sides. Someone asked me later how I felt watching the execution, and I said quite honestly that if I were a Saudi I would not commit adultery.

Another punishment carried out in Judiciary Square involved the cutting off of a thief's hand after repeated offenses. Riyadh was an astonishingly safe place to live. Several times I carelessly left my purse in a shop, and before I knew it was missing, someone had always returned it to me. Whatever one thinks of these punishments, displaying them publicly seems to have acted as a deterrent.

We started receiving invitations from Saudis to evening parties and picnics in nearby oases. One group of Saudi couples who had just returned from studying in the United States invited us for a picnic one day. I donned my conservative outfit and scarf only to find that the Saudi women were anything but conservative. One even wore a leopard miniskirt.

One unusual invitation was to a party of Saudi couples put on by a prominent minister. The minister pulled me aside and asked if I would teach English to one of the women at the gathering, a strikingly beautiful and vivacious Saudi woman. As usual I saw it as an opportunity to know Saudis but didn't want the minister to think I was a person to be hired, so I told him I would teach her for free. Knowing that Saudis are casual about time, I arranged to give the lessons at her home, where I could regulate the beginning and end of the sessions. She did indeed turn out to be fun, and it was only as the lessons were coming to an end that I learned she was the minister's mistress and that her husband was compensated with lucrative contracts from his ministry. Despite the fact that she learned very little, she showered gifts on me to reciprocate the favor I had done for her, thus saving face for both of us.

I was becoming known as a person who could teach English, probably as an extension of Bill's work. Soon I found myself teaching a princess, the daughter-in-law of former king Saud, who lived out of town in one of his palaces. I agreed on the basis that I would not charge but that I would need transport. Sunday afternoons her driver would arrive in a low-slung sports car and honk at my door. I would wedge myself into the back with one or more of the boys, and off we would fly across the desert to her palace. The boys would go off to ride horses with her sons, and I would be taken to a large plastic Quonset hut in the middle of her rose garden. Soon she would waft into the room, smelling of perfume from her bath, and accompanied by a retinue of relatives and servants who settled around her to listen to the lesson.

The princess, in her late twenties, had little education, and because she was unaccustomed to the written word, I stuck to spoken English. But after a year we had not progressed beyond lesson two in my primer. "This is a table." "What is it?" "It is a table." I attributed her slow progress to her lack of education, but I probably wasn't a very good teacher either, and certainly the venue was not conducive to learning.

Her husband, nicknamed the "Black Prince" because of his skin color, received his guests in a huge goat-hair tent outside the palace walls, so the women could have the freedom of the gardens. The Quonset hut served as an audience hall and as the afternoon progressed the lesson was interrupted by the arrival of guests. The lesson would start, "This is a pencil." "This a pencil," she would repeat. "Ahlaaan, I haven't seen you for so long; where have you been?" she would shout out to some newcomers. She'd rise to kiss them and send her servants scurrying to get drinks. After catching up with their news, she would fall silent, and I would come in with, "What is this?" "I don't know," she would mumble in Arabic. After several hours of these fits and starts, the lesson was over, and we would go into the palace for an elaborate feast. Other royal women would join us, including the slave mother of the Black Prince who, because she produced a son for the king, was given equal status at the table.

Once while waiting for dinner, the princess took me on a tour of the palace. Instead of the cushions found in the living areas of simpler Saudi homes, the huge rooms of the palace were lined with immense over-stuffed chairs along three walls. In the center opposite the entrance was an even more magnificent chair for King Saud. The king's bedroom had a picture of naked women hung behind the headboard of a huge bed and a ceiling covered in mirrors. After dinner the sports car would be waiting for me, and we would hurtle across the desert toward home.

Although the lessons were not productive, I gained a lot from the experience, not the least of which was a better understanding of Saudi Arabic. I grew to respect the princess's skills in managing the palace and the way she acted as a kind of tribal chieftain to solve the problems of her visitors. Among those who dropped by were rough Bedouin women, barefoot and masked in typical Bedouin fashion and smelling of wood smoke and goats. Some came to sell her gum Arabic (*mistika*) or frankincense (*luban*) and sandlewood (*oud*) that she burnt on smoldering coals to perfume the palace and pass to her guests. She picked through the pieces to find the best quality and then conducted a formidable bargaining. Women told her their complaints: one was abused by a husband; one had no money to feed her children; another had her property stolen. The onlookers clucked sympathetically while the princess listened respectfully and then found a way—usually financial—to console the victims. Also impressive was her dealings with the male manager of the palace. When he clapped his hands to announce his presence, the women hastily covered their faces. He would lay out his account book and receipts, and the princess behind her veil would review everything, questioning him closely about each price. I saw she was good with numbers, adding them in her head and correcting his mistakes. I imagined this came from years of running the palace rather than from her brief schooling.

Each time I left, I invited the princess to visit me in town. I didn't expect her to come because royal family members rarely visited commoners. But one day when I was alone, a horn blared at my gate. I went to see who it was, and there stood the driver informing me that the princess had come to visit. I immediately welcomed her, with more enthusiasm than I felt, and she and her retinue disgorged themselves with difficulty from the tiny sports car. I ushered them into the house, mentally ticking off the requirements of hospitality: cold drink, sweets, and ultimately coffee, none of which I was sure I had available. After they were seated, I asked them in the American way what they would like to drink and suggested a number of possibilities. They were used to having drinks presented on trays and looked surprised at my list. Each seemed to choose something different—a Coke, tea, lemonade, Sprite. Feeling helpless without Hamud, I nevertheless defrosted lemonade and cookies from the freezer, boiled water, opened drink cans, and set everything on various trays. It took time, but eventually I carried them into the living room. There the women were deep into the contents of a chest filled with various shawls and materials. Others had disappeared into adjacent rooms to examine the contents of my cupboards. They reassembled to drink the beverages and eat my cookies, which were a modest offering compared to the frosting-covered concoctions the princess served. Fortunately Hamud returned at this point and produced a coffee tray that in a Saudi household signaled the end of a gathering. I carried it out to them while he remained out of sight in the kitchen. I prayed they wouldn't wait for the incense any self-respecting hostess would offer since I didn't have any. To my relief they piled back into the car and left me to put my house in order.

I felt pleased they had come. Few Saudi women at the time had ever traveled outside the country, and it was probably an adventure to see how a foreigner lived. I'm sure the modesty of my house, the lack of servants, the simplicity of my food, and the plainness of my furnishings must have proved a disappointment. I in turn was surprised at how the mannered behavior I saw at the princess's majlis suddenly disappeared in their eagerness to explore my possessions.

In Riyadh I sometimes went to the afternoon gatherings of another princess who was known for her lesbian leanings. She always seated me next to her on the floor so "we could drink *lassi* (a yoghurt drink) together." I remember her exclaiming over the beauty of a Scandinavian woman who entered the hall, sounding much like a construction worker commenting on attractive females walking by. No matter how conservatively foreigners dressed, they always seemed half naked in comparison to local women, with too much hair or ankle or figure exposed. This same princess asked a Jordanian guest why she was leaving the party early, and when the woman whispered the reason, the princess announced loudly that this co-wife had to prepare for her turn with her husband. Rarely were such matters talked of so openly, especially matters related to homosexuality, which most Saudis felt was prohibited by Islam.

Heterosexual relations were a different matter and very much encouraged within the marital relationship. In Riyadh I attended gatherings of women where a particular attendant to the royal family was often present. She was from the slaves who had been imported to serve wealthy Saudis and stayed on in an ambiguous status after slavery was banned in 1963. She acted as a kind of court jester and was said to conduct sexual "training" for girls when they were about to marry. Presumably they were innocently unaware of sexual matters since married women were careful not to discuss such matters in front of them. I never saw her in her trainer role but frequently observed her playing the court jester. Part of her repertoire included stories that were sexual in content—some said to motivate the women to perform well for their husbands. One evening when she ran out of amusing stories, she turned to me for inspiration. She loudly asked conventional questions about where I came from, my family, and more. With each answer she mimicked my accented Arabic and distorted my mannerisms until everyone was convulsed with laughter. I was at a loss to know what to do. Should I refuse to answer and seem angry, or continue to let her mock me and join in the hilarity? My answers got shorter and shorter, and finally to my relief she turned to other subjects. She would never have insulted Saudi guests this way, but I was vulnerable as an outsider with no family to defend me. Often she made jokes at the expense of servants who, like me, were also vulnerable.

As in Jidda, I started receiving invitations to Saudi women's parties, where the talk was again about births, sickness, deaths, weddings, and divorces. I found the conversations boring, but stuck with them to improve my Arabic. I was beginning to realize that Bill's and my vocabularies were beginning to diverge. I understood "women's talk" but still found it difficult to understand "men's talk." At some point we accepted the differences and specialized in the areas where we were most proficient—he in the more educated men's talk and I in the women's talk of family and household.

A Saudi Bill knew one day asked if I could visit his French wife who was in the hospital. They had recently come back from studying abroad, and she had just had a baby who, although seemingly healthy, suddenly died. Far from home, she was feeling lonely with no one to talk to. We saw each other frequently after that, and the four of us took trips around Riyadh on weekends to find historic sites that Bill later wrote up in a small booklet. It was thrilling to visit a hillside where a battle had been fought with the Turks and find pieces of cannon balls lodged in the sand. They had several children, and we still visited them forty years later when he retired to Tunisia to be near a married daughter.

Two trips out of Riyadh gave us a new respect for desert dwellers. The first was arranged by a manager of Citibank whose children were friends of ours. David and I joined the trip, which had as its destination Medain Saleh, a remote valley with tombs left behind 2,000 years before by a little-known Nabatean civilization. The valley was virtually untouched by modern life except for the remnants of the Hejaz Railway made famous by Col. T. E. Lawrence during World War I. A railway station contained ancient locomotives and train carriages with bullet holes still visible. The valley was extraordinary beautiful with huge sweeping vistas interrupted only by cliff tombs scattered picturesquely at its edges.

We were greeted outside Medina by our guides in a fleet of pickup trucks piled high with tents and cooking gear. The men served us cups of cardomom-laced coffee and left us to wait. Since it was a full day's journey, the Westerners began asking when we would start. I reminded myself that it's not a good idea to ask too many questions about arrangements. The Bedouin don't know the answers, and their sense of time is highly flexible. The Western men, however, seem to have difficulty with such uncertainty.

Eventually a truck appeared carrying sheep and alfalfa. The rest of the day we careened along desert tracks at breakneck speeds as the drivers competed to take the lead. Sometimes they diverged around rocky outgrowths the size of mountains and emerged into the same open valley beyond. But every now and then we backtracked to rescue a vehicle that hadn't appeared within a reasonable time. Eventually night fell, and we became hopelessly lost. Each driver argued for a separate track and finally agreed on one. The moon came up so it was easier to see the open expanses of silvery desert. About midnight the guides stopped, even though we were still far from our destination. They erected huge tents— one for men and one for women. The Western men switched to the "quieter" women's tent to the amusement of the Saudis. The cook slaughtered a sheep and hours later a delicious stew was ready. But by that time the Westerners were asleep, including David, who had been content with my supply of peanut butter crackers.

The Bedouin do well with little sleep, and a few hours later at sunrise they were laying out carpets for the daybreak prayer. We Westerners straggled out of our tents still tired from the tensions of the day before and silently ate our breakfast of flat bread and white cheese and a concoction of dates and orange juice stirred into a black paste—all of it washed down with milk-tea perfumed by the smoke of the cooking fires. When I asked about the orange-date mixture, the cook said, "It stays in your stomach all day," and indeed with stops for tea we weren't hungry until the next sheep was slaughtered that evening.

We continued on toward Medain Saleh with the trucks moving every which way and requiring numerous stops to dig them out. While we waited for a punctured tire to be patched, one Bedouin asked me what it would cost to acquire an American bride. He phrased it in terms of the dowry, and I answered, "Nothing." When the others started looking interested, I dampened their ardor by saying American women wouldn't marry them if they couldn't provide the appliances Americans expected. As the water boiled, I enumerated a list of these items—washing machines, dryers, refrigerators—and at their request, added up the costs. Their faces fell. One finally said, "We only pay X for a dowry," and went away feeling the superiority of their own ways.

On a second trip to Medain Saleh, a friend Faisal came along with us, driving a low-slung sports car unsuited to the heavily rutted trails. The boys loved the car and took turns riding with him and listening to stories of his boyhood on the desert. One night as we were settling into our sleeping bags, gunshots rang out. Faisal investigated and found that tribesmen had seen our campfire and were announcing their arrival the traditional way in case women were about. Faisal invited them to sit next to the fire, while I started the kettle for tea—out of sight of course. They sat cross-legged on a carpet and began a series of comments and questions interspersed with long pauses as they digested the information. Had we seen rain? How far had we traveled and from where? In what direction were we going? Both sides were trying to figure out the identities of the other without directly asking. Much later they stood to embrace one another, relieved to know their tribes were not embroiled in a revenge cycle that might compel them to take some action.

Another time we saw a lone Bedouin, and Faisal warned us to hide our watches and other valuables, and to drive on if anything happened to him. The "dance" of the tea drinking resolved itself in another positive identification and we drove on. The area we were traveling through was less well-known to Faisal, and perhaps for this reason he was wary of strangers. We never knew exactly what he was thinking since in characteristic Saudi fashion he reported the conversation but without comment on its meaning. Unlike Americans who characteristically spill their innermost thoughts, Saudis never explained. Perhaps they felt it was too complicated for foreigners to understand. Or perhaps information was too valuable to be given lightly. In any case we became keener observers trying to fathom what was going on.

Of one thing we were certain: it took an act of courage every time Faisal met a stranger, and we began to understand why he carried a gun everywhere. As outsiders we were comparatively safe on the desert, where we were treated with courtesy and generosity. One anthropologist studying tribal behavior once commented that hospitality to foreigners gave the most credit to a host's reputation since they were unlikely to reciprocate. Listening to Faisal's stories of his childhood and observing his scrupulously mannered behavior made us respect the harsh world of the Bedouin and the sophisticated skill they seemed to possess for handling social relations.

One of our friends in Riyadh had an amazing story to tell. "Ahmad" was the son of a tribal chief in Saudi Arabia. When we first met him, he was just back from the United States with a university degree and an American wife, and lived in a modest house not much bigger than ours. Eventually he rose to become one of the highest officials in the Saudi government as well as one of the nation's richest men.

Ahmad grew up on the desert in his father's tent. As was the practice during the hot summer months, the tribe gathered around wells that were located in their *dirah* (rightful lands). The government was beginning to provide services such as health care and schools near the wells to encourage the nomads to settle, so Ahmad enrolled in one of these schools and became an excellent student. He related how when he saw the Syrian teacher for the first time with her face and ankles uncovered he rushed home to tell his mother he had seen a "naked" woman. When his tribe was ready to leave on the winter migration, he convinced his father to let him stay with a relative living near the school. This continued each year until he finished high school.

After graduation his father wanted him to take on the duties of a chief's son, but Ahmad resisted and went to live in a town on the Gulf. His father cut off his support so Ahmad took a job in an airline office to improve his English and earn a free ticket to the United States, where he hoped to enroll in a university. When he saved enough money, he flew to the United States where he was dismayed to find that the university in Washington where he enrolled was not the best in the United States. By the second semester he transferred to a university in Boston and lived in an international student dorm. Soon he ran out of money and for a time supported himself as a Fuller Brush man, but it still wasn't enough. He had only a few dollars left when he heard the Saudi king was visiting the United States and managed to speak to him in an elevator, asking for what was usual at the time, a government scholarship to study in an American university. The king discovered Ahmad's father didn't want him to receive any money. Desperate Ahmad wrote to a Mecca newspaper, and just as he was down to his last pennies, a large check came from a member of the royal family who was impressed by his initiative. Ahmad finished his studies, went back to Saudi Arabia, reconciled with his father, and later returned with his father's blessing to the United States to earn a Ph.D.

In Riyadh, I accompanied a journalist to see the agricultural lands that had been reserved to resettle the Bedouin. Ahmad described the futility of trying to make the Bedouin into agriculturalists. Nomads, he said, saw farm work as manual labor and therefore to be disdained. Tribesmen felt the nobility of their way of life could only be sustained in a desert environment outside government control. The Saudi authorities countered by saying that nomads couldn't be good Muslims if their children were unable to read the Koran or if they couldn't wash properly before prayer. Officials in the 1960s and 1970s managed to instill such a sense of shame in the Bedouin that many dropped their tribal names and moved to towns where they found jobs in the oil industry and the military. Eventually with airpower and vehicles, the government controlled the deserts, and the Bedouin realized there was no point in keeping up a nomadic way of life.

Recently we had lunch with Ahmad in Washington and had a chance to reminisce about our experiences during those early days in Riyadh. By that time he had become a tribal chief with members of his tribe living in a quarter of Riyadh near him. He described how tribalism was now reviving and flourishing albeit in an urban environment. Saudi policy recently changed when authorities saw the advantages in letting chiefs solve the problems of their people before they reached the government. Moreover, after 9/11 the government needed the tribal leaders to take responsibility for suppressing radicalism if it appeared among their young people. To track people, the government reinstated tribal names on identity cards. Ahmad says the government has conceded considerable autonomy to the tribal leaders, and tribal members are pleased to have their sense of dignity back. Moreover, he says with a smile, "our women feel secure in an urban quarter where they can work and move freely among their own kin."

In the 1960s, Riyadh was a central place from which to travel. We drove to the Gulf to see Dhahran and the Aramco oil company where a U.S.-style community with bowling allies, cinemas, swimming pools, and lawns created an American suburb in the desert. Sometimes we took picnics to the pink sands of the Al-Nafud, where the boys loved tumbling head over heels down the rosy slopes. Once we took a trip to the conservative town of Buraida to see the famous camel markets. Women there, including foreign women, had to wear trailing black cloaks that "erased their footsteps" as they walked.

Our longest trip was twelve days along the edges of the Rub al-Khali (the Empty Quarter). We set out with friends in three cars, believing with the arrogance of the ignorant, that we could emerge unscathed from open desert travel. In the end we did, but not without moments when it seemed we would never locate the barrels of gasoline that constituted the widely separated "filling stations" of the desert.

Ahead of us each day, tracks struck out in every direction, and we had to guess which ones to take. The Bedouin we met had no idea where our ultimate destination town of Najran was located, and so we asked from our inaccurate map how to find a "Green Mountain" or "Black Mountain" that turned out to be only descriptors of the mountains. Another common name on the U.S. Geological maps was Jabel Ma'arif, which some innocent mapmaker hadn't realized meant "I Don't Know Mountain." We got stuck a dozen times a day and had to dig ourselves out. Worse, our Chevy carryall had more than a dozen punctures from sharp basalt rocks, until finally the tires were worn so thin we had to use the extra ones from our friend's Toyota. Ahead of us each day storm clouds gathered menacingly on the horizon, and we knew enough about the dangers of flash floods to camp on dunes high above the plains where we would be safe if an avalanche of water cascaded through.

Luckily the rain held off until we turned north again. But one day we rounded a bend and in front of us lay an angrily roiling river, cutting off our road and leaving us with few happy options. Should we return the way we had come or wait days on the bank of the river until it became a dry gully again? We watched large Mercedes trucks making it through, but most passenger cars were waiting for the water to recede. We scouted out a place that seemed relatively shallow, and the Land Rover and Toyota, both with exhaust pipes on the roof, made it across easily. We started our Chevy in second gear and soon were struggling. Not realizing the danger, Bill shifted to first, and water rushed in the tail pipe. The car stopped dead, and the water rose up until it covered my knees. The car was about to roll over. Someone suddenly wrenched open my door and took Nicholas from my arms. I struggled out and was barely able to stand in the raging current. Hands pulled open the back doors and carried the two other boys to safety. While we watched from the bank, a group of Saudis and Yemenis hooked a chain to the car and attached it to a large Mercedes truck that winched it slowly out of the river. I was weeping uncontrollably with the Saudi drivers gathered around to console me. Our car started up again, but the brakes failed a few miles down the road so we squeezed into the other cars. The trip left me respectful of the perils of the desert and with a deep gratitude for the drivers who saved us.

Other parts of the trip from Riyadh to Najran to Taif left better memories. Nothing compares with the brilliance of the stars at night or waking up in the cool mornings and knowing from their tracks that scores of tiny insects and animals have come to investigate. We encountered Bedouin who wanted to slaughter sheep or camels for us. Emir Khalid Sidari, the governor of Najran, gave us his guesthouse and fed us royally for two days. During his evening majlis we heard of the death of King Saud in exile. Emir Khalid gave the boys a tiny gazelle that they desperately wanted to take back to Hamud. We couldn't refuse his gift and asked him to keep it until we came back.

Life as it was in the late 1960s is essentially gone now. The mud brick houses are replaced by lavish homes and palaces. Crisscrossing modern highways leave us as perplexed as the desert tracks did in the old days. Place names have no meaning, and I can no longer find our old home or even the road that used to lead to it.

When I visited Riyadh again in the late 1990s, the Syrian secretary of a princess guided me around a folkloric exhibit at the fairgrounds. It was ladies' day, and the grounds were filled with black-robed figures. In one tent I watched university students, graceful in their abayas and veils, buying cheap replicas of the old kitchen utensils we once used. "But what do you do with this?" I heard one ask the salesperson. She didn't know, so I stepped in to explain the art of coffee-making to the young women. "You take the coffee beans, and put them in this oversize metal spoon that you hold out to the fire, always stirring them with this long thin metal rod so they won't burn. You then put the roasted beans into this container (a mortar) and crush them with this pestle, adding cardamom if you like. The noise of the brass pestle makes a music that can be heard from a distance and it was the custom in those days for anyone who heard it to come for coffee. You know the rest, how the ground coffee and water are put in a pot and brought to a boil three times before it's poured into little cups." "Oh," they exclaimed, taking it all in, "Life must have been difficult in those days." I went away feeling I had come full circle, from learning like a clumsy child from Saudi women who seemed to know everything in the 1960s to instructing their granddaughters in skills I now knew better than they did.

5

RIMA: RIYADH, SAUDI ARABIA
(1967–1969)

My neighbor in Riyadh was a young Syrian woman married to a rising official in the Ministry of Petroleum. Several people suggested I knock on her door and introduce myself, even though in conservative Riyadh formal introductions were a more normal first step. The prospect of knowing a neighbor was appealing given the difficulties of transport and phone connections.

One sparkling winter day about mid-morning, I prepared a short introductory speech in Arabic and knocked at the iron gate of her compound. A small boy hesitantly opened the door, and I asked if the "Sitt" was home. Terrified at my foreignness, he nodded and closed the door quickly to prevent my entering. I heard him shouting urgently for someone to come. Soon there was a flurry of footsteps and a female voice reprimanding the boy for leaving me standing inhospitably in the sun. The door opened and there was Rima.

I don't know exactly what I expected—probably a more modestly cloaked and veiled woman like the Saudis I was used to. But whatever it was I momentarily forgot my carefully prepared speech and simply stared. She wore slacks, a blouse, and sandals instead of the traditional Saudi floor-length, waisted dress. Her light brown hair hung loosely down her back, not in the conventional tightly pinned bun at the nape of her neck. Her beautiful face with its alabaster complexion was already wreathed in a welcoming smile, while her gray-green eyes sparkled with sympathy as she saw me suddenly struck dumb by her appearance. I regained my composure and began my stumbling speech while she waited patiently for me to finish. She said simply, "Hi, you must be my neighbor. Please come in. I apologize for keeping you waiting in the sun." Her father had been a diplomat, and from living abroad she had learned enough English to let her natural loquaciousness take over. Sometimes at parties where she single-handedly tried to keep the conversation going with the English speakers, her mistakes brought the house down. She "raped a package for a friend's birthday." Or she didn't sleep well because of her husband's "sneering." She enjoyed these mistakes as much as we did. She also quickly polished her French because our neighbor from Lebanon—the daughter of a previous prime minister—couldn't speak any other language and Rima wanted to bring her into the conversation.

Rima ushered me into her modest concrete-block house, drew aside the heavy velvet drapes of the parlor, and threw open the creaky shutters to let in the air. A ray of sunlight lit up the disturbed dust particles dancing in the center of the room. I sat on a plush gilt sofa, upholstered in damascene tapestry. An intricate oriental rug covered the white marble floor and defined the sitting area. A number of gilt and marble tables were scattered around the room with their surfaces covered in knickknacks. I came to recognize in later years that this was the typical style of the Damascene middle and upper-middle classes. But here in Saudi Arabia it was a style beginning to be fashionable in the homes of wealthy Saudis. To my Western eye—still too judgmental of tastes that weren't mine—the room was a clash of colors and pretensions. I crossed my legs carefully to avoid endangering the bric-a-brac and waited while Rima brought lemonade and nuts and later sweet biscuits and tea. And thus began a wonderful friendship.

It was not easy to carry on a friendship with Rima for reasons that were typically Saudi. Our schedules conflicted to such a degree that there were few moments when we could get together. After waking her several times with my "early" morning calls, including that first day, I realized how difficult it would be, although out of hospitality she never admitted any time was inconvenient. I rose at 7:30 a.m., she at 10:30 a.m. I ate lunch at 12, she at 2:30 p.m. after a morning of preparations. She napped until 5:00 p.m. and went to bed about 2:00 a.m.

Her husband worked from about 10:00 a.m. until 2:00 p.m., ate and napped, and then visited or received his men friends until late in the evening. I learned it was not proper to call on women when their husbands were home or to stay if they returned home unexpectedly. Before I visited I assessed the situation at the door by the number of cars and, if the door was ajar, the sandals lined up in the courtyard. When Rima's husband was home the entire family and staff were completely absorbed in providing for him, preparing his foods, shushing the children so he could nap, or bringing his coffee. His schedule alone meant I could only conveniently visit Rima between 11:00 a.m. and 12:30 p.m., and even then she was constantly giving orders to her servants, buying vegetables for his lunch, or receiving phone calls about when he expected to be home.

On top of these activities there were prayer calls to contend with, including one around noon. She was fairly casual about the midday prayer, but I knew she tried to do them all and felt guilty when she missed any, especially the obligatory ones. And I in turn felt guilty when I prevented her from praying, which was apparent from the prayer call ringing loudly from the neighborhood mosque. Sometimes if there was a lull in our conversation, she would go into another room and roll out her prayer rug. With all this activity, we rarely had time for extended conversations—I just tried to fit in to the activity of the moment.

Another obstacle was that she could never reciprocate my calls because of the presence of my male Yemeni servant and the possibility that my husband or our office driver might drop in at any moment. Perhaps a more important reason was that foreigners were unreliable and ignorant about Saudi social rules. Better to avoid any hint of impropriety by not visiting me than to have Saudi neighbors talking about her. But also I was becoming aware that I was a nonentity in this society. With no social standing other than as a guest to whom hospitality was owed, I was in the embarrassing position of always taking and not giving. Was she really as eager to see me as she seemed? Or was I an inconvenience or, even worse, a duty? I never knew. I did know, though, that in terms of Rima's priorities I stood far behind other Arabs, Saudis, and family members. With these others, she impeccably kept up the reciprocity of favors and calls that are the basis of Arab society.

So since 11:00 a.m. turned out to be the best time for visiting, I would drop by then and share her breakfast of tea, olives, cheese, and Arab bread. If I stayed long enough I could help her prepare the noon meal and learn to make dishes I enjoyed in other households. Once I had expressed an interest in Arab cooking, Rima invited me to join her in the kitchen, and indeed she took it as an obligation to teach me what she knew. It was one of her talents to be able to instruct me in an elemental way that was rare in Arab women. Most would list "pinches of this and that," with no additional explanations about what to do with the pinches or when to add them.

I soaked up everything Rima taught me—in cooking as well as in human relations. "Look, Andrea, in cooking we have to follow the lead of the Hajja. She has long experience in these things." And I came to know that age breeds authority and wisdom. She would add, "It makes her feel good to know we can't get along without her advice." The Hajja had been her family's servant ever since Rima was a baby in Syria. When Rima had her second child, her mother sent Hajja to Saudi Arabia to help her out, even though by that time the Hajja was old and incapacitated and unable to do much more than give moral support. Rima would ask innocently, "How big should I cut the onions, Hajja, for the *fatet magdus*?" even though she had made the dish hundreds of times. And the Hajja would beam. No wonder she was willing to leave her family and travel thousands of miles to help Rima. Another time Rima telephoned her mother in Damascus. "Ummi, tell me do you put the sauce on first or the yoghurt for fatet magdus?" With a twinkle in her eye, she would say, "My mother loves to think I can't cook without her." She called her mother several times a week to make her feel indispensable to the workings of Rima's household.

When I was ready to go home, Rima would plead with me to stay. "But Andrea, you just came, it's too early to go." And I would list the numerous tasks I had to complete before my children returned from school. One day Rima sighed and said, "You know the difference between us is that you wake up in the morning and make a list of twenty things you hope to accomplish in the day, and if you only complete nineteen you're unhappy. I wake up knowing there are twenty things I should do and if I accomplish one I'm happy because I didn't expect to finish any." These words struck me as a metaphor not only to describe the differences between us but between our two cultures. Rima's list never gets accomplished because she takes advantage of the day's unexpected opportunities. Perhaps a neighbor comes for a visit, or a friend needs help with a party, or she plays with her son in the garden, or she hears someone is sick and goes to visit. Maybe she finds that the fruit has ripened on a tree in her garden and takes it to a friend to enjoy, or someone wants her to go shopping to meet her new dressmaker. I've seen Rima do all these things, and I know she gets more satisfaction from these encounters than she would ticking off impersonal lists of "to do" tasks. She welcomes the opportunities to tilt the balance to her side in the game of doing favors for others. I couldn't help envying the richness of her life—not in the negative "evil eye" way that would have made her recoil—but with admiration for a society that prioritized human contacts over impersonal accomplishments. I believed completely in the idea, but hard as I tried, I still felt better completing my lists than having my day interrupted with visitors. In the end my list became shorter, and I tried to make human relations more central. Only later in the United States did I realize how offensive my excuses must have been to Rima, when I invited a neighbor for a cup of coffee and she refused because she had to do her weekly shopping that day!

As I got to know her better, layers of her personality and philosophy unfolded. She believed deeply in her Muslim faith but didn't distinguish clearly between Islam and a world of superstitious evil that she was continually guarding herself and her family against. She had a saying for every action good or bad, and her children and house were hung with amulets to protect against bad luck. No sneeze or cough in my children or hers escaped attention, and she took pains to ward off any malevolent spirits that might be present. When two-year-old Nick was with me, she would exclaim, "Oh, Andrea, how could you have such an ugly son?" This hurt my feelings until I realized she was protecting him from an evil eye that might be attracted to a "pretty boy." Even knowing as she did that Westerners don't believe in such things, she still wouldn't take chances with a child she had grown to love.

She tried to live a life compatible with Koranic injunctions. "Andrea," she would say seriously, "we should be generous and if we are, our generosity will be returned many times over. Last winter when a Bedouin woman came begging at my door and I gave her my winter coat, the next day my husband brought me a fur coat from Europe. How could he have known? God must have directed his actions." Her sympathy was genuine. A ragtag Bedouin camp existed across the street. Her garden hose provided them water, her cast-off clothes covered them, and the leftovers from the meals she cooked in abundance fed them. They in turn showered her with blessings every time she emerged from her house, used their dogs to protect her property, and willingly did any odd jobs she needed. She frequently drank tea with the shepherdess, who became her special friend, and came back with copious information about the goings and comings of the neighborhood. She was genuinely fond of the Bedouin and full of admiration for the hard life they led. And although their status was at the other end of the scale from hers in terms of wealth, education, and social level, she used the respectful intimate terms *uxti* (sister) for women her age, *ammati* (father's sister) for those her mother's age, and *jiddati* (grandmother) for those much older.

Once trying to emulate Rima's goodness, I played hostess to a Bedouin group camped in the empty lot next to us. Their chief had been taken ill and came to the city to seek medical help, and much of his tribe had moved their tents next door to be near him. An American anthropologist living with the tribe had been caught up in the crisis. When he knocked at my door, I gladly allowed them to hook up a hose to my garden faucets and run it through a hole in our wall. Meanwhile the anthropologist scouted out wood and other necessities for "his" tribe. One day, after the tribe returned to the desert, I discovered a little shack with a padlock in the corner of the lot where they had been living. Someone had staked a claim to my water. Several days later the shack burned down, and we learned there had been a dispute between the local tribes over who had the right to the still flowing water. From that encounter I learned I would never know how to manage my relations with local people as Rima did. For me it ended in a shouting match, while with her it was always a mutually respectful exchange.

In the spring when the weather turned pleasant, I visited Rima more often. Each time she told me excitedly about a plant she had brought back from Syria. She explained that she had missed this fragrant flower when she came to live in Riyadh. In Syria the flower was used to celebrate happy events such as weddings and births because of its intensely sweet perfume. So when she returned to Riyadh, her mother gave her a bulb that she planted and tended carefully. First she showed me the pot with nothing appearing above the ground, and then the green tip emerged and became larger each week. Finally with great excitement, she announced that buds were forming and by the following week should flower. I made a point of visiting just when the flower would be in full bloom. Rima said nothing so I asked where it was. "Gone," she said sadly, and it was clear she didn't want to talk about it. But I pressed her. "I shouldn't be telling you what happened, because it will look as if I was against it. The Prophet shows us that when we give a gift we should give it wholeheartedly and without reservation. I am truly trying to feel this way." She explained that a young Canadian boy living in the neighborhood had come to play with Rima's son Hassan and seeing the beautiful flower had remarked that he knew his mother would love a flower like that. Rima saw his remark as a command to give up her flower. I tried to explain that a Western compliment was not meant as a request for the item, but she didn't see it my way and stopped me when I wanted to retrieve it from the boy's mother.

Rima and I frequently went shopping together. It was convenient because we could share transportation, alternating between her husband's car and Bill's. It was also better for propriety's sake for women to go together in the souk. She liked going with me because on her more daring days she could pretend she was a Westerner and leave her abaya and veils at home. There was always the danger of course that a mutawwa might overhear her speaking Arabic and realize she was a Muslim without coverings. That could mean a beating on the spot or a call to her husband to scold him for letting his wife out in immodest dress. Although her open-minded husband didn't mind, she tried not to embarrass him.

I benefited from Rima's bargaining skills although being softhearted, she weakened immediately at any sad story a salesperson told her. One day we were in the cloth souk looking for something appropriate for me to wear to Saudi parties. The simplicity of my clothes was becoming an embarrassment next to the glittery finery of the Saudi women, especially at weddings. I told Rima I would look down the row of stalls and pick out the flashiest cloth I could see. I chose a black cut-velvet piece with glittery strands running through it. We began our routine of showing interest in a variety of bolts so as not to attract attention to the one I wanted. Salesmen piled bolt after bolt around us, when Rima suddenly turned to me and began talking loudly in English. She wasn't making sense, and I was puzzled until I saw a cluster of heavily bearded men in ragtag brown cloaks watching us. Their look was full of contempt for the unredeemable Western morality we represented. Rima's ruse worked, and they continued on their way, banging on the shop shutters to close for prayer. "God protect us," said a shaky Rima. "It was the head of the religious police." The clerks also sighed with relief. They had enough trouble with prayer closings several times a day and didn't need new problems.

One of our ruses almost never worked. I would tell Rima what I wanted, and she would bargain for it as if buying for herself. Presumably as an Arab she would get a better price. I would wait around the corner, but invariably the shopkeepers knew we were together or decide since she was a foreigner to raise the price anyway. More often than not she came back having paid a higher price than I had been offered, saying, "But Andrea, the poor man has eight children and they don't have enough money to send them to school!" It was a story that in one form or another every shopkeeper inserted subtly into the pre-bargaining stages, and Rima never failed to fall for it. Still, they seemed genuinely glad to see her and pour their woes into her sympathetic ear. It was her childlike innocence and the respectful way she greeted all her "brothers" and "uncles" that protected her from the vulgar remarks sometimes directed at women in the souk. Although not resulting in many good buys, our trips to the souk provided a textbook lesson in personal relations, with Rima a superb teacher in the subtleties of these interactions.

I once took Nick with me to the souk to show my respectability as I'd seen other local women do. I was confident I could bargain successfully using Rima's techniques and adding my own stiffer backbone to the negotiations. I engaged a shopkeeper in polite conversation and showed interest in everything in his shop but the wooden chest I really wanted. I asked about the prices of various items, before finally asking about the chest I had in mind. Already I could feel him becoming irritated that I was asking prices for things I had no intention of buying. He was a taciturn fellow but I persisted, countering his price for the chest with roughly half his price (two-thirds I had been told was what I should pay), which was about all I could spend anyway. He went down slightly but I kept my price. He went down slightly more, but I didn't budge. He spat in the dust and turned his back and refused to have anything more to do with me. I walked out, thinking he would come after me and lower the price further, but when I passed by later he turned his back on me again. Whenever I returned to his shop in the souk, he refused to sell to me. From this experience I learned that the point of negotiations was accommodation and flexibility. I should have removed myself gracefully from the bargaining if I wasn't willing to meet him partway. Instead, I walked out without the gentle words that would have put us on friendly terms again. My emphasis was too focused on winning.

One day Rima and I were haggling over the price of a toy I wanted to buy for a birthday present. The shopkeeper insisted on 7 Saudi rials (SR) while I was sure I had been offered the toy in another shop for only 5SR. We had more shopping to do so I finally accepted his price, and we continued on our way. After several blocks I noticed he had given me the change as if for the 5SR figure. Since prices aren't fixed, I felt he unconsciously gave me the change for what he knew was the "right" amount, and I had no intention of returning the 2SR. But I had not taken Rima's conscience into account. "Oh no, Andrea, we have to go back immediately. Once you agree to a price you have to abide by it whether fair or not, and it would be 'a shame on us' not to give the man what he's owed." "OK, Rima, but we can give it to him on our way home," I said. "No, no, think how he will feel if he realizes what happened and thinks we are dishonorable people who don't keep a bargain." So back we went to return the money, and the man was exceedingly pleased. Rima's stock shot up another few notches. Often I had the uneasy feeling that my moral standards were not up to those of the saintly Rima.

Rima was not shy either about chastising improper behavior in the street—in particular that of adolescent boys and older men who made comments about our unholy "nakedness." With street urchins she took the role of an angry big sister appealing to their family honor and their sense of hospitality to foreigners. "My brothers, how can you do this sinful thing—revile women in the streets. It will drive your mothers and fathers into their graves knowing you have tarnished their honor." To my surprise, thinking of how adolescents in America would react, they would slink away, and the next time they saw us would vie with one another to carry our parcels, knowing full well that Rima would pay three times over to encourage improvements in their behavior. She also gently admonished shopkeepers about their outrageously high prices: "My uncle, how can you ask such a price? It's sinful! Can't you see that my friend is a guest in our country? You should give her the item free. What will she think about our lack of generosity—that we are all thieves and don't treat guests well"—all of this said in a tone of disappointment at the storekeeper in question. If the price were not immediately lowered, Rima would leave the shop muttering something to the effect that their lack of virtue would reap its own rewards. Few shopkeepers could resist Rima's sisterly reproaches, framed as they were to shame but not offend.

One day when I visited Rima, she asked if I planned to go to the wedding of the queen's niece at the palace the following week. I told her I hadn't been invited. It was only a month before we were due to be transferred back to Jidda, and I had never even seen the interior of the king's palace. I was not expecting to be invited to the wedding but hoped to hear the details from Rima. But once Rima detected the disappointment in my voice, she felt obliged to make my stay in Riyadh complete. "Andrea, it's easy, you can go to the wedding with my friends and me." "But I don't have an invitation. How can I get past the gate guards?" "That's easy, just get ready and come." I was reluctant to crash the party, but the opportunity was irresistible.

Promptly at the time she indicated, I arrived at Rima's house feeling awkward in my glittery new dress. I waited a half hour until she was ready, and then another half hour at the next house until that occupant was ready, and another half hour at the final house until there were four of us jammed into the back of the car. The driver sat comfortably alone in the front seat. Rima took this moment to admit that she had not located an extra invitation, but no one seemed concerned so I tried to relax, thinking only fleetingly of how it might affect Bill's career if I were discovered sneaking into the king's palace. At the gate Rima handed the driver our invitations, and he handed them to the guard, who counted them and then us and waved the car on to the palace grounds. "How did you do it?" I asked. They giggled. "We took one card out of the envelope and handed him three envelopes and an invitation, making four. Besides," Rima added, "he probably couldn't read anyway."

From then on the evening was pure enjoyment. We walked through the huge entryway where women were depositing their abayas in great heaps on the floor. Nannies squatted and cradled babies until they had to hurry them into the wedding hall to their mothers for nursing. In the hall, chairs were lined up in rows facing the platform where the bride and groom would sit. Most of the chairs were comfortable, but the most luxurious, overstuffed velvet ones were in the front row and obviously for royal family members. As the guests arrived, the women ushers judged their status and assigned them seats commensurate with their position—the nearer the front the higher the position. The women of the bride and groom's family were seated in the front rows along with the queen and her daughters and daughters-in-law. A woman would be offended if led to a place beneath her status, and to avoid this crisis many simply decided their own worth and chose seats up front. When the elite latecomers had to be seated in front, more chairs were found to accommodate them, and the crush eventually became almost intolerable. At previous parties, my foreignness always meant I was bodily dragged to the front by a perspiring hostess wanting to be safe since foreigner status was difficult to determine.

That evening our group entered the wedding hall looking as important as possible. We were led to seats directly behind the row where the queen would sit. I was still feeling like an interloper and sure everyone would know I had not been invited. As far as I could see I was the only non-Arab in the room—the other foreigners, like Rima, being Arabs married to Saudis. To reassure me, Rima pointed to a group of heavily veiled women sitting in the back. She explained that if someone was not invited and wanted to attend, she simply covered herself to hide her identity. "It's customary," she said, but didn't explain how they entered without invitations.

We had arrived several hours after the invitation stated, but still the hall was not filled. We watched the young unmarried girls showing off their attributes to the mothers of unmarried sons, who everyone knew were the ones who selected potential brides. The young women moved gracefully, greeting friends prettily with kisses and expressions of delight, answering questions sweetly, helping their hostesses usher in the guests, bringing sweet drinks or coffee, and running errands across the great hall where they would have maximum exposure. Indeed, they were a riveting sight—gaily colored flowers at the peak of their bloom. As the mother of three boys, I tried to assess the merchandise as I imagined a Saudi mother might, to find the right beauties with temperaments to fit those of my sons. When I mentioned my choices, my companions invariably disagreed. "Her skin is too dark," or "She is too thin," or "Her family is ordinary," or "She is too educated," or "Not educated enough." Having so dismally failed at these assessments, I began feeling as incompetent in my motherly duties as in social etiquette and moral standards.

We passed several hours with rounds of sweet drinks, tea, and coffee, and watching the palace servants singing and dancing in the African style. There was a women's band playing tambourines, drums, and the *oud* (lute) as background to the noisy conversations. I was relieved to find they didn't take up the usual collection for the bride and thought back to the first time I got caught at a wedding not knowing it was coming. Each guest had prepared herself with an elaborate handkerchief stuffed with cash to give to the usher walking up and down the aisle. She would hold up the exquisitely embroidered cloth and announce the owner's name and the amount of cash it contained. "Bint (daughter of) so and so gives 1,000SR." Before I had time to think, I was handing in my Kleenex with all the cash I had with me and hearing the usher announce, "Mrs. Rugh gives 10SR [about $2.00]." Everyone turned to see who had presented perhaps the most insignificant amount ever given at a Saudi wedding.

Queen Effat appeared and was greeted warmly by the other occupants of the front-row seats. As hostess, she moved through the crowd trying to greet as many women as possible and ensuring that her guests were comfortable. She stood out even in this glittering crowd. Her father was Saudi and her mother Turkish, thus giving her a pale complexion and honey blond hair. At the time she was in her late fifties but still exceedingly beautiful and meeting every expectation of how a queen should look and behave. Across the aisle from her sat relatives of the deposed king Saud, her husband's predecessor, who were of a distinctly coarser mold. They sat cross-legged with their bare feet tucked up under them on the chairs. One picked at her toes, and another spit the shells of sunflower seeds onto the floor. They were dressed in the conventional ill-fitting Saudi dresses that I was told were sewn tightly around them to show off their figures—and they looked very conservative next to the flashing glitter of the other guests.

Queen Effat and her daughters by contrast were beautifully dressed and had refined manners. Her dress was the flowing style Bedouins used for weddings but in the finest of materials, and her hair was arranged in a long plait down her back as thick as my arm. After King Faisal married her, he took no further wives. She was educated in European schools, as were her daughters, and they spoke several languages. Queen Effat had been the one who in 1960 pressed her husband to start public schools for girls despite the outcry from religious conservatives. Like his father before him who established a radio and telephone service, he arranged for the opening to include the chanting of Koranic verses. "How can a service be evil if it communicates the Koran more widely," observed the wise king.

Eventually the hours of waiting were over, and ripples of excitement passed through the hall. "The bride is coming." "No, the groom is late." At every wedding the groom was late—perhaps he was meant to show reluctance. We heard drums in the distance, and soon the drummers and several small children dressed in white appeared carrying candles and leading the procession. Then, barely visible, came the bride and groom surrounded by tearful mothers and aunts rearranging the bride's garments and veils as she passed slowly by. The groom looked terrified as well he might, since it was probably his first view of a roomful of unveiled women since his early childhood. Fathers and uncles of the couple joined the procession, and the women throw any cloth available over their heads to prevent the males from seeing them. In this case King Faisal also walked in the procession and as he neared, the stage, noticed an elderly aunt and bowed to kiss her hand to show his respect. Except for this procession of bride, groom, and members of the household, there was no ceremony since the male members of both families had signed the marriage agreement earlier.

The wedding party arrived at the throne-like chairs. The audience should have been able to see them, but the mothers, aunts, children, and photographers milling around them obscured their view. From my few glimpses of the couple they seemed incredibly attractive. The bride was dressed in a white gown and moved her head stiffly to avoid disturbing her elaborate hairdo plastered in place with hair spray. Her heavily made-up features even at a distance stood out against the white powder of her face. She maintained an air of dignity and grace, although surely she must have been close to panic thinking about the next few hours when she would leave her mother's home, go to a new household, and be subjected to her husband's advances. The groom was dressed in an immaculate white thobe (man's traditional long shirt-like dress) and headdress, and his now expressionless face masked what must also have been mixed emotions. He had been trained to avert his eyes in the presence of females, yet here he was in a roomful of women scurrying to cover themselves. He surely had to be curious about them, not to mention his bride whom he was seeing for the first time. Everyone was wondering—did he like her looks, did she meet his expectations? How would he treat her when they were alone together? Sitting on his throne, though, he didn't dare look around, even at his bride.

Photographers arranged the couple in various poses, alone and with an endless combination of wedding guests. I heard it claimed that some wedding photographers had never taken pictures before but crashed parties with cameras to get their only chance of a glimpse of young women. Between each pose there was a quick revamping of the bride's hair and a readjustment of her dress. All this made it seem more like a rehearsal than a real wedding.

When the pictures finished, the bridal couple led the way to the banquet tables set up in a nearby hall. Mothers and aunts burst into fresh orgies of tears, probably thinking of the terrifying experience of their own weddings. The guests rushed to the tables, pushing each other aside to get at the food. We pressed our way into the hall past showcases of silver ornaments that were gifts to the king and queen. The walls were wood-worked relief with tapestry insets. The dining hall was a fairyland of glittering lights and elegant table settings with huge platters of food lining the center of the table. The food was unrecognizable— chicken dishes in the shape of large birds, fish molded into flowers—with everything far too beautiful to eat. But the first several hundred who found seats dug in without hesitation, trying every dish and then leaving great mounds of unfinished food on their plates when they left. I tried dabs of everything but in American fashion felt I should finish it all. "Don't worry, Andrea, it's better to leave some," said Rima, "they'll feel better knowing they've more than satisfied your hunger." Otherwise, there was little conversation, except for, "The cook should have made the stuffed grape leaves more tart," or "The stuffed zucchini is the best I've ever eaten." "Oh no, my husband says mine are the best anywhere." "Really, the mutton is overdone and the camel meat a little tough." I sat there thinking everything was delicious and marveling at the effort that went into the meal. As the first wave of guests left, others poured through the doors and took their places. By this time my companions were picking at their food and laughing at my efforts to finish. "Really, Andrea, people will think you didn't get enough to eat," and one plunked a large glazed chicken breast down on what was left of my food "to make it look better."

The guests rapidly vacated the hall, and the servants cleared away the Sheffield silver, Rosenthal plates, and crystal goblets leaving nothing but the still half-full platters in the center of the table. "Uh, oh," said one of my friends, "come, we'd better get out of here." Looking back over my shoulder I saw the servants opening the doors to the terrace, and a horde of women—their cloaks and masks identifying them as Bedouin—rushed in. They began dumping food into the bags they carried, and in their haste seemed to be sweeping everything off the table. How did the food taste, I wondered, jumbled together like that when it appeared again from their sacks?

We had two more battles before we could go home. The first was finding our abayas from the heap in the entryway. The next was finding our car and driver. We gave our names to a man shouting into the cold winter air, "Daughter of the house of so and so," or "Family of the house of so and so," and eventually limousines untangled themselves from the mass of cars and drove up to the portico to take on their modestly covered cargo, finery and faces concealed under carefully arranged abayas and veils. Drivers, husbands, brothers, and unrelated males gathered around the door, hoping for a glimpse of a female figure under the clinging cloaks or, better still, a face behind a casually slipping veil. The unmarried men could perhaps attach this object of attraction to the announcement of a name and send their mothers out to investigate.

It was five in the morning by the time we dropped off our companions. They had several hours to sleep with their Saudi schedules while I was arriving home just in time to help my children get ready for school. Never mind, the wedding was worth it, and I still felt wide awake. Thank you, my friends, for a lovely evening that for you was commonplace but for me was an Arabian night's dream!

After I returned to Jidda, I saw little of Rima except when she occasionally visited her sister-in-law who was an official at the local girls' university in Jidda. More than a decade later, when we were living in Damascus, she came to see me when I was in bed with a case of hepatitis. She was the same old Rima—a little more sedate and dignified but with the same twinkle in her eye. Years later I learned that she and her husband had moved to Jidda, where she had joined the trend of greater religiosity and no longer attended ladies' parties unless their aim was to read the Koran or discuss religious topics. It was hard to think of the bubbly, empathetic Rima taking on a heavier mantle of religiosity. In Riyadh she had been the most inspiring example of a person living a religious faith I had ever seen, and it seemed incomprehensible she could become more pious. I have to believe the old Rima is still there beneath the surface of a more seriously religious Rima to shed light and laughter wherever she goes.

6

FAMILIAR TERRITORY: JIDDA AGAIN (1969–1971)

Bill's language center in Riyadh was doing well enough to leave it in the hands of a new Foreign Service officer, so we decided to extend our posting two more years and return to Jidda, this time with Bill as public affairs officer. Unfortunately the move meant leaving essential parts of our household behind. The two donkeys had grown too big for the confined space of a garden so we gave them away. The bigger loss was Hamud, who decided to stay in Riyadh with a family who offered him a higher salary. He felt so guilty about leaving us that several times I thought he might change his mind. But we couldn't afford to increase his salary to meet the one offered by his new employer nor did I have the heart to ask him to give up this better opportunity.

In Jidda we moved into a bigger house commensurate with Bill's status as a principal officer in the embassy. Again it was new and needing attention to gardens and trees but this time with help from the embassy gardeners. In place of Hamud we inherited Hassan. He was more competent at the elaborate cooking we needed with our expanded entertaining responsibilities but not as good at the cleaning. He was temperamental with me but good with the children as all Yemenis seemed to be. He helped the boys convert a wooden shipping crate into a playhouse equipped with screened windows, a doorbell, and lights. When they tired of it, he introduced them to the deliveryman bringing water to neighborhood gardens with his small donkey-drawn tanker. He let the boys ride the donkeys to his various customers. Hassan also brought them to meet the construction workers next door who with infinite patience let them slop around in cement and build the concrete foundations for our neighbor's house. When we finally returned to the United States, Legos and other plastic toys held little attraction for them after building real things.

Returning to Jidda held advantages and disadvantages. I was glad to renew my acquaintance with the Saudi women I already knew and meet new ones through the friendship circles I started attending again. One new acquaintance was a Saudi anthropologist back from the United States and working on her Ph.D. dissertation on the visiting patterns of Saudi women, many of them her relatives. Her insights helped me see that the endless chatter at parties about weddings, births, divorces, and deaths had significance in situating women in their social contexts. I began drawing up family trees to understand the implications. But my efforts were frustrated by the complicated ways they were related. The scribblings on my rolls of shelf paper were largely incomprehensible with dotted lines crisscrossing one another to denote their overlapping blood and marriage connections. At the edge the lines faded off into nothingness when an odd person married outside the family's usual pool of spouses. Despite the complexity, I discovered there were only about fifty main families in Jidda and that the nodes of crisscrossing relationships were not random, but rather gathered in knots that surely must be important. I felt that my inability to understand the meanings must be due to lack of training and the cumbersome methods I used to draw my trees. Still, I became interested in the new bits of information I could bring home with me.

Another anthropologist I met was the wife of the Japanese ambassador who was living and working in a village some distance from town. We dropped her off once and watched her small figure swathed in abayas and veils trudging off toward the distant village. She studied what happened to families when men migrated for work and discovered that the wives took their children to live with their own mothers rather than remain in their husbands' extended families. This suggested that the usual patrilateral focus of Arab society was not as rigid as it might seem. The work of these two anthropologists plus the one working near Riyadh inspired me to start thinking about taking anthropology courses if the opportunity ever arose.

I rejoined the coffee group consisting mainly of foreign wives of Saudis. Their in-laws would have been appalled by the stories they told about the intimate workings of their Saudi households—exposure being the worst nightmare of bringing a non-related bride into the home. Saudi wives protected such information, but few foreigners worried about the consequences enough to keep what they knew confidential. Saudi women's parties, I was finding, were about "image management," where they always depicted their families in ways that enhanced their reputations. Foreigners' parties were often the opposite, with disparaging glimpses of Saudi life and conjugal relations.

The foreign wives, as before, divided into the adapters and the criticizers. Even though they attended foreign parties like these, their husbands often didn't mix because of differences in social position. The women under normal circumstances probably wouldn't have been close, but their similar experiences in Saudi Arabia made them depend on one another to an almost desperate degree. Indeed, there was no question they were vulnerable in Saudi society without relatives to support them. The society depended on the checks and balances of kin to ensure the proper treatment of women. These foreign women only had one another and possibly the Saudi spouses of their friends, but even that recourse was a weak one since Saudis were unlikely to interfere in the private affairs of other families. The women couldn't leave the country or take their children out without the permission of their husbands. And there was nowhere to seek refuge if the marriage turned sour. Problems usually didn't reach this level, but when they did—and there were a few cases—even the embassy couldn't do much since foreigners had to follow Saudi law. It was surprising sometimes to think how little the foreigners knew beforehand about a country where they planned to spend the rest of their lives. Most didn't even know, for example, that unless they converted to Islam they could not legally inherit from their husbands. The coffee parties were a good place to share this kind of information and for me, of course, to learn more about the society.

Most of these couples lived in their own homes separate from their Saudi relatives—a practice still unusual at the time for newly married Saudi couples, but assumed to be a requirement for foreign wives who people knew did not adjust well to extended family living. The foreign wives invariably complained of two problems, both involving the amount of time their husbands put into fulfilling their "duties" to others. Those with nearby mothers stopped by every day to sit with them and constantly ran errands for them. In the evenings they sat with male relatives and friends while the wives sat at home. When some foreign wives accompanied their husbands to their in-laws', they found the hours of sitting around in the women's quarters so boring that most soon limited their visits to obligatory calls on feast days and special events. Marriages were often doomed if the foreign wives didn't find congenial friends of their own.

The second complaint was about the custom that men of a family combine their money in joint accounts from which family members drew what they needed. It meant the couples curtailed their own needs so the husband could meet his obligations to his family. The foreign wives complained of extravagant purchases by relatives at their expense. No matter how much their husbands earned, the money had to be shared with others. The Saudi men saw this as normal. Their foreign wives did not.

One Saudi woman I visited in Jidda was an artist. I was surprised to find the openness with which she pursued her art, given my experience in Riyadh of being sworn to secrecy about the artist who sculpted the bust of my French friend. Back in more tolerant Jidda, I was pleased to find Sophia—so clearly a respectable woman—exhibiting her art in carefully selected public places. Her large tableaux, in the Grandma Moses style, captured the traditions of everyday life in Jidda before they disappeared. By that time Saudis were using their petrodollars to spend lavishly on clothing and furnishings, and so it was soothing to find someone interested in older traditions. I loved to hear her talk about the paintings—the making of coffee, for example, or a series showing events leading up to marriage: the engagement, the henna night, and the wedding party. Each picture meticulously detailed the appropriate clothing, artifacts, and furnishings.

Her paintings made me look more carefully at the antiquities in the Jidda market: an old wedding chest "from the time of the earthquake in Medina," the silver Maria Theresa coins, the dresses and veils typical of various parts of the country—Taif, Abha, the desert Bedouin—and most of all the old silver jewelry that was rapidly being melted down and made into cheap, flashy "corrupted metals." Saudi women were turning in their silver as quickly as possible and buying gold. At the time, the carved wooden panels and intricate *mashrabia* screens on windows in the old houses were being torn down and smoothed over with cement. One day I asked my driver to stop and ask about a pile of wood next to a house under renovation. We filled the trunk with "firewood" of screens and wonderfully carved flower panels I had bought for a few coins.

Jidda's center was also being updated with asphalted streets and modern streetlights to replace the old gas lamps that a city employee lit each evening. I wanted to buy some of the beautiful old lamps and asked the mayor of Jidda if that would be possible. He took my request to the town council and after long deliberation they refused, saying that obviously the commerce-oriented Americans wanted to steal their designs and that I would put them out of business by making cheaper versions. The sophisticated mayor understood my interest and was very apologetic that he couldn't just give me one.

As a family we were delighted to be living near the sea again and resuming the pleasures of weekend camping in the desert. We joined our old friends at the same coral reefs that provided such a spectacular refuge from our claustrophobic compound walls. This time we also knew Saudi families well enough to spend weekends with them in their cabins on the sea. And we branched out to camp in new sites. One of these excursions was to the long lost harbor of Jar, mentioned in documents as one of the most important seaport towns in antiquity. An archaeologist from the Smithsonian Institution had asked the Saudis for permission to locate the site for future excavations, but he was denied permission because the Saudis at the time felt anything pre-Islamic, in the *jahaliyya* or "Age of Ignorance," was not worth investigating (they have since changed their minds). So with his directions, we set out to see if we could find any evidence of the old settlement near the present-day town of Rabigh. Others had found shards that suggested an ancient harbor so it didn't take long to find the site in a sandy area next to the sea with no sign of modern life anywhere. All that was left was a mound that probably covered the walls of either a fortress or a dock-like structure along a natural harbor. Strewn over the surface were broken bits of Roman glass, pottery shards, and small pieces of twisted metal. We took back samples that the archaeologist analyzed to confirm that it was the right spot.

A German friend from the camping group was missing for several weeks ,and when we asked where he had been, he replied, "In jail." He had been in a car accident in which the driver of the other car had been seriously hurt and eventually died. According to Saudi law, both drivers in an accident go to jail until they agree on a settlement. Even though our friend had not caused the accident, the victim's family was demanding blood money, and until they agreed on a sum, Werner stayed in jail. Through him we learned about the suggested compensation amounts with the highest payments for Saudi males, the next highest for females (presumably passengers since they didn't drive), and much further down the list foreigners and livestock. I began to see why the authorities were resistant to letting women drive. What self-respecting Saudi family would accept the imprisonment of its women until an accident was settled? And if women couldn't go to prison, presumably their male relatives would have to go in their place. I knew by that time that just because blood money was higher for males, it didn't necessarily reflect a difference in their value; rather, it recognized the greater financial loss when men died. Nothing was simple in Saudi Arabia ,and reform was much more complex than it seemed.

Bill spent much of his time calling on local functionaries. One of these, a Bedouin shaikh, invited our family to his encampment along the Red Sea one evening when he was entertaining other shaikhs. We camped several miles away in our own small tents and arrived just after sunset at the shaikh's large goat-hair tent. He greeted us and motioned Bill, the boys, and me to cushions near him. But when the congregation of chiefs arrived, I became uncomfortable as the only woman and asked the shaikh's permission to let me go to the women's tent. The boys and I spent the rest of the evening largely ignored, while the women prepared a sumptuous meal in big cooking pots. When the food was ready, the shaikh's sons carried the trays to the men's tent. The shaikh sent word for me to join them, but again I begged to stay where I was, and he agreed. We watched through the openings between the tent panels as the men ate from the fragrant meat heaped high on large mounds of rice. "Look, they like the meat. See how they are taking large chunks of it. No one roasts lamb like Aisha, or makes rice as well as Suraya. The guests will be satisfied with all we have cooked for them, and the shaikh will be happy that we have cooked such a good meal," the women said, clearly pleased with themselves. I was growing hungrier by the moment, thinking perhaps I should have accepted the shaikh's invitation. It was perhaps the only time in Saudi Arabia that I would have preferred the men's gathering to the livelier women's one. Eventually the men finished, and we ate from the half-depleted trays that were returned to us. The women critically eyed how much was eaten of each dish and complained when platters came back fuller than they felt they should be. The boys and I didn't waste time with these observations but ate until our stomachs were ready to burst—each dish seeming better than the last.

While renewing friendships was one advantage of returning to Jidda, the disadvantage was that with Bill's elevated position I was now called on more often to do diplomatic chores. Diplomatic life at the best of times made me feel vaguely uneasy. It was the never-ending list of people we owed invitations to, the worry that the food we offered might not be elaborate enough, that we might have invited the wrong mix of people or worked out the wrong protocol seating, or that the evening might be so boring no one would want to come again, or that my clothes might not be right, or any number of failings of ours that might be apparent. Worst of all, in Saudi Arabia there was the constant anxiety over whether local guests would show up at all or whether they might bring unexpected additional visitors. For some reason, like all diplomats, we used the Western formats for entertaining—large standing receptions or sit-down dinners—both of which didn't fit the Saudi lifestyle. Saudis didn't like standing for long periods at receptions nor did they drink alcohol in public, and when they arrived late, it threw our carefully planned seating arrangements into a shambles. In retrospect I don't see why we used these inconvenient forms of entertaining. Was it our protocol training that seemed to leave no other options open? I had to admit it felt more comfortable in Saudi homes sitting on cushions in their gardens than it did attending our own stiff parties.

The protocol rules we learned so carefully in Washington were invariably confounded by Saudi custom. Our knowledge of what should happen only made it embarrassing when through no fault of our own it became impossible to follow the rules. The ambassador's wife once asked me to accompany her and the assistant secretary of state's wife, Mrs. Sisco, to visit the queen in Riyadh. When the black limousine from the Saudi Protocol Office pulled up at the guest palace, we knew where we should sit: Mrs. Sisco on the back right seat, the ambassador's wife on the back left seat, and me in the seat next to the driver. But we hadn't counted on the security guard already occupying the right front seat; as a Saudi male, he saw it as his right. He unceremoniously directed us into the back seat, forcing Mrs. Sisco into the lowest protocol middle seat while the ambassador's wife scurried to the other side of the car, leaving me in the seat of honor. All I could think to do as we drove up to the palace was to leap out of the car and hold the door while Mrs. Sisco stepped onto the red carpet where the queen's aide was waiting.

Probably the worst duty was the yearly bazaars to raise money for local charities. We all had to contribute something to sell, as well as stand selling the pitiful items no one wanted. Once I made straw flowers from instructions in a craft book. Each flower took a half hour to make and sold for ten cents. I was assigned the job of finding a local recipient for the scholarship money that was to be the charity of the year. When I offered the headmistress of a local school a check for $500, her face fell, and she coolly accepted the donation as if it were an insult. I regretted the hours making the silly flowers.

I was lucky in our early years in Jidda to have as the ambassador's wife a woman who was intensely interested in local Arab culture. Whenever I was invited to a Saudi party that conflicted with an embassy event, I would informally tell her about the conflict, and she would encourage me to go to the Saudi event. This "favoritism" didn't endear me to other embassy wives. Looking back I know I talked too much to them about Saudi women's parties, but I was trying to show that my lukewarm participation in American events didn't mean I wasn't contributing to the embassy mission. But I must have stimulated another kind of guilt. Americans believe in being involved in the local community, but when faced with the reality of what that means, most don't have the persistence to stick with it. Involvement requires adjusting to different schedules and sitting through long parties that are exceedingly boring without an understanding of the language. Parents especially find it hard to attend parties at times when their children need them most. Others simply feel more comfortable sticking to familiar American activities.

Several times we visited Saudi families in the mountains of Taif, where Saudis go to escape the intense heat and humidity of the coast. One memorable weekend, our friend, Muhammad, took us to visit his large extended family there. He dropped me off at the "women's door," where young boys took my boys' hands protectively and guided them up the long flight of stairs to the women's quarters. Other boys carried the folding cot I brought for Nick and a bag with a three-day supply of diapers and baby food. I realized this enormous pile of stuff made it look suspiciously as if we were planning to stay forever. Then I remembered I had packed Bill's and my clothes in one suitcase that Bill was carrying off to the men's quarters. I sent a note back with the young boys telling Bill to send up the clothes I needed. These young boys—around seven or eight years old—spent their days conveying messages and goods back and forth between the men's and women's quarters. At that age they were old enough to take their responsibilities seriously but not so old that they posed a threat to the separation of the sexes.

In the large living rooms upstairs, I found roughly twenty-five or more women and numerous children tumbling among the cushions lining the wall. They all stood to greet us, and I felt overcome for a minute with the names and relationships they told me to explain their connections to one another. Our luggage was whisked away to a "matrimonial" room reserved for us on the floor above and a young woman brought us cool drinks and tea to revive us from the journey. The children tried unsuccessfully to entice my boys to play with them, and Nick especially resisted the idea of being passed from hand to hand like the other young children in the room.

Eventually I sorted out the relationships, starting with the matriarch who was treated with great deference by her adult daughters, daughters-in-law, and nieces. The small children were either grandchildren or belonged to visiting nieces. The girls ranged in age from toddlers to teenagers while the boys didn't exceed eight or nine years. The younger women occupied themselves with the babies, but when they became weary, the widows and unmarried aunts in the family rocked them to sleep. Once children became toddlers, they were turned over to children a few years older who carried them, fed them, wiped away their tears, and finally as a last resort took them to their mothers for nursing. The older children were severely reprimanded if anything went wrong with their charges and took their responsibilities seriously. Although sometimes looking longingly at the other children at play, they never left the little ones entrusted to their care.

For three days we lived in this whirl of activity that focused mainly on food and drinking never-ending cups of tea interspersed with small cups of Turkish coffee. At night the single women simply lay down on the cushions we used during the day, covered themselves with blankets, and slept soundly despite the noise and lights. The cushions provided an infinite amount of sleeping space for guests who dropped in.

At night the married women retired to the "couples' rooms" on the third floor, where mattresses and bedding were laid out on the floor. The husbands joined their wives by way of a back staircase that bypassed the women's quarters. I set up Nick's crib in our room at his usual bedtime while everyone stood around watching. They were shocked to see me feeding him a disgusting-looking dinner out of baby food jars and poking each mouthful through the bars of the playpen that, without a high chair, I was using to contain him. When he finished I asked them to leave so he could sleep. "Oh, no," they answered in chorus. "You can't leave him alone in the dark. We'll hold him until he falls asleep." When I insisted, they reluctantly left. But by this time Nick was wide awake and unable to sleep. I quieted him and, when he was almost asleep, left the room. Soon he renewed his wails, and I had to block the stairs to prevent the women from rushing to comfort him. I told the women not to worry, that he would soon fall asleep, and to show my confidence went down to sit in the women's hall. After ten minutes there were no further sounds. "See," I told them, "it only takes a few minutes for him to fall asleep." But they didn't seem convinced. After a few minutes the woman who had been most adamant about not leaving him alone entered the room and announced to the assembled group that she had just rocked Nick to sleep. On all accounts I realized what a totally inadequate and heartless mother I was—putting him in a "cage" to eat, feeding him disgusting food out of jars, confining him in a crib, and letting him cry himself to sleep.

The next morning I awoke early and found Muhammad had sent word that I could sit for a while in the men's majlis before his father and the older men arrived. I talked for a while with his brothers before rejoining the women again in the room upstairs. By that time a line of men—mostly sons and grandsons— had formed upstairs in an entryway to greet the matriarch who sat grandly in a chair receiving them. Their manner was so respectful that if I didn't know better I would have thought she was royalty. Some kissed her hand, others her shoulder, while she kissed their heads in return. All the women who shouldn't be seen— mostly daughters-in-law—had taken cover in other rooms. The rule was that males and females who could potentially marry shouldn't see one another while those who could not marry—a father, uncle, or brother, for example—could see her. The matriarch asked each male for their news, if they had plans to travel, and other details of their lives. Then later she conveyed this news to the rest of the women over cups of tea. I saw that although women remained in their own quarters they knew a great deal of what was going on in the outside world, perhaps even more than the men whose relations were more formal. It made me realize the importance of sons to a mother, for their wives either lived with her or spent most of their holidays in her house. A woman with only daughters would have an empty house after they married, and her holidays would lack the joyful feeling of a house full of people. Later, in the Gulf, I saw even more vividly how important women's networks were in enhancing their power even though they remained virtually invisible to anyone outside their families.

After the men left, we gathered around a cloth spread on the floor for a breakfast of yogurt cheese, fresh bread, olives, and dates and a sugary tea with spices and milk. At some point in the morning, the young boys brought in groceries the men brought from the souk, and the women spent the rest of the morning preparing the midday meal under the watchful eye of the matriarch. Their pace was relaxed but steady. I tried to help but was told as a guest I should just sit and drink tea.

By that time my boys were adjusting to the fun of having so many children around and before long realized it took little effort to become the center of attention. A few words in English sent the others into spasms of laughter. But their laughter was kindly, and the older children saw to it that the boys felt involved in everything going on. "Minders" from the older children tried to herd them around, but my independent-minded boys shrugged off their help. The minders still dogged their footsteps at a distance, feeling responsible for guests and children younger than themselves. Even Nick was getting used to being passed from hand to hand among the adults like the other babies. I felt relaxed and secure with all these hands to help and sat drinking my tea contentedly while watching the interesting panorama before me. I realized how stressed I normally felt with the responsibility of mothering three boys by myself. How would I feel as a daughter-in-law in one of these households? Would I appreciate the help, or would I feel resentful of the older women running my life? As a young woman would I hate the never-ending work or as an older woman taking care of never-ending guests?

By two o'clock after large platters of food had been sent down to the men's quarters, the oilcloth was again laid on the floor and small dishes set out artistically so each person was within reach of each kind of food. There was hummus, baba ghannouj, olives, tomato and cucumber salad, and large warm flat breads fetched from the baker just before we ate. In the middle of the cloth was a tray with a huge mound of rice and parts of a roasted sheep. I dug in like everyone else with my right hand, taking from the imaginary pie-shaped wedge that defined my space, while the hostess tore off select chunks of meat and placed them in my territory. When I could eat no more and needed to retreat before any more food was piled in front of me, I rose and a young girl gracefully poured water over my hands. Another girl handed me cologne to remove the smell of the meat. The plates were cleared, and new platters of cold sweet chunks of watermelon were brought. When these were finished, we retreated to cushions along the wall for mint tea while the young women and girls washed up the dishes.

We were quietly sipping our tea when suddenly everyone was running toward the balcony. Through the wooden mashrabia screens we could see cars driving up to the open porch where the men were sitting. The women whispered each man's name as he stepped out of the car and was greeted by the host. "There he is," one squealed as a tall, handsome young man in an immaculate white *thobe* walked over to greet the host. The women pointed to the blushing girl in the corner who was also straining to see him. One older woman explained that the man was the one she would marry. She of course wanted to see him, but according to convention, she was supposed to feign shyness.

We returned to the cushions where I asked more about the young man. They proudly noted that he was the perfect match for her. He was her paternal cousin, had graduated from the university, and would be starting a business soon with the help of his father and uncles. I asked the women if they all married cousins, and they replied that most did if there was a cousin of the right age when the time came to marry. I noticed that in describing their paternal cousins they used terms that included not just first cousins but cousins more removed—for example, the son of their father's uncle—so strictly speaking, the husbands were not always first-degree cousins. They explained that paternal cousins were the best marriage partners for women because then everyone in the family supported the couple and wanted the marriage to work. Cousin marriage also prevented a stranger from becoming part of the household as happened when the men married foreign wives or even Saudis from outside the family. The women went around the circle describing their relationships to their husbands and laughingly trying to outdo one another by naming the many other ways they were related through maternal and paternal links. The one woman not related to her husband seemed

Shaikh Abu Shakib and family
in the Druze village of Baysour,
Lebanon (1965)

Nick (second from left), Doug (third from left), and friends in Chemlan, Lebanon (1970)

Uncle Doug and Aunt Belle on
our balcony overlooking the
prison in Beirut (1964)

David and his guide on
a trek to the Cedars of
Lebanon (1965)

David, Doug, Nick, Andrea, and Pinocchio, our means of transport
in Riyadh (1969)

A palace in southern Arabia after a rare storm (1969)

Emir Khalid Sidari and his men greeting us near Najran (1969)

Bill running to help truck drivers rescue David in a flash flood near Abha (1969)

Preparing to stone an adulterer in the public square of Riyadh (1969)

Lunchtime on a main street in Bulaq (1978)

Andrea and Ansaf "insulting" one another (1977)

Ansaf at work in the
Bulaq Center (1978)

Andrea and kids
in a village in the
delta (1978)

Our boat tied up at the bank
of the Nile with paddle wheeler
in background (1980)

Our modest
house in the
Syrian village
(1982)

An older, traditional
village house (1982)

The Bedouin caretaker, Um Muhammad, and her daughter making my favorite bread (1983)

A public bath in Damascus (1983)

apologetic and described him earnestly as "like a paternal cousin," because their fathers were best friends. She called her father-in-law "Ammi" (uncle) because of the closeness.

I watched the newly engaged girl and wondered how she felt about the man she had seen briefly in the courtyard below. Although they were related, he hadn't seen her since their childhood when they were young enough to play together in the women's quarters. Could he be sure his mother had chosen the right woman for him? He would not know until the night of the wedding when he would talk to her for the first time. I could imagine the wedding night and the scared young girl facing intimacies that until now she had avoided on the pain of death. It might not be the best time to start a conversation with your life's partner. I wondered too about the children romping around us. How many of them would end up married to one another?

I asked Muhammad about this as we drove back to Jidda. He answered by describing his own two marriages, one to an American and one to a Saudi. He brought the American wife back with him from the United States, but life was too difficult for her in Saudi Arabia and eventually he divorced her. He explained that she insisted all the time on knowing everything he did and where he went. On top of that, she expected him to spend his time after work with her. "This isn't the way we do things here. She didn't realize that her place was with my mother and sisters, and that I have to spend afternoons and evenings with my male relatives and friends." After the divorce his mother arranged a traditional marriage for him with a Saudi relative, and that marriage succeeded. They lived separate lives during the day and saw each other nights and sometimes on weekends—he socialized with the men and she with the women. His mother was happy with her choice, and he was happy his wife got along well with his mother. "The way I think of it," he said, "is that in America love is at its height when you marry and it goes downhill from there. In Saudi Arabia you meet the girl for the first time at the wedding and love starts growing and only gets better." I could imagine his parents treating the American wife kindly while silently disapproving of her parents that cared so little about her that they let her go off with a total stranger to unknown circumstances. They might be thinking now with satisfaction about the young girl in their household whose husband had been chosen with great care to ensure her future happiness.

Although I didn't know all the intimate details of their lives, I could feel the warmth and sympathy for one another in Muhammad's family, and at least on the surface it seemed enviable. Everyone cooperated cheerfully in tasks, and no one demanded undue attention or seemed disagreeable in temperament. The atmosphere was light and playful, yet disciplined under the watchful eye of the matriarch. I heard Saudi men say they depended on their female relatives to provide the quality atmosphere in their home life, and from all I could see it was well worth the effort the women put into it. If this family was any example of what happens when all goes well, I could see what the men were talking about. At the same time, I could sympathize with Muhammad's American wife, unused to being cooped up with so many people day in and day out. By the end of three days, I was yearning to go outside alone and make my own decisions about the boys without anyone's advice. But I was an American and that's what felt right to me.

~~~

Our two-year assignment in Saudi Arabia had grown into five, yet even then we felt sad when it came time to leave. The boys were growing quickly, and with the exception of short home leaves for Bill to finish his Ph.D. at Columbia and a month in Woods Hole every other year, we had not seen much of the grandparents or other relatives. We asked to be posted to Washington to reacquaint the children with their own country before going out again on a foreign assignment.

7

RETOOLING:
HOME LEAVE (1971–1976)

I hadn't quite realized how many Arab-centric ideas the boys had picked up until we arrived in the States. Five-year-old Nick asked as we landed in Washington why all the people in America lived in tents, and I had to look out the window to realize how different peaked roofs looked from the flat roofs of Saudi Arabia. In the first few weeks, we took them on tours of the capital to see various points of interest, and the boys declared that "Ibrahim Blinken's" memorial was their favorite. Later after school started, Nick was invited to a classmate's house to celebrate Rosh Hashanah, and when his friend's mother asked his religion, he announced proudly that he was an Arab, presumably because he was born in Cairo.

Our first year was filled with finding a house, furnishing it, and becoming comfortable in our new environment. Without the Zeinabs, Hamuds, Hassans, and Abdus to make our lives easy, I had to learn to cook again and fit housework into convenient crevices so it wouldn't consume my entire life. The novelty of having our privacy back felt good. Bill, meanwhile, settled into commuting to work at the United States Information Agency (USIA), where he was in the Near East Bureau in charge of programs in North Africa, the Middle East, and South Asia. A year later he received a Council on Foreign Relations grant to take time off to write a book, *The Arab Press*. In 1972 he returned to USIA as director of the Near East Bureau.

A short time after we settled in, I received a phone call from a Saudi woman I had met at a women's party. She was visiting a brother studying at a U.S.

university and wanted to see me. Of course I dropped everything and invited her to tea. She complained that her brother was too busy with his studies to spend time with her, and she wondered if she could stay with me. I melted in the face of her tears and the still fresh memories of Saudi hospitality. She went off and returned with a stack of suitcases that I carried to Nick's bedroom. I assumed she planned to stay one or two days, but two weeks later there was still no talk of departure. Meanwhile, she made it clear she didn't like American food or the practice of having a small meal at midday, so I spent most of my time making food she liked at a time she was ready to eat it. I gave her breakfast when she arose around 11:00, made a special meal for her at about 2:00 and warmed it up again for my family at 6:00, and then prepared a light evening meal for her around 8:00. Throughout the day I made endless cups of tea prepared the way she liked it. Each night I fell exhausted into bed but was unwilling to admit defeat in what had become a matter of honor. When I thought I could bear it no longer, she said she would soon have to return to Saudi Arabia. Then ensued a series of expensive long-distance calls to her relatives on my phone and finally a request for me to loan her $800 to pay for her air ticket. I was ready to do almost anything to get her to leave, but we were having difficulty paying our own expenses after only recently paying settlement costs and the first installment of our mortgage. I explained truthfully that I didn't have more than $100 in our bank account, a fact that she probably didn't believe. In the end, the modesty of our house, the lack of servants, and the fact that we had no money must have made her realize she had not chosen a good place for her holiday. Her brother finally gave her the money, and the day came when she and her suitcases went off in a taxi never to be heard of again. I knew I hadn't handled the visit well but didn't see what else I could have done.

Free again I volunteered in art classes and at the library of the children's school, thinking careers in these areas might fit well with the boys' schedules. I soon realized that although I had enormous admiration for the women who filled these positions, it wasn't my kind of work. I joined a women's walking group that explored the parks around Washington and watched the vegetation change through the seasons, but this was a leisure-time activity that didn't take me any closer to finding a satisfying career. I joined a feminist consciousness-raising group, listened to members angrily express their private woes, and then watched as one by one they divorced their husbands. After years in the Foreign Service conforming to "women's roles" to meet embassy expectations, it was hard to take a 180-degree turn and become an outraged feminist. Besides, I didn't want to expose my personal woes in front of these strangers. I left the meetings feeling resentful and discontent, realizing that the child rearing I had taken on so willingly was not as challenging now that the boys were in school. Certainly it was unfair—to give it the cast of the group—that although I had graduated from college just as Bill had, he was engaged in activities that expanded his skills and gave him satisfaction while I did nothing but organize the household and transport the boys to their extracurricular activities. Life overseas had proved so infinitely distracting that these discontents had never surfaced, but now they were suddenly looming large in my life. In the highly charged atmosphere of the early 1970s, it was hard to feel satisfied in a wife/mother role when everyone asked, "What do you do?" and assumed that anyone with any intelligence was doing something interesting.

By the second year, I was ready for something more ambitious and decided to follow up on the interests I developed in Saudi Arabia. The struggles with the Saudi family trees, and the insights they eventually revealed, made me want to learn more about the mechanics of studying cultures. I made an appointment to visit the nearest graduate program in anthropology—at American University—to see if I could enroll in a few classes. I told the chair of the department that I wanted to learn the techniques of anthropology—for example, how to make family trees. She replied that there weren't any courses that just taught family trees. "But you can study ethnography or some other branch of anthropology." I didn't know what ethnography was but told her I wanted to study that. At home I looked up "ethnography" in *Webster's Dictionary* and learned that it meant "descriptive anthropology; sometimes loosely ethnology." Ethnology in turn is defined as "the science that treats of the division of mankind into races, their origin, distribution, relations, and peculiarities." I guessed my interest was "their peculiarities," but even at the time, I don't think I would have phrased it quite as negatively.

Ignorant as I must have seemed, I did learn some important things from the chair. I could take graduate courses as a "continuing education" student, and if I did well, I would automatically enter the master's program without taking the Graduate Record Exams. Furthermore, if I received high honors in the comprehensive exams for the master's—archaeology, linguistics, and theory—I could advance to the Ph.D. program. I didn't aspire to a Ph.D. but thought I might be able to do a master's degree before going overseas again.

One steamy fall day in 1972, I found myself standing in line with much younger students to register for graduate courses. I planned to take courses I would need for the comprehensive exams—archaeology, linguistics, and anthropological theory. I figured the first two would be more difficult since I had little interest in the subjects, but if I could complete them, I knew I could do the rest. Clutched in my hand was a $4,000 check, an amount that only a few years earlier had been enough to live on for two years. I suppressed the urge to step out of line and return to the secure life of motherhood, but I was encouraged by the thought that it would only take one semester to find out if I could succeed in an academic world I had left behind fifteen years earlier.

The boys were all in school, so I scheduled most of my courses in the morning and the rest at night when Bill was home. My mother-in-law gave me one afternoon of babysitting a week. On days the boys had soccer practice, I sat in the car writing seminar papers on pads of paper that I then typed late into the night. Each semester required one major paper a seminar—three in all. While other students wrote theirs in a crunch at the end, I completed one paper a month in addition to my reading and other assignments, so by the end of the semester all three papers were done. At least twice I became interested in another topic and squeezed in additional papers. Once when I already had turned in a paper, I asked the professor if I could submit a second one. He looked surprised but agreed. I begged him not to tell the other students who'd nicknamed me "the Ultimate Overachiever." My enjoyment of graduate work kept me in such a high state of elation that nothing seemed a burden.

I even found the linguistics and archaeology courses interesting. The linguistics professor assigned a problem before his course started. We were to analyze two lists of forty Native-American words from different tribes and decide whether they were languages that were totally separate or derived from one another and, if the latter, which came first. He cited books that explained how to analyze languages. I read the sources and wrote a twenty-page report of my conclusions. He gave me an A+, which he said was the first he'd ever given. He asked why I was in the continuing education program when I should be in the graduate program.

That encouraged me a lot, although my success, I felt, was more a matter of the seriousness with which I approached the assignment compared to other students. Other aspects of linguistics, such as phonemic distinctions, turned out to be as dull as I expected—mainly because I couldn't hear the differences. But I did love to read Benjamin Whorf on how language shapes behavior. My paper for the course described the subtleties of words Saudis use for objects that are important to them.

Archaeology, too, turned out better than I expected. The "digs" I visited overseas seemed the ultimate in boredom and discomfort—endless hours in the hot sun sieving through sand and debris, hoping to find objects that might prove significant. The course showed me that archaeology was basically the same as anthropology, just using different kinds of data. In our main textbook, the editor-author Louis Binford collected articles by the "new" archaeologists that read like mystery stories. Each researcher drew conclusions from the juxtaposition of artifacts—in one example, showing that the potters were women by the location of kilns close to their homes.

But it was anthropological theory that thrilled me the most. It raised questions that I sensed intuitively abroad but had not been able to articulate well. I examined the definitions of culture that various anthropologists used and settled on a definition that made sense to me: Culture is "the shared mental outlooks of a people that help them make sense of the world around them and react to it." Later I felt a large part of culture was the customary ways people have of relating to one another.

I liked to think of culture as like language, giving people a coherent set of "grammar rules" to organize their thinking. The rules were compatible within a culture but might differ dramatically across cultures. When people know two cultures well, they could move automatically from one to the other in the same way one might switch between languages. This shared knowledge of rules lets people communicate their intentions to one another and know their intentions will be understood. As anthropologists, our job is to extract the rules from the complexity of behavior. Thinking of culture as like language gives a somewhat more neutral way of dealing with a subject that, at its best, is fraught with emotional and moral overtones.

I learned from anthropological theory that a number of widely held beliefs about cultures had been largely discredited. One that has regained some currency recently is the idea that Westerners occupy the highest point on an evolutionary scale of civilizations. The implication is that with luck others might someday reach a similar pinnacle. With thinking like this, no wonder I was confused by Arabs like Rima whose moral standards made me feel inferior by comparison. Where was the superiority Americans assume?

Another implication of this "theory of civilization" was that universal measures existed to evaluate cultures, and we Westerners were somehow entitled to determine what those measures would be. This was the outlook of early anthropologists like Leslie White and his colleagues, and they seemed to hold the view of Americans who claim our differences from the Arab world are simply a time lag of 100 years or so—and "eventually they will catch up." The foremost critics of these unilinear approaches were the cultural relativists who called for judging cultures by their own values.

The techniques of anthropology also appealed to me: holism, comparison, and participation. Holism meant considering as much of a society's complexity as possible, knowing any piece of information might be relevant to an understanding of the whole. Holism also meant a topic could be entered from any vantage point—a person, a village, a custom, or an institution—and ultimately it would inform the whole topic.

The second technique, comparison, is what anyone confronting a new culture does—compares it with his or her own culture. It was what I was doing in Saudi Arabia, Egypt, and Lebanon, and, of course, what became most apparent were our differences. These differences—as in time concepts in Saudi Arabia—need to be understood to avoid misunderstandings and make social interactions easier. Anthropologists also compare the same phenomenon—say the behavior of a succession of rulers—over time to see how it changes. Or they might look at an activity like bread making in different contexts to see what is constant and what varies in the process.

The final technique, participation, is in many ways the most important. I especially learned its importance later in development work. Ideas developed at a desk invariably prove wrong when exposed to reality on the ground. Until a phenomenon becomes such a part of you that you know every detail, you will find it hard to speak authoritatively about it. But what kind and how much participation is necessary before you can say important things about cultures? It was what I was struggling to understand in getting involved with the people in countries where I lived.

There were also the practical questions of fieldwork that would confront me later on. How do you enter the field? What role do you fill? What kind of information do you collect? Does your outsider view differ from that of an insider? Whose perspective is most "true"? How do you report what you know? These are just some of the dilemmas of fieldwork.

Another issue that perplexed me was the matter of politics. Could an observer ever be neutral? Should anthropologists take sides at all, and if so which side? Many anthropologists have become involved in "moral" issues when, for example, they wanted to bring world attention to practices like female circumcision. I had wrestled many times in Egypt with practices I knew were unhealthy, or unfair, or should be reported and had done nothing. Was it wrong not to speak out even though, as in female circumcision, local people may see them as normal? All these questions stayed with me in my later work, including whether to attach myself to one school or branch of anthropology or another: Marxist, functionalist, structuralist, psychological, social, and cultural, among others. But each seemed too narrow to fully capture the complexities of cultures.

Academics (and others) today seem to be returning to the idea that universal values should be applied everywhere. And while there may indeed be taboos against murder or incest that are widespread, no two societies hold identical sets of beliefs. In my mind, therefore, they should not have to live up to the same standards, especially those introduced by self-promoting outsiders. It is differences that define us, not our similarities, even though the latter may be more numerous.

During my lifetime, anthropology has changed from a discipline whose books were widely read by the public to one where they are largely written for academic audiences. I believe this is a problem—and that anthropologists should do more to help the public understand the cultures they study. When anthropology turned away from the Margaret Meads, Ruth Benedicts, and others who were seeking distinctive patterns in cultures, it turned away, in my opinion, from the "grand" study of culture and focused narrowly on topics of interest mainly to academics. This has meant that anthropologists shy away from the larger picture the general public is curious about. Cultural relativism was discredited when other researchers started studying the same societies and drawing different conclusions. But instead of recognizing the failures of researchers, or contradictory results as differences in their subjects or the time periods in which they studied them, scholars dismissed relativism itself as too subjective. The deeper problem lay in believing that only one reality exists for any culture.

Anthropologists turned to postmodernism with its emphasis on collecting the self-expression of local people—their oral histories, practices, and beliefs—but with little analysis. Readers who had never been to these cultures found it difficult to grasp the significance of, say, children's games in explicating a larger society. Perhaps to give their work the impression of greater profundity, the postmodernists developed a new vocabulary that turned simple observations into impenetrable verbiage. The convoluted language further distanced academics from the general public, who have difficulty understanding it. In the case of women's studies, the language seemed to be used to make simple, albeit important, ideas seem more profound.

Middle Eastern scholarship took the hardest blow, becoming almost paralyzed by Edward Said's book on "Orientalism" that made non-Arab scholars self-conscious about anything they said—the implication of his book being that outsiders' views of the Middle East have distorted the reality. Many scholars retreated into safe topics and were fearful of criticizing anything Arabs said about themselves. Or they hid behind the language of postmodernism to make the cultures of the Middle East seem even more inexplicable.

The upshot of this evolution in anthropology was that when the United States invaded Iraq it was difficult to find an anthropologist anywhere willing to "explain" Arab culture. The field was thus open for other disciplines to explain Iraq in terms of their own agendas. We anthropologists should have been there to explain why the invasion was unlikely to succeed. But the excuse that covered this vacuum was that we shouldn't provide information that made it easier to manipulate local populations and that we would be aiding and abetting the military in their control of this country.

Through the study of anthropology, I grew to believe that human cultures are indeed more alike than different, but because the differences cause problems, it's important to understand them. I believe that understanding comes more easily from examples on the ground—with the best way being to experience a culture yourself, but next best is to read or hear about another person's experiences. I continue to believe certain elements of cultural relativism take us further than a perspective that decides which are "better or worse cultures or practices" based on a single set of values. I feel it's unfair to judge any society by measures that it doesn't hold for itself. Those who make these judgments only show their own cultural arrogance. I believe also that most people act rationally in their own best interest as they perceive it. Actions that surprise an outsider invariably indicate that something of importance is being preserved, nurtured, or sustained as a greater good for that society, and insights are waiting to be born in these puzzling pieces. If this seems too tidy a way of viewing cultures, my experiences in the Middle East should quickly show the messiness in pursuing the study of culture.

To make a long story short, I finished the first semester with the grades I needed to enter the master's program, and after two years when I passed the master's comprehensive exams with high honors, I entered the Ph.D. program. Each year about the time Foreign Service assignments were handed out, we held our breath, hoping we could stay in the United States just a little longer so I could complete my coursework. We were lucky. By 1976 when we couldn't delay an assignment any longer, my Ph.D. degree requirements were completed, including the French and German language exams, and I had only my dissertation left to do. I proposed a topic to my committee and was ready to leave in the fall of 1976 for Cairo.

It was an exciting move both for my research and because, after a hiatus of several years, the United States and Egypt were restoring diplomatic relations. We would be some of the first official Americans to be posted to an embassy that was rebuilding itself. The atmosphere would be different under President Sadat, who was turning to the West with his "open door" policy, which he hoped would improve the economy of his poverty-stricken nation.

The boys were more or less excited about going to Cairo, although it meant entering a new school and finding new friends. David was fifteen and in his last years of high school; Doug was at the vulnerable age of twelve—a time many Foreign Service families feel is not good to move—and in junior high; and Nick was ten and in elementary school. All three would attend the Cairo American College in the suburb of Maadi.

8

SECOND CHANCE: CAIRO AGAIN (1976–1978)

I was eager to apply the book learning I worked so hard to acquire in the United States. But in Cairo the task suddenly seemed fraught with difficulties. Where would I start, and how would I get permissions from the Egyptians for a study? I took a leisurely three months pondering these questions while we settled into our new home and the children started school.

The diplomatic part of my life had become easier. The State Department finally realized spouses were treated unfairly and ruled we no longer had to perform the tasks we were compelled to do before, such as the calling, the diplomatic functions, and the bazaars. In theory I could do what I wanted, but calling on spouses still seemed a good way to meet people, so I decided to visit the wives who accepted calls. Bill was higher in protocol rank now, which meant fewer spouses to visit, and this time I completed the calls in a few days with the convenience of Bill's official car. I also didn't need to attend diplomatic functions, but it was hard to opt out of parties with such high local standards for hospitality.

Bill's position this time required more entertaining responsibilities, but that duty was less arduous with a secretary who sent out invitations and kept our social calendar. We had also inherited a good cook, butler, gardener, and cleaning woman. Another plus was that our house was one of the most beautiful in Cairo, with large reception rooms, upstairs and downstairs kitchens, and a marble balcony that overlooked the garden. The garden stretched the width of a city block and contained mango trees of different varieties, kumquats, palms, frangipani, and flame trees—as well as a resident mongoose that chittered angrily when we disturbed him and a curlew that sent his haunting cry over the neighborhood each evening. The ancient gardener kept the paths of the yard lined with seasonal flowers—so many that our house on a quiet street in Dokki only minutes from downtown Cairo became known as the "House of the Flowers." The garden was a perfect place for large receptions or sit-down dinners. All I had to do was show up and check the cook's receipts. It felt strange to be so detached from the functioning of the household, but I knew it was good given the extensive research agenda I had planned.

Under President Sadat, Cairo had reverted to its vibrant, colorful self with traffic-filled streets and friendly, exuberant people. In our absence, however, many more women began wearing *zey islami* (Islamic dress), the modest, long, loose dress and cowl-like head cover that usually denoted a pious outlook. People explained that after the June 1967 War many Egyptians felt the Arab's humiliating defeat was Allah's way of punishing them for departing from traditional Islamic practice. In the mid-1960s when we lived in Cairo before, educated men and women wore Western dress. Now many students were donning Islamic dress, especially those studying at the Al-Azhar Islamic University.

Still, everyone was eager to welcome Americans back after the Russian-dominated Nasser era. Almost every shopkeeper we met told us how penurious and morose the Russians had been and added hopefully that they were pleased with the return of the more generous Americans. Our reputations had clearly gained in our absence.

With all this working for me, there was no excuse to hesitate any longer. So I set off one day to have tea with the new minister of social affairs. Meeting her had been one of those happy accidents that seemed too good to be true. During a party at the ambassador's home, she was standing alone—a shy and little-known lawyer—and like me trying to escape the meaningless chitchat that left such an unsatisfying feeling. We talked for some time, and when we parted she gave me her card and told me to come see her. Two weeks later she became minister of social affairs.

The reason our meeting was so fortuitous was that the topic I had proposed to my professor at American University was a study of her ministry. I hoped to look at it in the way anthropologists study a village—examining its organization, personnel, employee networks, and officials' strategies for getting things done. I was interested in this ministry because a woman minister often ran it, and many of its highest officials were women. Previous studies described the networking strategies of Egyptian male officials that took place in meetings that did not encouraged the presence of women. My study would look at the strategies women bureaucrats used to accomplish their goals and see whether they were similar to those of men. The gender cast of the research would fit well with the interest in women's studies at the time. But I also had an interest in the institutional culture of a society that depended on personal contacts to get things done.

Over tea and cakes we talked about general topics and what it was like being minister in the glare of media attention. I felt guilty taking advantage of our tenuous friendship but finally screwed up the courage to ask for permission to work in her ministry. I was convinced she would see the merits of my proposal and support it enthusiastically. I explained that I had selected her ministry because it had a number of powerful women in high positions supervising men, and I wanted to see how this unusual situation worked. I told her I knew male officials used *shilla* (friendship) groups to piggyback one another into positions of prominence and *duffaa* (alumni) groups of people who survived the period of schooling together and stayed close. Ministries dominated by men were soon staffed with networks of their own trusted acquaintances who could then be counted on to do tasks for their mentors. "But what about women," I posed the question rhetorically to her, "did they do the same?" I told her that if she would just arrange for me to occupy a desk in her ministry for several months, I would observe the interactions of her staff and, God willing, my findings might help her institute more efficient ways of running her ministry. It embarrasses me to think I phrased my request so naïvely. "*Inshalla* (God willing)," she replied, showing no sign of emotion. "I'll get back to you."

The upshot was that after several teas with the minister, I realized God was not willing to grant my request. All I did was ruin a budding friendship. My several years in the United States had made me forget that research and spying were almost synonymous in the Egyptian mind as people recovered from the distrust of foreigners engendered by the Russians in the Nasser period. My miscalculation taught me to listen more attentively to the messages behind the words and to move into sensitive conversations more slowly. Egyptians don't want to say no, and it was far better to test their inclinations before forcing them to decide. Luckily by then, I was losing interest in studying her ministry.

In the months awaiting her reply, I tried to make effective use of my time. It seemed a good preparation for studying educated women in the ministry to know more about Egyptian education in general. An Egyptian-American friend, Nayra, who had recently returned to Egypt, decided to try teaching kindergarteners in the creative ways she observed in the United States. She asked me to join her two days a week at the private school where she worked. The school was a complex of lovely, old, high-ceilinged buildings with beautiful moldings and heavily worn wooden stairs. The headmistress, Mary Salama, was a charismatic personality known throughout Cairo for keeping stern control over her charges and producing graduates who scored high on national exams, as well as developing proficiency in foreign languages and Arabic. She had to have been unusual to let Nayra and me experiment on a class of some fifty small kindergarten children. She gave us what we estimated to be the equivalent of twenty-five cents a student for materials for the year. It gave us the challenge of seeing how far we could make it go. In the souk Nayra found large sheets of newsprint, made cheap because of government subsidies on imported paper. We cut the paper into three-by-five-inch rectangles and bought crayons, scissors, and pencils.

Nayra established a rule that the children could draw or listen to stories or essentially do any activity they wanted as long as they were reasonably polite and orderly. Children who were ready to learn could start with alphabet letters and simple words. We covered the walls, somewhat untidily, with their artwork. But before long we realized we had seriously miscalculated the expectations of Egyptian parents. Complaints started pouring in: The children "weren't learning"—all they brought home were scribbled drawings and not the neatly colored-in outlines and pages of letters and numbers expected by the parents. Even within the school itself, we were causing an uproar. Teachers casually dropped by to offer advice on "controlling our class" and "the right way to teach." They criticized the messiness of the classroom and the way our children roared up the stairs after recess instead of marching in orderly lines. Our example was making students from other classes become disorderly. One teacher complained that we assigned girls as captains to lead the lines rather than boys, as had always been the practice. Furthermore, when our children went to music class, the teacher had trouble getting them to march in orderly lines. Often they came back crying from being disciplined. The last straw came on parents' night when the children's free-flow artwork (and little else) posted outside our classroom didn't stand up against the prodigious work of other classes—most of it neatly produced by teachers. The next day we were demoted to the art room, where our novel ideas might be less disruptive.

One incident in the art room pretty much stands for everything else that happened there. Nayra was determined to loosen the children up, and one day decided we would create such an enticing situation that they would immediately fall upon the materials and do some really creative work. We covered all the tables with oilcloth, bought with our own money, and arranged a few jars of brightly colored paint on top. The children marched in two by two and stood stiffly in their assigned places. We explained that they would do finger painting—that they should dip their hands into the paints and draw whatever they wanted on the tabletops. A look of horror came over their faces as they stood paralyzed at the idea of dirtying their hands and the tables. It took us bodily pushing their fingers into the paint before they would do it. Eventually they got the idea and left the class with "printed" versions of their artwork as well as cheerful spots of color all over their tidy uniforms. Before long the parents were complaining that the children were coming home with dirty smocks on art days, and soon our experiments in creativity were over. There was one small success though—a little girl who probably would be diagnosed autistic—refused to participate in any of her classes. She seemed to enjoy the art classes though, so we left the doors open during recess, and she would creep in and continue the drawings she started in class. We parted from the school amicably. The headmistress in her wisdom realized our ideas were before their time in Egypt.

I learned from this experience that these upper-middle- and upper-class children had already been conditioned before the age of five to behave properly and avoid anything dirty or disorderly. The mantra of the school was "color within the lines," stand in proper rows, boys lead, everyone progresses at the same rate and learns to read and write the 300 words mandated by the ministry for kindergarteners. Mannered behavior was being taught in the school and homes to separate these children from the masses of Egypt.

Meanwhile, I was spending three days a week in a social welfare center in the poorest quarter of Cairo. An American nurse I knew volunteered in the center and arranged for me to visit. By the end of the first day, I was so enamored with the director, Mme. Ansaf, that I asked if I could accompany her on visits to the residents of the area. When she urged me to join her as often as possible, I started coming three times a week and then five times after the school project failed.

Eventually I realized that Bulaq and its residents were more interesting as a research subject than the ministry was. But I worried whether I could get Egyptian government approval of my study, since I was told it rarely approved when it involved a topic like the poor that might prove an embarrassment to Egypt. I tackled the problem indirectly by going to the man in Bill's office known to work for Egyptian Security. I figured if he told me I could continue it would be all right. I explained that I was regularly visiting a welfare center in the heart of Bulaq and sometimes visited the community with the Egyptian social worker. I asked if that was acceptable and told him I wanted to make sure the government approved so no harm would come to my social-worker friend. He said he would think about it, which I took to mean he would ask his superiors. When he came back, he said there was no reason I couldn't do "charity work, since after all that was what embassy wives did." During the next five years, he was true to his words, and when I complained to him once when Ansaf was called to the police station, he intervened and made sure it didn't happen again. Egyptians were sympathetic to anyone who worked with the poor, and before long I had an undeserved reputation for "doing good." I explained my study to Ansaf, but she trusted me and didn't care what I did. When people in Bulaq asked why I was there, she replied that I was her friend and helping her. She didn't intentionally mislead them; it was simply the way she saw it.

Ansaf was a special person. The first day I met her I recognized how extraordinary she was by the sympathetic way she worked with the poor clients of the Bulaq Center and always followed up on her promises to them. A large part of her meager salary went to cases she felt needed more than the small amount the church doled out each month.

Ansaf was born in Upper Egypt in Assiut Governorate. Her father died while visiting Cairo when he stepped off a trolley into the path of another vehicle. His leg was severed, and he bled to death before medical attention arrived. Ansaf's mother had been educated in a school established by American missionaries in Assiut, where after her husband's death she found work and managed to raise and educate her three children. Ansaf attended the school until one day in the ninth grade a young man noticed her on the playground and asked her mother if he could marry her. She was fifteen years old.

Ibrahim was posted to a government school in Cairo, and Ansaf found a job teaching girls knitting in the Bulaq Center. This allowed the couple to support their four children—two girls and two boys—through university. The Bulaq Center that hired her belonged to the Anglican Church whose properties the Egyptians had taken over after the British left. While I was there the properties included a cathedral in Zamalak, a multistoried Bulaq Center on Ramsis Street, and in the middle of the slum areas a small center where the work with the poor was carried on under Ansaf's supervision. We spent most of our time in this small center. Even though the organization belonged to Egyptian Anglicans, the staff were Protestants like Ansaf or Copts like the teachers and janitor.

Just before I left Cairo in 1981, the church sold the larger Bulaq Center building on Ramsis to the *Al-Ahram* newspaper next door. By that time the Egyptian government decided to relocate the Bulaq families to dismal "Soviet-style" apartments on the edge of Cairo to clear space for a large cultural center for tourists on Bulaq's prime real estate. However, after the government disrupted the lives and livelihoods of the residents and tore down our small center, they never built the attractions they had planned. The priest in charge of the larger center over the years had managed to amass enough money to retire and build a substantial apartment in a suburb of Cairo.

But this is ahead of the story. When Ansaf came to work as the knitting instructor, her coworker was a woman who ran the center and visited poor families. The families complained to the bishop that she demanded food and drink in return for keeping them on the registers of the center. Registration was required to receive the small monthly stipends and gifts at Christmas and Easter that the center gave out. The bishop investigated their complaints and fired her. No one but Ansaf knew the families so she became the center's social worker despite her lack of academic qualifications. Ansaf always refused tea, coffee, or food, except on visits to the homes of more affluent families (some of whom were store owners or drug dealers). This shows how exceptional she was since "gatekeepers" in Egypt inevitably took advantage of their positions.

From the beginning I tried to maintain an observer's role, even though I was often impatient with the inefficiencies of the center and would have liked to figure out long-term solutions rather than rely on handouts. My research demanded an inconspicuous role and I didn't want to compete with Ansaf whose empathy endeared her to the community.

There was no job description for Ansaf's work or limitations on what she could do other than the meager five cents a day she received to solve problems. The center also housed services paid for separately through the church: literacy and vocational classes (handicraft and knitting) every weekday, baby weighing and inoculations on Tuesdays, religious instruction on Wednesdays, and visits to families twice a week. We stopped by the homes of people who were ill; who suffered a death, or had a crisis in income, or wanted to marry a child; or who needed a mediator for a conflict between neighbors; or sometimes just to cheer up a lonely old woman or encourage someone who was coping well with her difficulties. Ansaf's most valuable assets were her store of people who provided free services and information about where other services could be obtained.

I discovered we had visited over 250 families in Bulaq when I instituted records for my research. I thought Ansaf might find the records useful to show others what we were doing, or to keep straight which families had benefited from our help, but every detail of these matters resided in her prodigious memory. Records were just a nuisance.

Some of the inhabitants and their problems I remember vividly. Um Dawud—whose name she claimed proudly was the same as mine—had a tennis ball-size cancer in her breast. She sought help at the free government hospital but was repeatedly turned away until we went with her and were conspicuous enough in line for the doctors to notice. Out of sheer embarrassment, they admitted her to the hospital. In the crowded ward we found two patients to a bed, lying head to toe, on sheets too dirty to describe. The nurses hurriedly dismissed another patient to make a place available—a fact that was discomfiting as the patient pleaded to remain. We visited Um Dawud frequently to ensure she would receive attention and bribed the attendants to change her sheets and bring her food. The doctors cut out the cancer, and she lived for many more years.

There were the black-clad women holding hands nervously whom we took on their first trolley ride to visit a doctor friend of Ansaf. They had ingrown eyelashes—a common problem in Bulaq that led to blindness if left untreated.

Ansaf had a list of doctors who would operate free for this and other problems. On the trolley they squatted on the floor to the amusement of the other passengers. They returned to Bulaq in the same lines with their eyes bandaged. Our postoperative treat was freshly squeezed orange juice. Several had eaten whole oranges, but had not had the luxury of orange juice.

Each woman in Bulaq had a story that identified her. "Remember this woman," Ansaf would say, "the one whose husband planted hashish on her and she went to jail for six years," or, "We're going to visit the woman whose son died in that horrible car accident." They told their compelling stories to help us remember them the next time, and indeed it was often the story that was the reason for our visits. "We must go see this Muslim woman to thank her for caring for her Christian neighbor," Ansaf would say.

Sometimes Ansaf poked fun at the women in a playful way. She would say, "Can you imagine she paid five piasters for tomatoes when everyone knows they cost only four." The person would be secretly pleased by the attention, and they both would laugh heartily over the incident. Ansaf rarely left a house without a joke to cheer the inhabitants.

I am trying to think how to describe what Ansaf and I were to each other. We were different in every way—in physical appearance, education, economic level, and, of course, nationality. She had the dark skin of the Egyptian south against my anemically pale skin; she was sturdily stout, and I reed thin. In personality, she was vibrant and engaging, while I was quietly introverted. Her life experience was deep and focused, while mine was broad and superficial. I was childlike in this environment against her confident adult. I was the observer not wanting to be drawn into the conversation; she the person of action always knowing the right thing to say. We never stood in line or took a tram without Ansaf talking to everyone around us—I holding on to my reticence, she almost missing her stop. She used me as a foil, an excuse to connect with others who of course always wondered what an American was doing on the dilapidated transportation system. She would tell the person next to her my story, embellished to make me a paragon of virtue, and the story would pass up and down the bus. I was her proud possession—I made her feel "big," she said. And I was happy to listen to the things she found out about people. Each newcomer's life was a story to her, and each story elicited such a depth of sympathy from her that they were encouraged to continue.

Ansaf also demanded respectful behavior and could answer with a sharp retort to anyone who was not proper. I have seen her straighten up and go quiet in situations where people of a higher class rudely dismissed her. She never overstepped the bounds of class yet wasn't submissive or obsequious either. My unuttered response was, "She is worth a hundred of you." But she would not have wanted me to breach her code of conduct by expressing such comments. She was a person of peace and moderation.

We needed each other in so many ways it's difficult to relate them all. Her son told me many years later that she always said I had been the most important influence in her life and had made her feel "important" for the first time. And I don't challenge his statement. I wrote a front-page article about her and the miracles she performed in Bulaq for the *Al-Ahram* newspaper. Everywhere she went people recognized her from the picture and story—even her butcher, she pointed out. She still tells me many years later that she thinks of me every day. Instead of President Hosni Mubarak's picture hanging over her desk, it is my portrait that hangs there, with pink cheeks she had a photographer paint in.

For me she was the perfect mentor in Bulaq, and in life, I later realized. Ansaf was the confident female who didn't flinch from any situation—always knew what the moment required. I was her child in Bulaq, not understanding fully what I was seeing, nor knowing how to solve problems we faced together, nor even communicating properly. She took it upon herself to explain everything to me, to translate the parts I didn't understand, and to shield me from the pleas for money that inevitably followed someone who looked as rich as I did. I saw how sophisticated her knowledge of certain things was, how she could read people's faces and understand the nuances of their emotions. She did it without even knowing how she knew. We would emerge from someone's home—I moved by the person's story and she scoffing at what she knew was a tale to impress us.

Meanwhile, I had a broader experience about what we might do to help the people of Bulaq. Her vision was grounded in the morality of charity, mine in longer-term goals of sustainability. Near the end of my stay, I convinced her that loans might be a more long-lasting and effective way to solve people's problems rather than just giving them money. She adopted the idea wholeheartedly. I helped her amass a large fund but within a few years she had spent the whole amount on needy cases.

I have to mention our way of communicating in a strange mixture of Arabic and English—a language we developed for ourselves that made us almost unintelligible to anyone else. Having gone to the missionary school in Assiut, where the course was partly in English, she understood English at an elementary level and spoke it at an even lower level. After a time I understood the Bulaq women's Arabic quite well—involving as it invariably did issues of home and family—but I never fully developed the vocabulary for complicated discussions. She wanted to practice her English; I wanted to practice Arabic. The result was conversations where I spoke Arabic and she English interspersed with words we didn't know using our own languages. I don't remember that we ever had difficulty understanding one another. We had our own ways of insulting each other too. "Liar woman," I would hurl at her when she went overboard cooking for me after promising only to make my favorite *mulakiya* soup if I came to lunch. She loved that insult that no one else could get away with—another indication of our close relations.

Two stories in particular about Ansaf show her "centeredness" in situations that would have unbalanced a less secure person. After I turned my attention to working full time in Bulaq, we spent nearly every day together with the kind of teamwork only women who love their work achieve. She knew my thoughts and I knew hers, even though a gulf of culture and experiences prevented us from entirely entering each other's worlds. Soon though I began to feel that I was letting her bear too much of the burden of our relationship. We would work from 8:00 a.m. to 2:00 p.m. in Bulaq and then head off to our respective homes in different parts of town. I knew her world of Bulaq and had visited her family in their homes and had even taken trips by train to see a daughter in Upper Egypt and another in Alexandria. It was months into our work, and she hadn't been to my house in Dokki or met my family. She had not asked to go there, but knowing Ansaf, she probably saw in my silence a reason I had not invited her. And to tell the truth I didn't want to show her my palatial house for fear it might change her feelings about me.

The first day of many days I visited her stands out. She needed to leave work early because a relative had come to town and she needed to prepare a special meal. She was running late and seemed anxious about getting the food ready so I volunteered to help. Her home was not far away on the high ground at the beginning of mainly Christian Shubra. We stopped at the corner to purchase meat, probably costing a third of her monthly salary. Her building was halfway down an alley. That day garbage filled the stairwell, and the banister sagged in dangerous loops. One could tell the building had once been modestly grand from the high ceilings, ornately carved doorways, and the curve of the marble stairs. But now Cairo's overlay of sticky silt shrouded the walls and painted the corners of the stairs black. Her apartment by Bulaq standards was spacious, but an earthquake had caused such cracks in the walls that the government inspectors had condemned it—but a few Egyptian pounds to them allowed her to remain. She had two small living rooms, two bedrooms, a kitchen, and a bath—a middle-class format that differed from the homes of the poor with their one or two rooms that were always multifunctional. The two narrow bedrooms led out to small balconies encumbered with washing lines rigged to drip water onto the street. As I came more often to visit, she would be waving frantically from the balcony, sure I would lose my way and not turn left at the butcher's.

One of the two sitting rooms was a formal parlor that barely accommodated her curved upholstered chairs and love seat and doilies scattered here and there to keep off the dirt but just as grimy as everything else in Cairo's pollution. In the center stood a coffee table with a cracked glass top on which now sits a chunk of plastic with seashells from Woods Hole I made one summer. Covering a wall were pictures: one of her parents and siblings, with her father wearing the old-style red *tarboush*; the second of herself standing with Ibrahim after they were married, when she looked so young and vulnerable; then of her children and their families and friends; later of me and my children, and eventually of grandchildren. The wall was as infinitely expandable as was her heart. Her house had the character of Ansaf, organized and tidy—not prettified—but muddled enough to show family and friends came before interior design and matching colors. The inner sitting room had a dining table pushed to the wall, a buffet, and refrigerator, and another wall of pictures. Finally there was a small kitchen, and beside it a bathroom that I tried to avoid at all costs. The room was barely big enough to contain the Western-style toilet with the standard flush chain attached to a tank near the ceiling. My hesitation was due to the lack of a door. Ansaf had decorously hung a curtain, but no matter how I arranged my knees, they always stuck out into the hall.

During that first visit, we were intent on the kitchen—a tiny room with sink, hot plate, and little else. The menu was salad, chicken, and lentil soup. I tackled the only job where my skills might work—chopping the onions—and she began boiling the chicken to make a broth before she gave it a final pan-fry. Thus began an argument that lasted thirty years. "Dr. Andrea (she never got over that formality), onions have to be chopped very fine or it's bad for the stomach," she would say. And I would answer that I couldn't do them as fine as she wanted, and besides she was cooking them in too much oil. We managed to get the meal ready that day. But the visit began my dilemma of how to reciprocate her hospitality without overwhelming her with our differences in wealth. I thought it was easier for me to adapt to Bulaq with its poverty and disease than for Ansaf to adjust to my world of overabundance. But I didn't know Ansaf.

It took six months before I had the courage to invite her. To ease the tensions I asked her to bring her family on her day off. They came dressed in their best, but even so my staff was confused by the differences between Ansaf's family and the upper-class Egyptians they were used to seeing in our home. Ansaf looked around and said, "So this is your home. It's very nice." And that was the end of it. It didn't change our relationship or make a difference in the way we worked together. Ansaf never saw me as rich and never let the Bulaq people plead for money—that kept our relationships dignified. Indeed, in all the time I knew her, she never asked me for anything. So in my palatial house on that day, she collected herself and made sure we laughed a lot and had a good time.

The other story is similar. I told her one day that the British ambassador's wife was leaving Cairo for another post. Ghislaine had helped us sell the handiwork of the Bulaq women at every bazaar. Ansaf had marveled at how such "a big person" had worked with so little fanfare and decided to give her a going-away gift. After consultation she decided on a cardigan that she would make on a knitting machine. We chose the color of yarn together, and she set about completing the sweater. When she was done, she wrapped it and handed it to me to give to Ghislaine. I reminded her that she always made me give the small gifts I brought to Bulaq—a sack of oranges, for example—to the recipients myself. "You said a gift should come from the hand of the giver, so you have to give the present to Ghislaine yourself."

I called Ghislaine, and she invited us for tea at the enormous British residence next to the Nile. A doorman helped us out of our car and onto a red carpet that led up the stairs to the entrance, where a butler ushered us into a reception room and went to call Ghislaine. She appeared and sensing what was appropriate, showed us around the rooms of the lower floor. In the study— probably once belonging to him—was Lord Kitchener's picture. One has to be an Egyptian to appreciate the effect on Ansaf of standing in the room where so much history had taken place before Egypt became independent of Britain. We returned to the reception area for tea, and Ghislaine thanked Ansaf profusely for her gift. The car arrived, and we descended the red carpet again. In the car, tears streamed down Ansaf's face. "What's wrong?" I asked. And she replied, "I have never had such a thing happen to me before, where a big person treated me as if I were the same. I've learned a lesson that I'll never forget. I'll never treat the poor in Bulaq as if they are anything less than myself." Nor did I see her treat them as less before or after the visit. That was what made her unique in a society that never forgot class distinctions.

<center>~~~</center>

Much later in the summer of 1987, I invited Ansaf to spend a month with us in Woods Hole. That summer was the first after Ansaf's husband, Ibrahim, died, and I hoped the visit would distract her. I wasn't sure how she would react to this first venture out of her own country. And, indeed, I was brought up short several times when I saw how much she had to learn of even the most basic routines. Escalators at the airport were particularly trying, and I had to grasp her firmly by the arm and pull her on at the right moment. In Woods Hole the night she arrived, she went without washing because she couldn't figure out how to work the lever-type faucet. Before long, however, she mastered the intricacies of American life, if not perfectly at least enough to get along.

Our roles reversed in the United States, and I think we both felt un- comfortable in our new positions. She recognized the change when she said, "Now I'm the anthropologist and have to ask you questions." And she did. "What waters all this?" she asked, noticing the greenery when she landed in Boston. "Is this a mountain?" she asked, seeing the small ravines along the railroad track on our way to North Carolina. She marveled at the drive-in bank teller—"In three minutes you can get money from the bank while it takes us half a day." She loved the cash register that automatically knew the price of goods in the supermarket without having to bargain. And she told everyone when she returned home that my eighty-year-old neighbor rode her bicycle to shop as though that were the most bizarre thing she had ever seen. I loved seeing America through her eyes as a place of marvels having to do with organization and material goods. Prior to her coming, I had often been disgusted by the wastefulness of our society, the overflowing trashcans, and the constant buying of new things before the old had worn out. Ansaf made me see another side: the orderliness of the society, the law-abiding nature of most Americans, and how those factors made life immeasurably easier than in Egypt.

An unexpected insight was my realization that we Americans (or was it me?) lack the patience and sensitivity for prolonged social interactions, especially where it takes self-sacrifice and suppressing our own desires to make others comfortable. We get satisfaction from accomplishments—as Rima in Riyadh showed me. We need space for solitary pastimes that we feel deprived of when there are too many interruptions. We are impatient when days go by and we don't accomplish the tasks we feel are important.

Ansaf and I were as close as sisters could be in her context of Egypt, but in America the differences in our worlds became all too apparent. I normally swam and walked each day and spent long hours reading and carrying out other pastimes. She neither swam nor walked, couldn't read English with any fluency, and from morning until night wanted to be visiting my friends. She sat in a lawn chair on the beach—a solitary figure in her black widow's garb—under an umbrella to keep her already dark skin from becoming darker, watching while I swam. She sat in the living room staring into space until I returned from even the most abbreviated walk. The highlight of her day was trips to the supermarket that I tried to keep to a minimum. She tried to help prepare our meals but knew little of our foods, and when making Egyptian food, she used so much oil we could barely eat it. To cut down on work in our household in the summer, everyone made breakfasts and lunches for themselves from food available in the refrigerator, but Ansaf was too polite to help herself to our food without being invited, and I ended up preparing every meal for her. She scolded me for letting Bill prepare his own lunches and felt I was not attentive enough to his needs. It made me feel resentful to spend so much time on "inconsequential" matters that to Ansaf were a woman's duty.

I racked my brain for ways to entertain her. I brought her wool and knitting needles. I turned the TV to soap operas she could understand from watching the expressions on the actors' faces. But unless I sat with her, she wasn't happy. If I tried to do housework, she felt she should be helping, but she didn't know how to use washers or dryers or vacuum cleaners and had never seen a dish-washing machine.

In desperation I decided we would take the train to visit Bill's mother in Washington and then my parents in North Carolina. That worked for her since we were spending all day together and the passing scenery entertained her. The visits also worked well because she was seeing my family and we were going out to meals together. My stepmother, Mayhew, had a wonderful ability to put people at ease. And Daddy, trying to act the generous host, insisted Ansaf could have anything she wanted on the menu. Previously I had ordered for her from the unfamiliar foods, but this time my father read out the items. Not knowing what he was saying, she politely agreed to everything and then was aghast when she found she had ordered three times what she could eat. However, Daddy's generosity and hospitality were fully affirmed by providing so much.

These few diversions helped for a while, but then we were back to days of not having enough to do. She sensed my growing irritation and would ask if everything was all right, and I found there was no way to explain how our different lifestyles were getting in the way. Her culture was accustomed to lots of sociability and mine was not. Furthermore, I was frustrated that I wasn't preparing for upcoming projects in the fall because of my anxiety over how she was reacting. Part of the problem was feeling guilty at how well I had been treated in Egypt. There, people found me an interesting diversion, and we never lacked for something to do. The sociability often was too much for me, but certainly easier to manage when I could return to my house each evening. America didn't keep her busy enough, and nothing in her complex life prepared her for such isolation.

There were several lessons in this experience, beyond the obvious ones. In her own context Ansaf was brilliant—surpassing even the most extravagant expectations for a person in her situation. In my context she was adrift, unable to cope. In her context I was the helpless one, and she reached out to help me. I was too embedded in my own culture and its values to do the same for her. We had somehow overcome other major differences between us in becoming friends, but there remained these differences of culture that we had not known existed. As I thought about it, my other close Arab women friends never became close to Ansaf perhaps because of the socioeconomic differences that separated them as inexorably as the cultural values did Ansaf and me. I couldn't help but think of the millions of immigrants who felt the same alienation in the isolating context of America without ever being able to return to people who understood them.

That summer seemed endless, and I was relieved when I finally put Ansaf on the plane for Cairo. A month of eating our salads and less heavy foods had made her sleek and healthy-looking to my eye, but her son Hanna complained that she looked too thin when she came back from the United States "as if she hadn't eaten very well." Eventually Ansaf and I both recovered our warm friendship, and when the long stretches of boredom and frustration faded from our memories, we looked back on the experience as a good one. Bill's gift of an album of pictures helped reduce the painful lows to a series of highs. She dubbed it "Queen Ansaf in America." I know the visit was a highlight of her life, but I also know she would never exchange her life in Egypt for all the conveniences of the United States.

I'm glad my annual visits to see her now take place in Egypt, where long ago we established a comfortable relationship. There, she takes charge of me and orchestrates our activities to her liking. It works infinitely better, and we are both happier. As two people we could not be more different, but neither of us at the time was complete without the other. Long after those years in Bulaq, we still know that a magical friendship occurred and has stayed with us ever since.

9

IMMERSION:
BULAQ, EGYPT (1976–1978)

Bulaq Abu Aila is a difficult place to describe to anyone who hasn't been there. Each day brought emotionally wrenching experiences to me of human tragedy mixed with doses of overwhelming humanity. A visitor who accompanied me there once wondered why people seemed so happy and children so full of laughter. To him, the catastrophe of living under such conditions called for endless despair.

My feelings about Bulaq changed from being appalled at the miserable lives of the people to becoming angry at the government for failing to provide decent services or cheating people out of the ones they were eligible for. Eventually I stopped noticing the peeling plaster and felt at home in the warmth and friendliness of the people—the cocoon effect was as alive in Bulaq as anywhere else in the Middle East. Bulaq became home to people I grew to love, admire, and become furious with, all at the same time. Describing the physical aspects of their neighborhood is only one part of a very complex picture.

I got used to the smell—a smell that followed me even after I left Bulaq. The smell was a combination of rot, mold, urine, and feces from sewage that oozed out of poorly connected pipes and into the streets. A United States Agency for International Development (USAID) contractor told me that when they installed new drinking-water pipes, they found previous contractors had simply run sewage pipes (with the same leaky connections) through the middle of the water pipes. The Bulaq smell clung to my clothing to such an extent that I would dab perfumes all over myself to avoid offending others at diplomatic functions. More irritating even were the fleas, and once bedbugs made our nights a misery until we figured out how to get rid of them. On my return from Bulaq each day, I stepped into the bathtub fully dressed and let my clothes drop to the ground before turning on the shower. The fleas would hop up my legs to where I could see and squash them. Despite these discomforts, the most lasting impression was the sheer hopelessness that neither the people of Bulaq nor I could do much to change things. Some days it reduced me to screaming fury when I reached home. Fortunately the Bulaq people faced their problems with more equanimity. Being constantly surrounded with problems, they got used to them.

Days in Bulaq juxtaposed against evenings at diplomatic dinners with their wasteful extravagance made mine a schizophrenic world. One evening sitting next to the Egyptian minister of health, I decided to describe an incident that happened that day. Ansaf and I were visiting an elderly widow when there was a loud knock on her door. She took a few coins and in a few minutes came back with a newspaper cone of white powder. "Who was that?" Ansaf asked, and the widow explained it was the woman from the Ministry of Health whose job it was to eradicate cockroaches. She was supposed to dissolve the powder and spray it herself but instead sold it to those who wanted to avoid the noxious fumes. Ansaf told me about incidents of people dying because the powder had been mistaken for sugar and stirred into tea. Only a week before, she said, a young man rejected by the girl he loved took the powder and died. All this I told the minister, even though I could see his face reddening with suppressed anger. When I finished, he burst out, "Why don't you foreigners mind your own business. You don't understand what you see and make a lot of problems for us." This outburst taught me a lesson I should have known—that the local bureaucracy wasn't accountable for anything. It was the inability to correct situations like this that ate at my soul.

In the previous century, Bulaq had been a fashionable part of Cairo. Situ-ated on a swampy area that had been drained to provide middle-class housing close to the Nile, the early buildings of stone and brick fronted narrow dirt streets built on top of what were originally drainage canals. Some of the better buildings—constructed originally as substantial one-family dwellings— were at least 100 years old with entrances several feet lower than the debris-elevated roadways. Subsequent generations had subdivided the houses to the point where many families lived in a single room and shared a bathroom on a central staircase with a number of other families. Walking into downstairs rooms usually meant descending into permanent darkness with sewage welling up and over the floor. When the water was at its highest, residents used elevated walkways made from planks and stones to get to their homes. These downstairs rooms were the cheapest rentals available—perhaps an Egyptian pound or less a month—and therefore were occupied by the poorest of the poor, mainly for the elderly and widowed. Some lay handicapped in the gloom, day and night, on beds with legs submerged in water. They kept their food tightly contained in metal cans because of the rats.

In drier buildings, the area beneath the stairs was prime real estate for the elderly. I knew one, Kokub, a cheerful kindly woman who lived in such an alcove with her beautiful fair-haired granddaughter and their single possession, a rickety bed. I used to have dreams of adopting this little girl but hesitated at least partly because I knew no one would ever match the loving care she received from her grandmother. Mornings I would see Kokub combing the girl's hair and adding a large colored bow before she took her to school. Other widows who couldn't afford even the price of such a space lived in broken bread ovens, abandoned chicken coops, or any small corner they could find.

The largest numbers of those Ansaf and I visited were widows. Although a system of pensions existed in Egypt, it was largely reserved for people in civil service jobs. Meager as the salaries and pensions were, civil service jobs were coveted because they were so secure. Parents at the time would rather marry their daughter to a securely situated civil servant than a man in the private sector who might be earning ten times more. Most of our Bulaq widows had been married to men with only pick-up jobs as porters and laborers, and once their husbands were gone, they had no income unless a son or daughter gave them something. Most of these adult children were so poor themselves they had little left over for aging parents. The Bulaq Center gave the widows fifty piasters (about seventy cents) a month if they regularly attended religious services. At the time Ansaf estimated that a family of four with 12L.E. ($16.80) a month didn't need our help.

Ansaf and I were excited one day to hear the government was offering "Sadat pensions" of 10L.E. a month to widows. All they had to do was apply. So we took one of our widows to the Mugamma building to test the system. This was the towering building on the edge of Tahrir Square, where most dealings with the government take place. Kafka would have found inspiration in this nightmare of a building. Filthy marble stairs worn into concave grooves circled up floor after floor around a central atrium. We took the stairs because they were reassuringly more substantial than the grille-cage elevators that lines of people waited for on the ground floor. The light became brighter once we climbed above the heaps of discarded trash that filled the central core of the building. For years workers tossed their refuse down this hole until the piles rose several stories high.

On an upper level, we searched for the right office and saw what is a common sight in the Mugamma—offices with wall-to-wall desks, each shared by several employees, the men sipping tea and reading newspapers, and the women knitting or shelling peas or otherwise readying themselves for the midday meal. Perhaps one clerk in the room would have a ledger open. To do business meant getting the signatures of at least half the occupants of an office, one or two of whom would be out on errands so you had to come back. We found the right office and stood in line. When it was our turn, we thrust the widow's identity card through the grille. "Oh, so sorry," the clerk said, looking at me out of the corner of his eye. "We need your marriage certificate and the certificate of your husband's death." We returned a few days later with the papers. "Ah," said the clerk, "I see the name is spelled differently on these two documents. We can't give you a pension since we have no way of knowing that you are the right person." After several more tries with different women, each having some "irregularity" with her papers, we realized the Sadat pensions were mainly for show.

Almost worse than the swampy lower floors in Bulaq, where people lived in perpetual gloom, were the roof-top dwellings. They were thrown together from flattened ghee (clarified oil) cans and were cold in winter and unbearably hot in summer. They took up a small portion of the roof space while the rest was covered with old tires, broken furniture, cracked pots, discarded plastic—anything that might prove useful some day. Access to these dwellings was by improvised ladder that shifted as you climbed and usually was missing critical rungs. The flat roofs had no perimeter walls and it was painful to watch children tumbling near the edge with no adult noticing, so confident were they that nothing could happen if "their time had not come."

The outward signs of chaos in Bulaq masked what was really a highly organized way of life. The day started with housewives sweeping the paths in front of their doorways and sprinkling them with water to keep down the dust. Water was precious, and so each pan of washing water ended up damping the dust of the roadway. The people in nicer neighborhoods of Cairo disdained Bulaq residents for the filth in their streets, but without regular trash pickup, they had little recourse but to dump it somewhere outside of their homes. The Christian *Zebalin* (garbage collectors), whose donkey carts plied the streets of prosperous parts of the city and recycled virtually every bit of garbage down to food scraps for their pigs, found nothing of interest in Bulaq. So people deposited garbage in derelict buildings or open spaces but not near their homes or on the roadways. The *Baladiya* (municipality) excused itself from removing rubbish by saying its trucks were too big to enter Bulaq's narrow alleyways. There was, in any case, little left after the inhabitants devoured every scrap of food and sold every piece of paper to fuel the fires of bakeries, but enough of a rich porridge remained to reach the second floors in some areas.

For a few minutes each morning, Bulaq was orderly until people on their way to work began throwing their castoffs in the street. Neighbors greeted one another on their way to fetch water from the public spigots, sometimes paying a penny or two to a self-appointed guard to turn the water on and off. The last few meters to the spigots meant wading through a murky soup of garbage—cold in winter and unbelievably pungent in summer. A coveted job for the poorest women was bringing *tanakas* (metal tins) of water to the homes of the slightly richer for a few pennies. One of our women made her living this way. A young widow, she spent mornings coming and going while her chubby baby stayed with her neighbor. One morning she was weeping uncontrollably, for the baby had died during the night. "Why didn't you take him to a doctor?" we asked. "I didn't have the money," she said. We told her we would have helped. Most likely the baby contracted some illness from the murky water where his mother waded. She was a good worker and unlike other women not ashamed of letting people know she worked. Ansaf found her a janitorial job in a nearby church.

Each morning the black-garbed widows rounded up neighborhood children to escort them to school. Never having sufficient income, the widows took on this chore and other errands to reciprocate for meals their neighbors provided them. The neighbors shrugged off their gratitude, saying some day they might need help and as long as God provided enough they would share with others. Once a USAID officer suggested the Egyptian government start a "meals on wheels" program for the elderly in Bulaq, but happily the idea failed. I could imagine the disruptions such a program would cause to the networks of neighborly help.

The men would go off to the nearby railway station to find work as porters—the total of their tips determining what the family ate the next day: lentils and bread if they were lucky; cheaper onions, tomatoes, and bread if they were not. Others fixed used furniture, repaired shoes, and peddled foods. Women bought cases of fruits or vegetables in the wholesale market to sell for a small profit. Others positioned themselves in the main alleys with kerosene stoves and made *tamiya* sandwiches that workers bought on their way home. Soon the smell of garlic and onions—the poor man's spice—wafted deliciously through the air, almost drowning out the other smells. Other women sold pasta made with machines financed from the loans we provided. One enterprising woman gathered clothes to wash in a machine she also bought with a loan. Ansaf was dubious at first, but we let her do it, and in the end she made a good living and repaid the money. Other women went door to door with cloth, underwear, hair ornaments, and other items bought at wholesale and sold for a profit. Bulaq was alive with their creative hustling.

A woman—not one of our clients—leaned out her window, "Won't you come for tea? You haven't been for a long time. I'll make you a good coffee," she upped the ante. A child arrived running, "Auntie says come, they just sent her the kind of village bread you like and wants you to have it while it's fresh." We went and she pulled the bread out of a container under her bed. In the half gloom she lighted a candle in an extravagant gesture of hospitality. The next day we brought her fruit, keeping the dignity in our relationship.

A month after I began spending full time in Bulaq, I sent a new proposal to my adviser. I was not sure where my study would lead but felt the new topic—"Religious Community and Social Control in a Low-Income Quarter of Cairo"—would cover about anything. I wanted to look at the part religion played in the life of the poor. Was it an opiate, as the Marxists claimed, or something else, and how did Muslims and Christians interact in this poor neighborhood? It was too sensitive to ask questions directly, but I knew I would learn a lot just following Ansaf around.

Most of our work had little to do with my research, but overall it gave me an idea of what it was like to be poor in Bulaq and especially how women coped with poverty. Convention said they shouldn't work—that men should support their families—and most of them adhered to this ideal. Poverty wasn't the only problem in Bulaq. There was the mother trying to marry off her daughter or another with a son ready to marry. We arranged a meeting between the two families but then had to bring the bad news that the potential groom was not impressed. One success was a marriage Ansaf arranged between a blind shaikh and a woman who had been badly burned from a kerosene stove explosion. They had been married for some time when the shaikh's family began agitating for him to marry a more attractive wife. He was on the verge of divorcing her when Ansaf reminded him that she had been a good wife and mother and didn't deserve his rejection. She arranged a reconciliation, and when I left Bulaq they were still married.

Another of our duties was to console people when there was a death in the family. More than any other ritual—births, engagements, marriages, holidays, and homecomings—it was important to visit the bereaved. The pattern was the same—the visitors would wear black and burst into tears when they entered the room. The bereaved would describe the last days and hours of the deceased, how the family sought out doctors and bought expensive medicines, and did everything in their power to save the person, but alas it was God's Will that he or she was taken. The story would be retold with each newcomer, emphasizing the point that everything possible had been done. I had the feeling the bereaved were working out the story they wanted to remember. We would stay a while, drink some bitter coffee if it was offered, and then go on our way. Close neighbors and nearby kin passed by every day the first week, bringing food and toning down their music or any parties that might offend her. These friends and relatives had to visit during the first seven days, on the fortieth day, the hundredth day, and a year later. Scrupulously paying these visits showed the closeness of a relationship.

I gained other insights from Bulaq. I found, for example, that links among poor women where there was little property to inherit were more important than the paternal relations I saw in Saudi Arabia. The Bulaq women disproportionately married maternal relatives who helped one another with household tasks and economic crises. I saw how important it was for men to provide sufficiently for their families; being a macho male was less about sex in Bulaq and more about earning power. Their neighbors and wives ridiculed men who brought in little income. And although the families frequently needed additional income, women usually refused to work or, if they accepted, would do it secretly so as not to reflect on their husbands' abilities to support them. I was impressed at how families stayed together even with the tensions of poverty. With their different roles to perform, men and women needed one another to accomplish the tasks they couldn't do respectably for themselves.

I saw there were times in their lives when poverty affected them most. The first was when they wanted to marry. Men had to accumulate enough to pay a dowry and furnish an apartment before families would agree to let their daughters marry them. Women's families bore the expense of linens and cooking items and the white outfit the bride wore. We couldn't help much with the men's expenses, but we recycled dresses, shoes, veils, and household items donated by affluent Egyptians and foreigners. After the wedding, the couple was usually reasonably well-off until children came and with them the high costs of "free" schooling. Many couldn't afford the fees, the uniforms, the supplies, and the cost of tutoring that children needed to succeed. I was surprised that parents often sent girls to school longer because of their better academic performance. If they continued through university, they might even become eligible for a civil service job. The boys dropped out early to apprentice with mechanics, electricians, or plumbers, where once they gained a skill they earned more than civil servants.

I watched Ansaf negotiating crises in Bulaq and learned the typical negotiating patterns for resolving problems from the most minor to the most complex. Even Sadat used this approach in his historic trip to Jerusalem in 1979, but his generous concession in going was never reciprocated by the Israelis who had different expectations about negotiations. The pattern involved four steps: (1) the disputants would first agree that they wanted to resolve the problem; (2) then they would express in the strongest way how each had been wronged; (3) eventually one side would give a generous concession, followed by an equal or greater concession by the other side; and (4) then both would agree on the terms and drink a cup of coffee to reestablish the relationship.

For example, a girl from the literacy class borrowed some donated clothes "to try them out." We sold these clothes inexpensively to support the center's programs, and Ansaf asked the girl to either pay for or return the clothes. For a week she was absent from class, and since she was a good student, Ansaf wanted her back. The next day we went to the parents and told them we wanted to resolve the problem so the girl could return to class. The parents agreed but then said the price of the clothing was too high, and Ansaf replied that they shouldn't quarrel over money meant for the poor. Ansaf offered to reduce the price by half, and the parents said they would pay two-thirds of the original price. They invited us for coffee, and the next day the girl returned to school.

Ansaf and I were on the lookout for services that might help the Bulaq people. We inspected old people's homes and orphanages that might take our cases and found them generally dismal places. One day we stopped by the home of a Muslim woman who told us she had raised a Christian girl, Samia, after her parents died. When Samia reached her teen years, she became blind with a problem doctors couldn't cure. The woman said she worried because her own sons were becoming adolescents, and it was unseemly to have an unrelated girl in the house. We found a Christian orphanage where Samia was admitted for a fee and visited her from time to time to make her feel people cared about her. Once we asked if she needed anything, and she asked for some silk lingerie—a strange request but nonetheless one we honored. A few months later, the administrator informed us Samia was pregnant by another orphan at the institution. When the baby was born, they told Samia it died and gave the baby to a Christian family. When she became pregnant again, we used the excuse to transfer her to a better orphanage.

One topic that interested me was the interactions between Muslims and Christians. Ansaf, although a Christian, made a point of occasionally helping poor Muslims, but for the most part she did it as a goodwill gesture because they had access to more substantial charity through their mosques. When Muslims and Christians talked about one another publicly, they were always complimentary. But in private the Christians talked about their discrimination at the hands of the Muslims—how they were unable to find work, how Muslim men harassed their daughters, or how their sons were offered jobs if they would convert to Islam. I couldn't help noticing, though, that when there was an especially generous act, it was invariably a Muslim being kind to a Christian and not the other way around. I felt it was partly the defensiveness that minorities feel in a sea of others. While

I remained in Bulaq, relations between the two communities were carefully regulated through mutual flattery and separate institutions, but elsewhere in Egypt conflicts between the two groups were beginning to emerge.

~~~~

Egyptians are careful about discussing subjects that might give foreigners a negative impression of Egypt. "Um al-Dunya" (mother of the world), as Egyptians call their country, has the most glorious civilization, the most delicious food, and the nicest people. This conviction comes from a strong sense of pride in their culture and, I suppose, decades of insensitive remarks by foreigners. Among taboo subjects is the topic of superstitions that Egyptians believe foreigners think show ignorance.

Ansaf and I were working together for a year before she revealed a side of Bulaq I barely knew existed—the world of spirits. By then she trusted me not to ridicule practices that were strange to my Western beliefs. She herself approached these issues with sympathy for anything the poor did to relieve their suffering, but she wouldn't say whether she believed in them herself. From time to time, the Bulaq women would say that someone suffered from *afrits* (spirits), which I assumed meant psychological illness. One day we visited a woman, Suad, who suffered the symptoms of possession because, her neighbors said, her husband threatened to leave if she didn't have children.

Ansaf explained that each person has two guardian angels, one on the right shoulder recording "good deeds" and one on the left recording "bad deeds," so when the person died there would be a record of his or her life on earth. These personal spirits accompanied people wherever they went. In addition, good and bad spirits inhabit the world around us and cause difficulties in vulnerable people—if they show off their wealth, or behave badly, or if the spirits became jealous, often of a woman's husband. Sometimes another person, through sheer maliciousness, casts an evil eye on a victim and activates a bad spirit. To avoid being accused of instigating a problem, people avoid praising another person's possessions or children, or if they do, they added the phrase, *mashalla* (with God's protection) to offset any damage.

Bad spirits are especially liable to enter a person when he or she (usually she) is unprotected—in the dark, in the toilet, after childbirth, or when she is upset by a quarrel. The symptoms of possession can be alarming—swooning, fits, irrational speech and behavior, attempts at suicide, and other severe mental and physical illnesses. At the first sign of possession friends and relatives gather to support the possessed person, considering the problem inflicted from the outside rather than of her own making. If the possession is mild, the concern of supporters may be enough to cure her. If not and the symptoms are severe, the victim is taken to a practitioner to resolve the problem.

Muslim and Christian possessions take different forms. Muslims spirits are usually jealous and demanding. The afrit (usually a he) may cause his victim to behave contrary to role expectations. The victim may, for example, have been a dutiful wife and daughter-in-law but suddenly starts saying disrespectful things to her mother-in-law or neglects her wifely duties. What she does is not her fault but brought on by her afrit. Christian spirits are more inclined to cause physical illness or mental suffering. The line is not always clear, and it becomes less clear when the victim looks for a solution. Most people seek help within their own religious institutions, but sometimes Muslims consult Christian practitioners and occasionally Christians try Muslim remedies. If the problem persists, the victim's family may feel someone has cursed her and go to a practitioner who removes curses, or they threaten the instigator until she removes the curse.

I wondered how Suad would get rid of her afrit, and Ansaf reminded me that since she was a Muslim her first recourse would be to attend a *zar*. Zars were frequent occurrences in Bulaq as well as in other parts of the city, even though the government outlawed the practice as superstition and Muslim clerics said they were un-Islamic. Zars are believed to have come from African countries, such as Sudan and Somalia, and only later became popular in Egypt. We found that Suad planned to attend a zar in a few days.

Ansaf and I were the first of the 100 or so people to crowd into the two-room flat rented by the *muallima*, or organizer of the zar. She was a heavy-set, self-confident woman energetically ushering in her guests while simultaneously shooing away the children trying to get inside. People paid a small entry fee and more each time the band played the special drum beat of their afrit. The muallima's helpers were two men—one, dark skinned, on the drums and the other, light skinned, with the tambourine—while the muallima played the castanets. The men's skin color later became a factor in Suad's cure. The band started a rhythm to appeal to the afrits. At the sound of a favored beat, the afrit takes over the woman, and she staggers around the room, slowly at first and then faster until she whirls in a frenzy as the beat increases. Suddenly the music stops, and she sinks into the arms of her supporters. She may continue to dance this way through several rounds of music. The dancers and spectators are all women, some possessed but the majority there to help the victims. They surround her, encourage her to dance, and then provide physical support when she falls. By the time they've danced for hours, the victims gleam with perspiration, their eyes close dreamily, and their motions become erratic.

I was used to the decorous behavior of Bulaq women, and it was shocking to see their abandonment in this unusual environment. Even more surprising was the lack of criticism from onlookers for acts that would have elicited strong disapproval under normal circumstances. The zar was clearly a place where the restraints of polite society were dropped and women could vent their frustrations safe from censure. But still it was surprising to see women dancing seductively in front of male musicians or, for that matter, wearing thin and form-revealing clothing. It was shocking, too, to see women acting out sexual fantasies as they responded to the quickening beat of the drum and then collapsing with a violent shaking as the music stopped. Later, the women talked about their sexual encounters with their afrits and the spirits' jealousy when they slept with their husbands. The extreme physical exertion of the dancing must have provided temporary relief from their frustrations.

Later in the evening, the muallima consulted with Suad, telling her that if she wanted to rid herself of her afrit she must do two things: first, she must make some excuse to her husband and spend a night in the zar room "drinking with a black man and a white man"; and, second, she must tell her husband that the afrit would not leave until she wore a new red dress for him. Ansaf took this advice at face value, but I felt Suad was being told she should sleep with the two men, in which case she might indeed solve her problem if the childlessness was the fault of her husband. We never learned if it worked.

I was curious to know what Christians did if they became possessed, and Ansaf, as usual, indulged my curiosity. The following week we set off for a church near Cairo's main railway station. This church had a special dispensation from the Coptic hierarchy to exorcize demons. A well-known priest performed the ceremonies three times a week. He would hold holy symbols—a cross, holy oil, or a picture of Mary and Jesus—in front of the victim, and the spirit inside would "burn up" with a cry of agony. What was particularly strange was that the Christian holy symbols had the same effect on the few Muslims present. A crucial difference between Islam and Christianity is the issue of Jesus Christ's divinity. Adherents of both religions believe Jesus is a prophet, but only Christians believe he is the Son of God. Muslims are not supposed to worship idols or believe in supernatural powers. And yet here were Muslims responding in the same way as Christians did to the Virgin Mary, Jesus, and other sacred objects. The priest entered swinging his smoking censer, and a wave of muttering and grumblings interspersed with shrieks arose from the assembled afrits to show their displeasure at the holy objects. The priest approached each victim one by one and asked about her symptoms. The spirit's voice answered—"I want her for myself," or, "She doesn't pay enough attention to me"—and the victim would writhe and screech to show the extent of her anguish. Then the priest would grab her hair roughly and begin shaking her, meanwhile inserting wads of cotton wet with holy oil in her mouth, nose, eyes, and ears—the holes where demons were mostly likely to exit. He would twist her head to force her to look at his cross or push her to the front of the church to touch a picture of Jesus or Mary. The moment she looked at or touched a holy object, the spirit shrieked and with a horrible gasp "burned up" as he exited through her orifices. There would be a moment of silence while everyone waited to see if there were other Ibrahims or Ahmads still lurking inside her, and indicating whether she was ready to give up her possession. If the afrit was particularly stubborn or she was possessed with more than one, the priest would tell her to come back the next week.

The woman next to us became possessed, her supporters told us, after a traumatic birth in which she nearly died. Since then, she had refused to sleep with her husband for fear of getting pregnant again. When she jumped off a wardrobe trying to kill herself, her family and her husband's family brought her to the church. They clearly sympathized with her plight, stroking her gently and trying to calm her. The problem, as they expressed it, was that her afrit wouldn't let her sleep with her husband because the afrit wanted her for himself. The priest exorcized a demon from her but there were still more.

Her problem made me think of a case where we tried to mediate a reconciliation between two families. A young Christian woman, Sana, had been married without full realization of what was entailed. After the festivities when she and her husband retired to their room in her parents-in-law's cramped apartment to consummate the marriage, she was horrified by what happened, and the horror was compounded the next day when she found she had to take care of the household for her husband's parents and six brothers. A week later she fled to her parents' house and refused to return. Since the couple was Christian, there was no chance of divorce. We spent hours trying to get her to return since she had no future other than as a wife and eventually mother. Everyone was furious—her husband's family because of the money they spent on her dowry and her own family because she had dishonored them. The two cases were similar, but the possessed woman seemed to have found a better way to express her unwillingness to sleep with her husband. Her "misbehavior" was an affliction rather than, as in Sana's case, stubbornness, and the whole family was committed to overcoming her problem.

Another practitioner existed in Bulaq that I learned about one day when Ansaf came to me with a worried look. Her favorite niece had been introduced to a number of prospective suitors, and each time she had been so rude that the young man had not returned. Ansaf's sister was at her wit's end, and Ansaf wanted to help. So that afternoon we went to see Sayyida Antoinette, the soothsayer. Her powers became evident one day when a visitor noticed oil dripping from the eyes of the Virgin Mary in a picture on her wall. The visitor ran out into the street and announced the miracle. From that time on, Sayyida Antoinette gained a reputation for solving problems.

When we arrived, she was in the middle of a session with two women. They had given money to a friend to buy a washing machine, and she had disappeared. They wanted Sayyida Antoinette to tell them where in Egypt the money might be found. She mentioned a village in the delta but said it had already been spent. The women left, and we explained to Sayyida Antoinette the many disasters related to finding a husband for Suzy. The most recent suitor had gone off to his village and was expected to return the following weekend. Ansaf needed a way to make Suzy say "yes" this time. Sayyida Antoinette prayed with Ansaf and then gave her oil from the holy picture to sprinkle on a threshold Suzy would step over. The suitor married a woman in his village and never returned, but a few weeks later Suzy fell in love with a man at her church and eventually married him. Everyone gave much of the credit to Sayyida Antoinette.

Discovering these practices and practitioners gave a boost to my research. Up to this point I was drifting—gathering good information but nothing particularly new. Suddenly with these spirit activities, I could show the separate tracks Christians and Muslims took to solving important problems in their lives. Each community had a consistent approach that linked the causes of possession, the religious explanations, the way problems were solved, and even the kinds of institutions that restored order. The Koran, for example, says that spirits are not necessarily incompatible with a religious life since they can be good or bad. They may only need placation to restore stability to the person. One Sura (LV:15) says spirits typify "the hidden forces and capacities of men" while another warns people against "using spirits as an excuse for their weaknesses" (LXXII:6). Although this sounds as if afrits are manifestations of human tendencies, the Bulaq people like to think of them as sentient beings with minds of their own.

The Bible sees possession differently. It says people become possessed when they are weak in faith, and therefore possession is antithetical to a religious life. People must rid themselves of spirits to restore their standing in the church. To placate spirits as the Muslims do would be flirting with evil. A relevant passage in the Bible speaks of Jesus casting out demons from possessed people (Luke 11:19, 20) while another (Peter 5:89) says devils can be resisted if a person's faith is firm.

The theology is reinforced for Muslims and Christians by a difference in their points of family tension. In Muslim families, women know their husbands can divorce them easily or take a second, third, or even fourth wife. Even though it doesn't happen often, Muslim women strive to be good wives and mothers by keeping clean houses, making good meals, and raising well-behaved children—so there will be no reason for their husbands to want to marry again. Suad's problem was of this kind—she was not a good wife because she didn't produce children. The demands of her afrit for a dress were a short-term solution since her husband would have to pay out money that he might be saving for a dowry for a new wife. If her childlessness continued, she could easily resurrect the afrit again to counter her husband's threats.

The tension in Christian families wasn't from fear that the husband-wife relation would dissolve since Christians cannot divorce in Egypt except under certain circumstances. What is needed when spirit possession occurs is to restore peace and stability to the family. This happens only by ridding the victim of her troublesome afrit. The problem may arise because women can't discuss their frustrations openly and therefore resort to afrits. Possession elicits attention, which may be enough to restore equilibrium. Or, if not, she can have multiple afrits to express her frustrations. Each afrit must be painstakingly exorcized to restore her faith.

The parallels consequently work this way: Muslim wives are anxious over easy divorce; religious documents see spirits as good and bad; rituals placate misbehaving spirits to keep problems under control; placation costs money and that makes it hard for men to marry again, thus helping to relieve women's anxieties; but if the need arises, she can become possessed again. In Christianity divorce is difficult, if not impossible; spirits disrupt households that legally can't be dissolved; and they must be exorcized immediately to restore family harmony and the individual's faith as the Bible exhorts. As a vulnerable minority, Christians face stronger censure if they cross over and attend Muslim zars, where they might be seen as flirting with conversion, whereas Muslims as a confident majority often attend Christian ceremonies when they want to end their possession.

These observations were not the only way the religious community was important to the poor, but this material with the rest made me feel I finally had something important to say. By June 1978 my dissertation was ready to defend before my committee.

10

A NEW DIRECTION:
CAIRO AFTER GRADUATE SCHOOL
(1978–1981)

At the age of forty-three I had completed my Ph.D. With my new "tools" for studying culture, all I had to do was find an opportunity to use them. I applied to the United States Agency for International Development for local contract work. Despite my degree I wasn't competitive since I had no experience in development and no real specialty. Although anthropology should be important in such work, few openings specified general expertise. Moreover, in the embassy's eyes, I was a Foreign Service spouse, qualified for secretarial jobs perhaps but not for a position that required professional expertise.

Then, suddenly, just as I was giving up hope, a USAID official from Washington who knew me asked the Cairo Mission if I could accompany her to evaluate the impact of USAID projects on women. They agreed, and we visited projects in different parts of Egypt. At the end of that time I helped write up our observations. Our report called for USAID to review new projects for their potential impact on women. Studies had shown that, dollar for dollar, assistance spent on women had the greatest impact on such indicators as literacy, fertility, child mortality, and health, all of which show a country's relative development. USAID was just beginning to address women's issues seriously.

On the side I wrote a stronger report entitled "An Anthropologist in AID-Land," expressing my dismay at the projects we had seen. I felt the "specialist" consultants had been unaware of the potentially negative consequences of their projects on women. In one case, USAID promoted a small-loans project that let businesses in the souk use their buildings as collateral to expand the size and inventory of their shops. These shop owners, already well-to-do by local standards, increased their wealth at the expense of poorer merchants who rented shops or peddled their wares in the street. Women were often among these poorest peddlers. In a brave moment I gave my report to the director of USAID, and I heard him tell someone that the reason it didn't hire more anthropologists was "because they always tell you what's wrong but never tell you how to make it right." I remembered his words and from then on never criticized a project without making practical suggestions for correcting problems.

This brief assignment gave me something to write when forms asked for previous experience. Perhaps more important, local USAID officials respected the fact that "headquarters" had asked me to accompany a senior officer. On one point, though, the work turned out to be a liability. I didn't realize that payment rates for USAID contracts are based on compensation for previous jobs, and raises only came when substantial new work was completed or a year had lapsed since the last raise. Because I had no relevant work history, the mission started me at the salary of a beginning secretary, mentioning it several times that they couldn't justify paying more to a Foreign Service spouse.

The second opportunity for work came just as the first, totally unexpectedly, and gave me as an anthropologist what I needed most, a development specialty. A team of fifteen experts, Americans and Egyptians, was hired through a contractor to complete a major assessment of primary education. They were given three months to travel around the country and produce a report with recommendations for how USAID money should be spent on education. I gave the team a briefing, and afterward, to my surprise, the team leader asked if I would join the team "to help them understand what they were seeing."

Two months later, we were on a bus in a remote area of Upper Egypt, speeding along an unlighted country road after dark with the horn blaring to compensate for the headlights that didn't work. Before we reached the hotel, there were a number of close misses, despite the driver's constant invocations for Allah to protect us. The hotel, the best in town, was filthy with floorboards that in some cases had rotted away so we could see the rooms below. But everyone was hungry and quickly assembled in the dining room before an unappetizing array of food covering a dirty table—cooling mutton in pools of grease, gray-green peas from cans, and other undistinguishable plates of food. As we neared the table, a cloud of flies rose off the food. Our team leader mentioned the flies to the hotel owner who went out and returned with a large can of DDT. He sprayed at the flies until they dropped dead onto the platters. A few brave team members tried to scrape food out from the bottom layers while the rest retreated to their rooms to eat the reserves they had brought with them. The team asked for a meeting, and most of the Americans decided they were no longer willing to "risk their health." The next day they left Egypt.

That left one team member to write the report. Hearing the team had deserted, the USAID education officer left for vacation, leaving his young assistant in charge. The consulting company sent out a writer from the United States, promoted the remaining team member as leader, and as a last resort, hired me since I had been present at most of the interviews. Although brilliantly eloquent at speaking, the team leader unfortunately had difficulty transferring his eloquence to paper. Each morning he would suggest content, and the writer and I would fearlessly write whole chapters on Egyptian education.

In the end, the report was much better than USAID ever expected. The consulting company was happy we had completed their contract, and more to the point, we saved the careers of at least two USAID officers who continued to hire us on similar jobs. Out of my crash course in education, I had become an expert in educational development. As a specialization it suited me well since education reforms require understanding the social values that underlie teaching, learning, and the way people view the goals of education.

For the time being, I was out of a job again. And then another lucky break occurred—I met a husband and wife team of irrigation engineers at a party. Newly graduated from college they were on a Watson fellowship to enhance their careers. They chose to sail up the Nile and investigate the Egyptian irrigation system. They had outfitted a small *falucca* sailboat with a butagas stove, padded seats for sleeping, and a frame for mosquito netting that could be pulled down at night. Bathroom facilities consisted of a chamber pot that was so inconvenient it was easier to sit out over the gunwales. The costs of outfitting the boat and the delay in obtaining permits from a suspicious Ministry of the Interior had exhausted their fellowship money. So they applied to USAID for a grant to study field practices. USAID gave them $2,500, and I agreed to go along and help with interviews.

We set off in the month of February when the wind in Egypt is strong enough to push a sailboat against the Nile's strong current. Accompanying us was a hired boatman, Ramadan, who had lost his boat and cargo in an accident on the Nile. I had my own interest in the trip. For a long time I had been impressed by the way Ansaf looked at complete strangers and said, "Oh she is a Christian from the countryside in Upper Egypt," or "She is a Muslim from Sharqiya Governorate in the delta," or "She is a Bedouin from the Sinai." Ansaf could never explain how she knew, although we both felt it must be from the details of their dress. The Nile trip came just as I was starting to take notes on dress and wondering how I could systematically cover Egypt to discover the patterns myself. The trip would let me collect dress details along a good part of the Nile.

We discovered that the wind stopped regularly in late afternoon and picked up the next day in the late morning. When it stopped, we tied up at the closest bank since we had no motor. This made a fine way of "randomly sampling" the farmers. We realized there was no point in refusing the hospitality of the person whose land we tied up at, or he might be uncooperative in the interviews the next morning. One night the wind died just as we reached the very small farm of a landowner, and of course he invited us for dinner. "Come after the Maghreb prayer," he said, and we dutifully followed the path through his fields just after the sun dipped below the horizon. We easily found his small shack and his family of eight children squatting quietly outside on a tattered mat. Our dinner was cooking in a large blackened pot on a wood fire. The children one by one shook our hands politely and then retreated to the warmth of the fire, covering their limbs and bare feet with their tattered clothes. Their eyes shifted frequently from the spectacle we provided to the steaming pot. After a decent interval the farmer's wife ladled out large bowls of soup and handed them to us along with coarse *baladi* bread. The soup comprised water in which onions had cooked. The children watched as we ate. To be polite we took our time. Finally we put down our half-full bowls and half-eaten bread, thanked our hosts for so much food that we couldn't finish all we'd been given, and started home. From the darkness of the path we could see the children descending hungrily on our bowls. The next day, the man helped us arrange interviews with his neighbors, and in gratitude for his help—not his hospitality—we left tea and sugar as gifts.

Our days followed a routine—up early in the morning, following the canals inland on foot; talking to farmers, engineers, and canal gate guards; and then setting sail before noon when the winds came up. It was important to leave before an animal had to be slaughtered for our meal. Every few days we stopped at a village to buy fresh vegetables, fill our water tanakas, and visit the local irrigation office. When the wind died far from houses, we drew up by fishing boats and bought fish just pulled from the Nile. Our dining reached new heights when Nayra joined us for a week and prepared delectable banquets.

Meanwhile, during the day I kept track of women's dresses and shawls and began to see a pattern emerging. Whenever we entered a region with a new political, economic, or social identity, the dresses would change. The most obvious difference was in the alternation of waisted and loose granny dresses—starting with a waisted dress along the Mediterranean coast; then a granny dress in the delta; again a waisted dress in Christian Middle Egypt south of Cairo; and granny again in Upper Egypt in the far south. Smaller details such as sleeve tucks, horizontal or vertical, identified women from different villages. I found styles in remote villages that were identical to styles of 100 years before in a regional town—the last gasp in a ripple of fashion that spread out to peasant wives. I saw how the Nile Valley dresses contrasted with dresses of the oasis and desert dwellers, so you could identify them at a glance. I found villages in the delta where an "embire" style existed that was patterned after the *empire* dresses of Napoleon's camp followers 200 years before, but with discretely added insets to cover the décolleté neckline. Later I learned the subtle differences in embroidery that distinguished tribes of the Sinai and the marital status of women. I saw how the dress of rural Egyptian men changed after they returned from work in Saudi Arabia to show off their newfound affluence. I even saw a remote island in the Nile where women dressed like men, presumably to ward off males from boats that grounded on nearby shoals.

The three of us, meanwhile, were also finding that Egypt's irrigation system was much more complicated than we thought. The waters of the Nile move north, passing over barrages that regulate its flow. In a moment of candor, an engineer told us that the ledgers in the offices of the Irrigation Department had been falsified for so long that when a new engineer arrived, he didn't dare make corrections for fear the "lost" water might be blamed on him. This might explain why estimates in a larger USAID study based on barrage figures made it appear no water at all came out at the Mediterranean coast!

Irrigation control has both a visible and an invisible face. From the Nile, water is diverted into large feeder canals (*tira*) before they branch off and deposit their loads into smaller canals that, in turn, branch off farther into the countryside and feed the farmers' fields. At most points, gates can be raised and lowered to control water flow in the amounts specified by government rules. Yet there are numerous ways farmers can circumvent the rules. They are not supposed to take water from the main tira feeder canals, but they do—with pumps. The smaller canals are only open at specified intervals for an amount of time decided by the government. But farmers can bribe the gatekeeper to leave the gates open longer, or use pumps that bypass the gates, or draw water off more quickly during scheduled openings. Water flow also depends on where the farmer's field is located and whether he gets along with his neighbors who, because of inheritance laws, are often his kin. If the farmers owning property between his fields and the main canals keep their canals free of silt, the water flows smoothly and adequately, but if these farmers are lazy or ornery and their canals silt up, little flows to the fields behind them. Any rise in the field level from absolutely flat also means less water reaches crops in the elevated areas. Although land in Egypt cannot be inherited or sold without a minimum water right, which theoretically prevents fragmenting the land into pieces too uneconomical to farm, as with anything else in Egypt people figure out ways to get around the rules.

This is only the tip of the iceberg with regard to irrigation. After the Aswan Dam (completed in the 1960s) held back the annual floods and with it the fertile silt, formal control of the water became easier. People argue whether the net effects were positive. On the plus side, controlling the water flow meant up to three crops could be planted each year in some areas that previously had only one, and devastating droughts were avoided. There were also the benefits of more electricity, new industries, and more land becoming available. On the negative side, without the silt the land under irrigation produced poor quality crops, and farmers had to start using chemical fertilizers. Moreover, the major canals were no longer flushed out by the floods and thus required extensive dredging in the January *khafaf* (the drying out time) when water is drained from the canals. With the greater abundance of water, farmers irrigated excessively, and the land soon became waterlogged and mineral encrusted, further reducing the productivity of the land. The existing drainage canals were not extensive enough to wash away the salts, especially in areas like Upper Egypt, where the problem was occurring for the first time.

Other problems also became apparent. Many of the trees that shaded the paths along the canals and prevented erosion were dying from waterlogged roots, and the treasured antiquities of Upper Egypt started deteriorating as the moisture from the higher water table seeped into underground tombs and climbed the ancient walls. Still, despite these drawbacks, most people believe the benefits of the Aswan Dam outweigh the disadvantages if only because of the famines it averted.

I returned to Cairo eager to show off my new skills in dress identification to Ansaf. "OK," she said with a twinkle in her eye, "we will test you." One day she spied a woman in an unusual dress that was unlike the ones in Bulaq. I thought the dress was from a village just south of Bani Suef, in an area where the patterns suddenly changed from a northern to a modified Middle Egyptian style. Ansaf asked the woman where she came from, and she replied promptly, "From Cairo." "Oh," said Ansaf, "we wondered if you came from near Bani Suef because of the dress you're wearing." "No," she said, "but my mother came from that area and she taught me to sew." My disappointment turned to glee at Ansaf's surprise. "You now know Egypt better than I do," she exclaimed generously.

~~~

While I waited for the awarding of a USAID-funded education project —where I thought I might have a chance to participate—I jumped at every opportunity to travel in Egypt. One opportunity was to tag along with a group of Al-Azhar medical students on a weeklong visit to a village in the delta. Their enlightened professors—one a medical doctor and one a psychiatrist—felt the students needed to learn the common diseases of rural Egypt. The mother of the psychiatrist, Muhammad, living in the village invited the wife of the doctor, Tarek, and myself into her home and plied us with comforts that included great pillowy beds and extravagant breakfasts of *fatayer* (honey-infused pancakes) topped with thick cream from her cow. I understood for the first time the Arabic greeting "May you have a morning of honey" or "a morning of cream."

We accompanied the students each day as they interviewed residents and completed their questionnaires. The most common ailments they found were bilharzias—a parasitic illness whose cycle involves snails, standing water, and humans—and respiratory illnesses, including tuberculosis and chronic bronchitis aggravated by the smoke from cooking fires and the damp cold of winter. Psychological illnesses were more difficult to identify because of the reticence of villagers to talk about them.

In the evenings we held focus groups—some sex-segregated and some mixed, to discuss problems such as husband-wife difficulties, birth control, and the means by which the villagers might take a more active role in resolving their own health problems. A number of the women felt they had had enough children and complained that their husbands were unwilling to prevent more. The medical students were trained in nondirective methods and role playing, and they soon had the participants acting out their problems in an entertaining way while conveying important health information.

We also visited the village school to see what children knew about common illnesses. The medical students would call out a class and ask, for example, what the children knew about bilharzias, where it came from, and how to prevent it. Their eager replies were full of misinformation that the medical students corrected. Then they posed a variety of hypothetical situations, such as, "What would you do if you found your little sister had been wading in an irrigation canal?" The correct answer was that the child would bring her out of the canal and vigorously wipe any area of her body that had touched the water. This would remove the parasites before they had time to burrow into her skin. When all the children correctly answered the questions, the medical students called out another class and let the first class teach the correct information and pose the hypothetical questions. They repeated this until all the classes had learned about bilharzias. It was an effective teaching device that clearly delighted the children, with the added benefit that the teachers also absorbed the information.

After working in the village for several days, we were suddenly challenged by some university students home on holiday. They had heard about our activities and construed them as threatening village morality. It didn't help to have foreigners present, although to the rural villagers the Cairo students probably seemed as foreign as Bill and I did. The students said they objected to discussions of birth control in mixed gatherings and to the fact that a Christian medical student had joined the Muslim students for prayers in the mosque. It was around 1980, and it was the first time I had seen protests of this kind based on religious rationales. The atmosphere was ominous until the medical students defused the crisis by asking the local students to explain specifically what bothered them. Their objections boiled down to a semantic complaint about the use of the Arabic phrase *taqdid al usra*, meaning "to limit the family." They said it was against religion to talk about limiting families since only God knew how many children a couple should have. They eventually accepted the phrase *tanzim al usra*, meaning "to plan the spacing of children," as terminology that didn't challenge God's prerogatives. In the end, they supported the work of our students and later joined in some of the discussions.

I was relieved the challenge ended peacefully. Several times I had seen Egyptian crowds become quite dangerous, and the embassy had warned us to lock our car doors and drive away immediately if we were ever involved in an accident. Once I saw crowds gathering around the body of a man who had been hit. They smashed nearby cars and tried to get at the driver of the car who had hit the man. Another time I saw the driver of a trolley that had accidentally run over a woman near Bulaq running for his life with an angry mob after him. Another time when a driver in a Mercedes knocked down a little girl in the street, he only saved himself by jumping out of the car and slapping his face the way women mourn loved ones to show his remorse. The crowd turned from angry to sympathetic almost instantly and began to console him, pointing out that in fact the little girl had not been hurt. On my way to Bulaq one day in 1979, I got caught in the bread riots of Cairo. I was in Bill's car when suddenly the narrow street filled with angry protestors rushing toward us. Ibrahim reversed the car and sped backward down the street, which luckily was empty, and we managed to escape. I had been unaware that the government had announced higher prices for flour, and the bakeries in protest refused to bake bread. When the people found their staple food unavailable, they rioted all over Cairo, smashing shops and burning government buildings. The government eventually compromised, and everything went back to normal.

Still waiting for work, I decided to launch another small study. I had been impressed in Bulaq at the extent to which families remained intact despite their grinding poverty. It made me realize how pivotal family life was to Egyptians. The question that nagged me, however, was, if family is so important, why do orphanages and homes for the elderly exist when relatives are supposed to take over and care for such people? Egyptians always expressed horror at hearing that many elderly Americans ended up in retirement homes when "their families should take care of them." And yet I knew homes for the elderly also existed in Egypt. It seemed a good idea to explore this question further. But to know about the clients of these institutions, I needed access to their files, and that was difficult for me as a foreigner to achieve. I had good access to Christian institutions with Ansaf, but neither of us would receive the same kind of welcome in a Muslim institution. Luckily, I found a Muslim student who agreed to go out on her own and ask my questions. Through her I accumulated data on eight orphanages and five homes for the elderly.

These institutions turned out to be quite different from Western ones. They generally catered to people who fell inconveniently outside the safety nets of family. Most of the orphans came from poor families where either their relatives couldn't support them, or one parent was missing and the other worked and could only care for them on weekends. Another group of children were those who had been dropped off at places of worship or police stations as newborns and were assumed to be the product of illegitimate liaisons. The "orphaned" poor could eventually marry and lead normal lives because their family backgrounds were known, but the children of unknown parentage had a much more difficult time because of the assumed immorality of their parents. Often they married one another, or a boy of little means might come to ask for a girl.

A related issue we explored was adoption. We knew it was illegal under Islam but wondered if the government had rules about it. That meant a trip to the ministry office that deals with children's affairs. There after a few minutes, the friendly official said, "Oh, but we have ways of seeing that newborns are taken care of." She explained that when childless couples came looking for a baby, the ministry helped the woman go through a "pregnancy" with wads of foam padding until the child was "born." The baby's name was registered in the couple's name, and according to her, even the couple's relatives didn't know what had happened. The couple avoided the stigma of childlessness, and the child obtained the benefits of normal family membership, including a portion of the inheritance.

The homes for the elderly were of two kinds—a lower-level institution that catered to the poor without families to support them and a higher-level institution where the elderly could elect to go. Some elderly with the means to do so sought to live separately from their adult children, many of whom lived in cramped urban apartments. Or sometimes their employed children paid for their care during the week and brought them home on weekends. A final group resided there because their children were working in the oil countries and they had no other choice. In that case, too, the relatives of the elderly often paid for their care. In most cases, family links remained intact, even among the poor, and it was only circumstance that required them to reside in institutions.

The day finally came when I joined the consulting team for the first major education project in Egypt. Our report had recommended both qualitative and quantitative improvements in Egyptian education, so it was dismaying to find that USAID earmarked the bulk of the funds for school construction and little for improving the quality of the school program. The reason, it seemed, was that vast sums of money could be expended quickly without much direct supervision by USAID officials. In the Camp David agreements of 1979, Egypt was promised large sums of money roughly equal to the nonmilitary grants given to Israel. However, the money given to Israel was handed over in check form while the Egyptian aid had to be overseen by the Americans. USAID had a relatively small staff in Cairo and needed a project that was big and costly where most of the oversight could be subcontracted out to engineering companies.

USAID officials felt quality issues could be addressed with a few teacher training programs and a "basic skills" course introduced at the primary level. Consequently, schools received hardware for home economics, carpentry, electricity, agriculture, and maritime courses based on the needs of particular regions. In most schools, the girls took the home economics courses and the boys the other courses.

It was difficult to argue against building more schools in Egypt, since almost no schools had been added since the 1960s. Most parents were enthusiastic about educating their children, and schools everywhere were overcrowded. After independence in 1952, President Nasser promised education opportunities to all Egyptian children rich and poor, urban and rural. For a few years education became the main vehicle into the middle classes for any rural and poor children who persisted to the end of university. Nasser guaranteed government jobs for all university graduates, but when they came in droves, the bureaucracy was overwhelmed. Pay scales for civil servants remained low compared to the pay of plumbers and other skilled workers.

By the early 1980s when we began working on the Primary Education Development Project, if children remained at home it was because there weren't enough spaces, schools were too distant, or no middle or secondary schools existed near enough to qualify for university entry and subsequent jobs. The Ministry of Education tried ingenious ways to accommodate as many children as possible. Class size rose to more than fifty students in many schools, with two and even three shifts of students over the course of the day. Teachers often taught more than one shift and were exhausted by the end of the day. Some schools had a "flying class" where students rotated periods of physical education so the "flying class" could occupy their empty seats while they were outside. One minister in the mid-1980s did away with grade six, thereby opening up an extra room in every school. Instead of solving the problem, it created a crisis as the double class bulge wound its way through the secondary and university levels. The missing year meant children learned less and failed exams more, and eventually the idea was abandoned, causing yet another crisis when an extra year was added.

Many of those prevented from enrolling in rural areas were, of course, girls. Communities invariably favored boys if space was limited since education was equated with earning power and males were the financial supporters of families. Conventional wisdom said girls didn't go because of their parents' conservative views, but our experience suggested that was not true in many cases. We proposed a study to see the effects of constructing the 2,000 that schools USAID eventually funded. Did resistant parents change their minds about enrolling daughters once schools were conveniently nearby? How near did the schools have to be? What other obstacles were there to girls' education? We thought we could answer these questions by combining a large statistical study of school catchment areas with an in-depth study of some new school communities.

Our team consisted of three Americans (two education specialists and me), an Egyptian statistician, and a group of Egyptian students to act as researchers (four men and four women). I was in charge of the in-depth study of ten new school communities chosen from near urban centers, remote villages, farming and industrial sites, and from conservative and more liberal areas. For five years our researchers visited the villages, once in the spring and once in the fall, to collect data on enrollments.

Although we stayed in poorly maintained government hostels and ate the starchy food they served there, the student researchers saw our trips as a glorious lark. Each night I had to call a curfew at 10:00 p.m. to stop their singing and hilarity and remind them that the next day we had work to do. The researchers were conscientious and got along well with the villagers, but each day brought its share of problems—most of them boy-girl difficulties that were surprising considering that the sexes kept at arm's lenght. Even from a distance they developed crushes on one another, and at one point I even had to turn away a prospective suitor—a pharmacist who asked to marry one of the girls after she stopped by his store for medicine. The supervisors of the girls' and boys' teams fell in love and went through a tumultuous time when her father refused to let her marry him because he didn't have a secure job. I began to feel like a marriage counselor.

Each day we stopped by the education office to pick up the government minders who accompanied us to the village. They didn't much enjoy the trips and tried to prolong their welcoming cups of tea. After arriving in villages too late to complete our questionnaires, we changed our tactics. I would spend the first day drinking as many cups of tea as they wanted, and thereafter I stayed in the car while a researcher fetched the minder.

The female researchers and I visited families in the communities while our male colleagues visited the schools, collected statistics on enrollments and teacher characteristics, and observed the "basic courses." The experience taught us a lot about conducting and analyzing interviews in the Egyptian context. Teachers invariably blamed girls' poor enrollments and attendance on the parents while the parents blamed them on the teachers. The truth probably was a combination of both—parents kept girls home to help with siblings and housework and didn't take homework or attendance seriously. On their side, teachers were often harsh and didn't prepare the girls to pass exams, so many dropped out or repeated grades. Parents reported that the teachers encouraged poorer students to drop out because they took too much of their time.

Incidental to our study, we observed rural children dressed in the garb of religious shaikhs attending the parallel Al-Azhar religious schools, the fastest-growing education system in Egypt. Rural parents liked these schools because the incidental costs were lower and because children moved up through the system automatically until they were admitted to Al-Azhar University. The university had the same departments as the national system that prepared students for a variety of professions. A friend teaching in the medical school told us stories about the restrictions he faced in his classes. For example, the women medical students were not allowed to see naked male bodies or study the sexual organs. And as in the education system overall, the work was largely rote. The students could recite the memorized symptoms of disease but could not identify the disease from a patient's symptoms. The rush of children to the Al-Azhar system was almost certainly a reaction to problems in the government schools—their poor quality, costliness, and ultimately the difficulty of passing exams to move to the next stage.

Our study produced findings that helped USAID establish education policy for projects later on. We found that although parents often said they would not educate daughters, almost all of them changed their minds once schools were built in their villages. One and a half kilometers, however, was about the limit girls would walk to school. If boys were already going to distant schools, parents would often let them continue there, in what they felt were "more established" schools. Parents were more likely to send girls to the new "untested" schools with higher quotas of inexperienced teachers since "it didn't matter so much to them." If we found villages with unusually high enrollments, it was almost always the result of an enlightened leader in the past.

In many villages it was a pleasure to talk to community elders, most of whom were "unspoiled" by public education. They invariably spoke intelligently about their problems and about the history of education in their areas. I was struck with their grasp of a wide range of subjects and the logic with which they spoke. This kind of intelligence often seemed missing in the village schools. Once I was looking over enrollment figures in a principal's office when I noticed that the fourth grade class had more girls than boys, an anomaly rarely found in rural schools. When I asked about this oddity, the principal said the figures were correct, and the teachers sitting there agreed. When I asked why, and one teacher replied nervously that more girls were born that year; the others nodded in agreement. The next day when nearby schools didn't have unusual fourth grade classes I returned to the first and found the figures for boys and girls had been reversed.

In looking at enrollments, we discovered we had to count students in an entire catchment area to see if there was a net increase, since many students transferred out of crowded schools into new schools closer to home. Despite that finding, USAID took credit for all the increases in enrollment in Egypt during the decade they constructed schools, without making allowance for children transferring from existing schools, the addition of shifts, or increases in class size. It was a claim designed to impress Congress with the way U.S. tax money had been spent.

There were other problems. The schools cost about a third more than normal ones because of dishonest local contractors and the fact that they had to be "overbuilt" because of shoddy materials that might bring the roofs tumbling down on children. The ministry never honored its agreement to pay for maintenance, and the schools quickly deteriorated. In addition, the practical courses never worked out—some of the tools were inappropriate (a lawn edger for agriculture) or required utilities where none existed (stoves for home economics). Teachers were not trained sufficiently to teach the skills and reverted to rote teaching styles they knew best ("Children, repeat after me: This is a hammer and it is used to hammer nails into wood"). Even if they were prepared to let children use tools, there was no budget for materials—again, a ministry failure to honor its agreements. Finally, parents complained that they didn't send children to school to learn manual skills and that basic classes took time from studies that led to jobs. "We can teach farming," parents said. "The schools should help them pass exams."

USAID can't be faulted entirely for this mistake. The UN's emphasis on "basic education"—giving children rudimentary technical skills that would be useful in their lives—seemed a good idea, but it should have been tested on a limited scale before introducing it all over Egypt. It was the first in a string of examples I saw of interventions that proved ineffective and had to be abandoned after much effort and expense. The Egypt project was my first experience in a large development project. Indeed, to my knowledge it was the first major education project funded anywhere by USAID. I couldn't have asked for a better opportunity to see education in a "holistic" way from the perspective of parents, teachers, managers, and developers.

11

CHANGE: ABDUL WAHHAB
AND THE RELIGIOUS SHAIKHS

One of the people I came to admire while living in Egypt was Abdul Wahhab al-Mutawwa. Reading his column in *Al-Ahram* was for many Egyptians as much a ritual as Friday prayers. He was Egypt's equivalent of Ann Landers—only better. I started following his columns when I realized they were an important topic of conversation for Egyptians. At first I read out of curiosity, but then like everyone else, I became addicted to them. After painstakingly translating a few of them, I enlisted a friend, Samira, to help.[1] We spent several weeks in the Dar al-Khutab Archives unearthing his early columns.

The columns ranged from short pieces to full pages. The joy in reading them came from the colorful way writers described their intractable problems and the often unpredictable but sound advice offered by Abdul Wahhab. Through these letters I felt as if I was entering the private life of Egyptians in a way that was not possible in real life. The letters were of two kinds: requests for advice and descriptions of behaviors that serve as a model for others. On January 20, 1989, a writer offers her example as the best approach to marriage:

> I am the only child of parents who raised me well. After I completed
> my studies at the Faculty of Law many suitors came asking to marry me
> because of my father's good reputation. One young man visited my father
> and I was attracted to him. But from the beginning he tried to control my

---

1. I want to thank Samira Megalli who helped me translate the columns. Here they are paraphrased.

every move—from what I should wear to whom I should see. My father thought the man had no right to control me in this way and threw him out.

A number of years passed while I remained single. During this time I worked as a lawyer. One day my relatives were talking about a couple who were struck by tragedy—the wife was injured in an accident and their child killed. I was impressed at the extraordinary efforts the husband made to try to save his wife.

No one who could be called a suitor visited me during those years, until one day I met a man in his forties with a face radiating goodness. I soon realized he was the one my relatives had spoken of whose story had so impressed me. I was immediately attracted to him and invited him to have a cup of tea with me. We talked and talked all night until dawn. He wanted to marry me but was afraid to ask for my hand because of the twenty-two-year difference in our ages. I hoped my father would accept the marriage despite this problem. As it turned out, even though several relatives opposed the idea, my father consented and in fifteen days we were married.

Unfortunately we didn't have a child at first and my parents were disappointed not to have grandchildren. It was only after my father died, God rest his soul, and we had been married six years that I became pregnant. And then I became pregnant again, and again, until I had five children. You can see the power and wisdom of God. I left my work to stay home with my children. My husband had a stroke but came through it, thank God. He loved us so much he stayed home rather than go to a hospital.

The point of my letter is to show others that a woman needs to follow her own instincts in love even when it means opposing relatives to find her happiness. If she doesn't she may be tempted to love someone outside of marriage. Also I want to show that having children is in the hands of God and their timing can't be predicted.

Abdul Wahhab answers:

I thank you for your letter and the feeling of happiness it projects. I agree with you in some parts and disagree in others. Let me begin with the agreement. The ear sometimes loves before the eye. Because you were touched by what you heard about this man, you put him on a pedestal before you met him. The pores of your mind were already open. That is clear from the fact that you married in fifteen days. You did the right thing since you felt such a strong desire for him.

With respect to the children coming from God, that is true and I approve of having children. But did you consider your husband's age? Since you are a lawyer, you are an educated woman. Yet you had five children! Two or three children would have been enough. Don't blame God entirely—you also bear responsibility for having so many. You want to set an example for others, but you should know that the reasons for happiness are an enigma that can't be generalized to everyone. Heart and reason must be combined. You took a risk and it worked. You were fortunate.

One of the most poignant of Abdul Wahhab's columns shows the difficulties of rural children caught between the traditional ways of their villages and their new lives in cities. The letter writer says (May 5, 1989):

I came from a modest village family. My mother and father were illiterate. As a child, I went to the *madrasa* [religious school] to learn to read and recite the Koran. Eventually I obtained a diploma from secondary school and was accepted in the Faculty of Medicine. I rented a small apartment and began my medical studies.

After a few weeks I met a young woman and felt attracted to her at first sight. This girl, however, was detested by all her schoolmates because she was so pretentious. She was not beautiful yet I loved her and thought of nothing else but her day and night. She didn't encourage me and after a while I became so depressed I failed my exams while she succeeded in hers. My father did his best to help me according to his understanding of the world. He sent me to holy saints and sheikhs and finally to doctors. In trying to cure me, he spent all his money. Every night my mother sat by my side comforting me. Eventually I got better and was able to complete my degree. During this time, even though I had no news of the young woman, she was always in my thoughts.

I was appointed an intern in a hospital and was surprised to find that she was my supervisor. Even though she was not very popular I asked her to marry me, and she accepted. I returned to the village to announce the news to my parents. They knew she caused my depression and were against my marrying her. My father refused to help financially but she came from a wealthy family and her parents didn't ask for much [dowry]. I quarreled with my parents but they continued to be patient with me. One day I became so angry I hit my mother in front of my father and brother. They were shocked by my behavior. Later that night I passed my mother's room and heard her asking God to bless me. This blessing still rings in my ears today.

I told my fiancée what I had done and she replied, "It was the least you could do." After that I dropped all contact with my parents and concentrated on supporting my wife and our three children. Soon my wife started causing me all sorts of misery and I wanted to divorce her but reconsidered when I thought of the children.

The two eldest boys are like their mother and close to her. One day the eldest son smoked a cigarette in front of me. I told him he was rude and raised my hand to hit him. He caught my hand and spat in my face. My wife and another son intervened but I was furious. In the middle of this episode I saw my mother's gentle face and heard her speak to me. I left the room and went to bed. When I got up in the morning I could no longer move my arms, legs or body. I thought this paralysis must be God's punishment. Even after three months of physical therapy, I still have headaches the doctors say are a figment of my imagination. Now here I am in my fifties, humiliated by my wife and children, sick, and a burden to them. I can't stop crying. I repent the past and ask God to forgive me for my behavior toward my parents who are now dead. The message I want to convey to your readers is that children should always respect their parents.

Abdul Wahhab answers:

We only reflect on our bad deeds when they lead to sorrow. We learn to be wise after the fact. You began to think about your deeds after your son struck you. God's punishment actually began when happiness deserted you. You married a bad woman of poor character—hated by everyone who knew her. She even supported you in your mistreatment of your mother. Your children will likely know the same suffering when they marry since, as Sharif Hussain [the Shaikh of Mecca] says, the sins of the parents are punished in this world. There is a vast difference between good and bad, between a pious man and one who is motivated like an animal by his worst instincts.

I don't want to be cruel to you but your letter may make others aware of what is in store for them. Everyone who has children or shares this kind of misfortune should consider their weaknesses and refrain from criticizing you. As far as your parents are concerned—they died without forgiving you. Your suffering atones for that. You will be punished in the next world but we cannot predict what form that punishment will take. True contrition, however, is always accepted by God. Go to your brothers and sisters and send one of them on the Pilgrimage to Mecca. You can give them what you could not give your parents. Go yourself if possible. I will pray to God to forgive you.

One final letter shows that life was not easy for middle-class urban dwellers, either. The writer describes his situation (January 1, 1985):

I am a young man of twenty-nine. My father was an ordinary civil servant and we all lived a modest life together. My father taught me to be self-reliant by showing me how to fix electrical and plumbing problems around the house. Life was going well until inflation hit. My father decided to take early retirement from his government job and work in an Arab oil country to make a better life for us. The first year he regularly sent letters with money inside, but they were less frequent the second year and finally stopped altogether the third year. People said he must have moved to another country, or changed his address, or perhaps he married and had children by a new wife. We would have died of hunger if we had not received his small pension.

I was sixteen and suddenly responsible for the family. So I went to the owner of an electric shop nearby and asked if I could take orders for repairs in front of his shop three hours a day. In return he would receive the profits from items I would buy in his shop. The man agreed. After school I ate quickly and then stood in front of the shop until 7:00 p.m., studied until 10:00, and then went to sleep. My job paid for our clothing and rent.

My studies however suffered and my last year I received passing although low grades. The storekeeper offered sweet drinks to all the neighbors, saying how proud he was of me. I was surprised to find a person unrelated to me celebrating my success. I accepted the fate my low grades held for me and entered a technical institute where after two years I would be guaranteed a government job.

One day in the lecture hall, the light went out and the professor asked for a specialist to repair it. I told him I would do it. The professor asked how I knew this kind of work and when I told him about my job he exclaimed before the class, "The person who knows how to make everyday repairs is someone who can be relied upon." This instantly made me an expert in the eyes of my classmates.

One day a young girl asked me to repair her tape recorder and I returned it in good condition without asking for money. Thus began a friendship that deepened into a sentimental relationship. She asked about my circumstances and I answered truthfully. I learned that she was the daughter of an inspector in the Ministry of Education who was nearing retirement. She graduated from the institute with high grades and I with modest grades because of my work. Our relationship continued by way of the telephone in the shop where I worked, and soon we were making plans for a future together. She suggested I ask her father for permission to marry. My mother warned me that I wasn't financially ready for marriage and might be refused. But I went to see her father, and explained that I was supporting my family but had enough income left over to start thinking about my future. I told him we could live in my mother's large apartment for three or four years until I could rent my own apartment. He promised to think it over and answer me soon.

On the appointed day I returned and was surprised that her father talked about general subjects without referring to marriage. After a while he asked me to rewire part of his apartment. I did the rewiring and left without an answer. My friend contacted me and asked me to go to her father again since a relative was asking for her hand. This time he wanted me to repair the fridge and again left me with no answer. This situation lasted a year, I going to him, he not replying, and I always fixing things. When I returned home each time, my mother greeted me with pity in her eyes.

I worked harder at my repairs and tried to forget my friend's father. I made sure my sister and brother received a good education so they would find good careers. After a time my friend contacted me to say that her parents had refused my proposal because I had no apartment, my family was a burden to me, and because my father was absent. I was surprised to hear that I, the victim, was suddenly responsible for my father's absence. But I resigned myself and told my friend I would establish a life that met her family's conditions.

By some miracle I was given a big contract in one of the new cities near Cairo and, after a few months, I could afford a two-room apartment with furnishings and a motor scooter for transportation. The next time my friend contacted me, I told her I had been hurt by her family's treatment of me and would never go again to them unless she guaranteed they would accept my proposal. She replied that the situation had become critical since they were pressing her to accept the proposal of the relative. So I got up my courage, forgot about my dignity and went to meet her father. After we made small talk for a while, I broached the subject of marriage but he only wanted me to repair his television. I cut him off politely, saying I had not come to talk about television sets. I told him we had loved each other for five years during which time I struggled to work myself into a better position. My father had been a government employee like he was, and our family was a good one even though of simple means. I told him I too was a government employee but that I had other activities to support a family. I asked why he deprived us of our happiness.

Finally he answered that he had taken my situation into consideration, but as a father it was his duty to ensure the welfare of his daughter. He went on about the reasons for his refusal, counting the points out on the fingers of his hand as if he were giving a lesson in school. Each finger penetrated my heart like a dagger and I left his house paralyzed by my failure. My mother immediately saw the results of the visit on my face. I told her I wanted to go live in my new apartment and asked her to visit me every weekend.

I lived alone in my apartment in the village and didn't return to Cairo. Every time my family visited, my brother who was working in the electric shop would tell me about my friend who called to ask about me. She became engaged to her relative but some time later called my brother to say the engagement had been broken off.

I continued with my job until one morning while I was supervising a repair in the new city, a workman told me someone was looking for me. My friend stood there with a suitcase in her hand looking at me with downcast yet accusatory eyes. I greeted her warmly and took her to the administrative building. She began to cry and soon I was crying too. Minutes passed before we could speak. Her fiancé had broken the engagement himself after feeling her coldness toward him.

Finally she asked if I would go to a *mazun* [marriage official] with her to get married and present her family with the fact of our marriage. This was the only solution left to us she felt. I assured her that I would never abandon her, whatever happened, but that I had suffered from the last refusal and now couldn't marry without her family's approval. She would have to return home and I would meet with her father one more time. This would be more dignified for both of us. But I warned her that if he talked about fixing the television, I would break it. She collapsed and cried, accusing me of deserting her. Finally she set off to take a bus back to town. I ran after her to give her a ride on my motor scooter. She accepted angrily but called me "Betrayer." She left me in front of her house swearing to refuse me even if her father accepted the marriage.

Sir, I have taken a vacation from my job to put an end to this affair. Was I wrong not to marry her without her father's consent? Or am I a coward as she says? Will her father ever consent to our marriage and if so will she carry out her threat to refuse me?

Abdul Wahhab answers:

My friend, you were not wrong when you refused to end your suffering by marrying her. You behaved responsibly when you rejected for your friend what you would have rejected for your sister. You also avoided embarrassing her father, even though no one would have blamed you for doing so. You have behaved nobly. Because you have borne family responsibility from an early age, it has given you a maturity well beyond what is expected of one of your years. A person like you shouldn't be refused by any reasonable person. Is it logical that you should be prevented from marrying when you have struggled to meet their demands for five years? Is it right that her father rejects you yet finds nothing wrong in exploiting you for repairs? You speak about his daughter and he speaks about fuses.

I feel it is important to obtain parents' approval in marriage, and I believe too in the dignity of the father's position in the house and his responsibility toward his children. I have always liked what Confucius said about the father's position in the home being like an Emperor. But even an emperor must build his relationships on love and justice and understanding of his children's feelings if he is to deserve his position. The Prophet, praise be to his name, called for children to obey their fathers and noted the father's obligation to care for his children. But what kind of care does this man take of his daughter? We are not able, however wise we are, to feel what our children feel, or to choose for them what they reject. Why so much suffering when the way to happiness is clear? You are not a coward. Go to her father for the last time, and explain what happened. Tell him you could have put him in an embarrassing position but you know the responsibility of a family member and have refused to do to her what you would have rejected for your own family. If he accepts, then good. If not, you have the right to behave in whatever way you want. And if he talks about his television you have a right to break it on his hard head. Your friend's threat to refuse you was said to express her suffering. She will make it up with contrition when she realizes her dreams. Contrition [prayers] is a small effort to pay for happiness.

~~~~~

After reading Abdul Wahhab's advice I became curious about him. From the columns I knew he had a "red agenda"—a list of deserving people he would try to help. Once a week in his office in the *Al-Ahram* newspaper building, he held an open house to solve the problems of his readers with money, jobs, and other help contributed by anonymous benefactors. One evening Samira and I showed up on "red agenda" night and were graciously received by Abdul Wahhab. He looked to be in his fifties, softly rotund, of medium height, and with a receding hairline. He was soft-spoken and clearly more used to listening than to being the center of attention. I told him I found a profound wisdom in many of his columns and wanted to know more about how he wrote them. With prompting he explained.

AW: I usually select one or two letters from the two hundred or so letters I receive each week. I choose ones that represent problems common to a number of writers. Then I read the letters and rewrite them. This is because people often can express their suffering but can't tell their story in a coherent way. Either their style is poor or they have difficulty arranging the action in a proper sequence. I only rearrange the events to tell the story better. Then I sit down and think for a long time about a solution to the problem. When I decide on an answer, I write the column. Altogether it takes about five hours to write a column.

Q: What made you start writing the column?

AW: I started working for *Al-Ahram* when I was eighteen and in my second year of the Faculty of Arts. The newspaper decided to send me to England for a twelve-week training course in journalism. On my day off I used to read the Sunday papers to practice my English, especially the advice columns. I found them interesting even though I couldn't always understand the answers, but I discovered that mankind is basically the same everywhere—facing the same problems: death, poverty, disease, and losing family, friends, and lovers. I began thinking about doing a column like this in Egypt although I knew it would be different. I felt the answers in the English columns, even to very complicated problems, were too short to be helpful and often simply advised the person to "seek psychiatric help" or "go to a counselor." That didn't seem enough to respond to the suffering in the letters. I place a great deal of importance in the role of feelings and my own emotional response to the person who writes. In this matter I consult both my brain and my heart, and then rely on my heart when there is a contradiction. You have to feel sympathy toward people to be able to help them.

People of course present their own side of the story in a better light than might be true, and certainly better than the side of the person opposing them. This was a problem for me at first, but soon I decided to accept as true whatever they write in their letters. For one thing, you can't help a person unless you believe in him. So I say in the column, "According to the facts you have given me, the solution is so and so." If they are lying, then they probably won't accept my advice anyway. And since the answer is for a wider audience, they expect my answer to respond to the facts.

When I started the column the editors at *Al-Ahram* gave me the freedom to do what I wanted, but I decided to refrain from giving advice on religion, ethics, and law, although there are elements of all these in the columns. I guess my approach is humanistic, rather than based on any set of organized beliefs.

Since I started the column, people's problems have changed. Six or seven years ago the main problem was dealing with the family apartment in the case of divorce. The 1979 changes in personal status laws required a man who divorced his wife to leave the family apartment to her. Many men asked where they would live in such a case, and some claimed their wives acted like dictators knowing they would get the apartment. The situation changed when the law was revoked; now the man can stay in the apartment if he finds an equivalent place for his family.

A problem of the 1970s and early 1980s came from the *infitah* [Egypt's opening to foreign economic influences], when a whole new class of nouveau riche suddenly turned Egypt's social order upside down. Those who had been rich became poor, while the poor became rich selling goods

Egyptians suddenly wanted. The infitah is only indirectly important these days because of the many Egyptians who work in Arab oil countries. But the effects are starting to show up in children who grew up with one or more parents absent most of the time, or who were raised abroad in a different culture. Recently I received a letter from two young men who complained that their father worked in the Gulf States for eighteen years and only came home infrequently. When he retired, the sons saw their father as a stranger. I urged them to remember that he sent money back all these years to support his family, and that he suffered more from being absent from his family. They should treat him with the respect and love due a father.

These days the main problems for young people are jobs and marriage. The average age at first marriage used to be about twenty-two or twenty-three but now it's around twenty-seven. The main reason is economic. When young people are physically ready to marry and are meeting the right kinds of people at the university, the young men have no money. Ten years later when they are financially ready to marry, they can't find the right person. I finally had to open a file on marriage because I received so many letters from both men and women.

I believe the tendency to be more religious today is beneficial. It encourages young people to find happiness in marriage and family life, yet gives them more freedom to manage their own lives. Religion affects young men's choices about which young women to marry. If they see a veiled girl, they are propelled into marriage because she looks modest and moral. Education is also beneficial because it encourages people to stress reason and logic. Parents no longer control the lives of their children as they once did. Young people commonly marry without the permission of their parents. Part of the reason is that parents are no longer able to finance the apartments and furnishings needed for marriage and therefore they can't control their children's futures. Most marriages, now are love marriages, and most failed marriages are those not built on love. Even though there are many factors in successful marriage, the most important is love.

The more I read Abdul Wahhab's columns the more I felt something was going on in Egyptian society that observers seemed to have missed. Most of the writers were men, and certainly the most disturbed were men. They complained that although they did their best to be good husbands and fathers, they felt they were unable to live up to others' expectations. Economic factors, as Abdul Wahhab noted, were a major factor, and it seemed to particularly eat away at the self-image of men when they couldn't support their families. The situation was different for women. Now they had choices. They attended schools and universities, and many were working. The expectation that men would still support them meant they weren't obligated to contribute in a major way to household expenses. The conventional view of "oppressed women" in Arab society was not one supported by the letters. Instead, one might say it was the men who felt oppressed by the burden of supporting families in an economy that didn't allow them to do it properly.

Abdul Wahhab retired from *Al-Ahram* sometime in the 1990s and died shortly thereafter. Along with him went a remarkably tolerant and wise mind. Although he claimed to refrain from giving religious advice (he was a Muslim), he drew eclectically on the wisdom of Christian, Jewish, Greek, Chinese, Muslim, Buddhist, and Hindu traditions, giving him a flexibility to respond appropriately to the heart-felt complaints he received.

I have to compare the tolerant Abdul Wahhab with another group of advice columnists. These were religious shaikhs answering readers' questions about correct Islamic behavior. Almost every major newspaper featured a column written by one of these shaikhs, and like Abdul Wahhab's columns, they also served as a commentary on social change. In the late 1980s I received a small grant to travel to Egypt to look at the way the new "fundamentalist" religious philosophy was changing social values.[1] Interviews yielded little that was new so I started searching for evidence of how conservative religious views might be affecting society. It was then I noticed how much the religious shaikhs' columns had proliferated and expanded since the 1970s when we lived in Egypt. I collected columns from seven

---

1. My chapter entitled "Reshaping Personal Relations in Egypt" appeared in *Fundamentalisms and Society*, Martin E. Marty and R. Scott Appleby, eds. (Chicago: University of Chicago Press, 1993).

local newspapers over a four-month period and translated their content. I should warn that many moderate Muslims looked upon the shaikhs' pronouncements disapprovingly and considered them misinterpretation.

The most common questions posed to the shaikhs concerned the proper observance of religion—whether certain behaviors were obligatory, prohibited, recommended, or forbidden under Islam. Next most common were questions about family relations, mainly husband-wife and parent-child obligations. If the questions were tallied by gender, the largest number concerned the proper roles and responsibilities of women in modern life. Finally, another important group of questions concerned the relationship of Muslims to other religious groups and cultures.

Examples give a flavor of the shaikhs' advice. According to one shaikh, the seven deadly sins were: denying the oneness of God, black magic, murder, usury, taking money from orphans, neglecting jihad, and accusing women falsely of adultery. Acts that were forbidden or not to be recommended included hunger strikes if the purpose was suicide, which was forbidden; working in places where alcohol was served; taking drugs that affect the mind; and smoking because of its addictive qualities.

Concern was expressed by the letter writers about the observance of ritual ablutions—whether stones or sand might be used if water was not available—and prayer: was it necessary when traveling and was it valid when a person's clothing was soiled (not if one-third of the dress was soiled), or when a man accidently touched a woman after washing (the shaikhs were divided on whether he must wash again).

Permitted acts included music and singing, if carried out in a proper way, and the display of family photos if not sexually provocative or meant to venerate a person unduly. The shaikhs strongly supported family roles although admitted that there were new factors in modern life. Husbands and wives had the right to enjoy each other sexually, and men had the indisputable right to sex in marriage. A man who in every way followed Islamic rites was not a good husband if he abused his wife. A wife should be obedient in all that doesn't contradict Islam. If she disobeyed her husband, he should first appeal to her good sense; if she continues to disobey him, he should leave the marital bed; and finally he could give her "a good but gentle beating." Man is in charge of women, said one shaikh, because Allah made him to excel her.

The columns devoted to women stressed their obligations and rarely their rights. One writer said a man had no right to manage his wife's money without her permission or insist that she accompany him abroad without her consent. If the man provided sufficient income, he could refuse to let his wife work. Islam did not require her to pay household expenses, but she could if she wanted to. Her husband should not ask her to remove her veil in public if she was following the Islamic injunction to conceal her attractions. Several writers wrote about the importance of modesty in dress, and in this regard they applied higher standards of morality to women. A woman should not encourage her husband to commit sinful activities (for example, selling drugs), or she would have sinned three times: against him, her children, and society. Even a fully veiled woman sinned if she aroused men's lust by wearing perfume.

Parents and children should be close. Allah showed more concern for mothers because of the greater time and effort they put into raising children. The father who failed to support his family committed evil to himself, to his children, and to society. After prayer, the best deed is to revere one's parents.

As to other religious groups, the shaikhs were divided. Some believed a person should be tolerant to religious groups defined as "people of the book" (Christians, Jews, and Muslims) while others said it was "dangerous to reveal your secrets to people who conceal their hostility to Muslims." Wearing Western clothes, said another, does not mean a person is drawing away from Islam.

Sometimes the letter writers asked questions that would have been amusing if they were not asked so earnestly. One woman asked if it would be a sin for a male dog to see her naked when she emerged from the shower, and the shaikh answered it would not.

From my perspective, these letters showed an important new trend in Egyptian society that differed from the 1960s and 1970s. A significant segment of the younger generation now seemed to be turning to religious shaikhs rather than to their parents for advice on moral issues. Parents previously set and enforced standards for family behavior, and families vied with one another to have sterling reputations—to be viewed as families one could safely marry one's children into or do business with. As piety increasingly became the vogue, children didn't feel their parents knew enough to advise them on correct Islamic practice. Indeed, many parents resisted the religious trend in its initial phases, even while finding it hard to criticize children who were taking religion more seriously.

The second change was that children who previously subordinated their interests to those of their families were suddenly taking an independent stand about their religious obligations. As Abdul Wahhab commented from the perspective of economic factors, parents no longer had much control over the futures of their children. In urban and even rural communities, like-minded young people were gathering in groups to study religion. Private mosques, not under the control of the government, encouraged more pious views and at the same time served people's needs by providing them subsidized food, clothing, health care, and even transportation so female university students wouldn't have to endure the crowded public transportation system. In certain ways, this was reminiscent of early Islamic communities where religious brotherhood was considered a more solid basis for community than tribal or family ties with their parochial interests and constant conflicts.

The columns of Abdul Wahhab and the religious shaikhs offered contrasting approaches to the ills of Egyptians. Both, however, confirmed the basic fact that society was changing in important ways. Men were finding it more difficult to carry out their financial support roles because of the poor economy, while women enjoyed expanded opportunities. Women could remain at home and follow traditional roles, or they could move into the public world of education, employment, and even politics. Simultaneously, Egyptian parents were losing control over their children, whose longer education, technological skills, and interest in religion often left the older generation feeling irrelevant. Religious leaders took up the slack by becoming the arbiters of moral behavior and, in private mosques, by serving basic needs and providing a place where young people could congregate with like-minded peers.

12

FINDING A NICHE:
SYRIA (1981–1984)

We were lucky again, and Bill was appointed deputy chief of mission in Syria, a slot normally given to State Department officers. By this time David was off to Stanford University, and Doug was just finishing at the Putney School in Vermont. With no school for Nick in Syria, he enrolled in the Sandy Spring Friends School near his grandmother in Maryland.

We arrived in Damascus in September 1981 to a city totally unlike Cairo —subdued, orderly, and more like Europe with its organized boulevards, trees, and well-tended parks. I missed the messiness of Cairo. By comparison the dour population seemed tight lipped and silent. I was turned off by the cookie-cutter women in black coats and kerchiefs stalking the streets on shopping runs each morning. I longed for the rollicking ways of the fun-loving Egyptians, the cheerful encounters on the streets, the taxi drivers ready to give me a lecture on any subject—including "the loss of true love since the death of Um Kalsum," the great romantic singer. In Cairo I started out well collected in the morning and moved through a gamut of emotions—love for the raggedy vender offering a free taste of his food, tenderness for the beggar children moving in and out among the cars, amusement at the jokes of students on their way to university, sadness for a needless loss of life in Bulaq, and anger at a man shouting expletives for no reason at all. In Egypt you hated, loved, and felt sad in the space of moments.

After the roller-coaster ride of Egypt, I should have welcomed the calm predictability of Damascenes. But instead I only foresaw difficulty in getting involved. It even seemed harder to relate to people who normally mixed with

169

embassy officers. Local sophisticates invited us to parties, but I didn't pass muster sufficiently to be included in the long-term activities of the wives. "You don't speak French, oh my!" they exclaimed incredulously. "How about bridge? You must play bridge! No? My dear, what a pity; we have such a nice group that plays several times a week." Some invited me to tea where in their splendid homes I sat in velvet darkened rooms on gilt Louis XV (or was it XIV or XVI) chairs and tried to talk about French cosmetics, clothes, shoes, perfumes, etc. One glance at my clothes and jewelry made it all too apparent that these were not my areas. After a few tiresome coffees, we both gave up. But I nevertheless felt a sense of failure. Surely I shared common interests with someone, somewhere in this country.

The first breakthrough came with an invitation to join a group of Syrian women who were graduates of the American University of Beirut. Not only did they speak English—the upper classes didn't speak Arabic in public—but they also had a book club that read and discussed modern American novels. AUB, like many foreign universities, had imbued them with admiration for things American—furniture, clothes, a devotion to good works, and thankfully, a disdain for personal adornment. Not once did they mention Gucci. Their kitchens were full of quaint pot holders and spoon rests and other American objects picked up while their husbands studied in the United States. Although not really my taste, they were a relief from the bridge-playing Francophiles.

We had fun with such books as Anne Tyler's *Morgan's Passing* with its weird characters that needed explaining to the Syrian women. They could forgive any trait in protagonists as long as they were "family oriented," and Morgan fortunately was. One character in the book feigned illness to prevent a child from leaving home and taking advantage of an opportunity that was perfect for her. We Americans sighed and blamed the parent for undermining the child's chances, while the Syrians rejoiced to find there was some humanity left in the Western world. One said, "When my son was going to return to his studies in Germany, I pretended I was ill, and slept with him in my arms the whole night before his departure." The Americans rolled their eyes. I loved my time with them, but a book group that met once a month to discuss things American didn't lift my spirits for long. I started thinking of renting a room away from Damascus.

At a cocktail party one evening, I confessed my dream to a Syrian doctor and explained how I wanted to get to know "authentic" Syrians. She was sympathetic and asked what I wanted to do. I said I wanted to rent a room in a village. She replied, "I can arrange that if you're serious. Come see me at our house in the mountains. I know the 'unofficial mayor' of the village and am sure he'll rent a room to you." I was overjoyed.

But the plan soon gave me second thoughts. Every aspect of this adventure had the potential for going wrong. Would the ambassador allow me to go? He agreed almost instantly. What would Syrian security do—would they let me stay in the village? They didn't seem to mind although a member of the Baath Party visited me once when Bill happened to be there, even though regulations on both sides said that neither was supposed to meet. Would my host suffer consequences by sheltering a foreigner from a country that by media accounts was the implacable enemy of the Syrian state? He didn't seem concerned. Would the dour Syrians be any friendlier in the village than in Damascus? Was my Arabic up to the odd country accents of the villagers?

All these concerns occupied me as we approached the village the following weekend. I imagined a village of cozy mud houses surrounding a village well and a donkey or two scattered across the landscape. But this was Syria and my image was left over from Egypt. The entry road into Wusta was lined with luxurious mansions—the "summer homes" of rich Damascene officials and professionals. The saving grace was the substantial two-storied stone houses clustered in the center of the village. These old house had storerooms and workshops at street level and living quarters above. The stone arches that framed the second floors led out to spacious balconies that were the natural play areas for young children. I would have loved to live in one of these houses.

Ours, however, turned out to be a small concrete-block house on one of the few roads that branched off from the village's main road. Next to it was the modern house of the *doctora* who was helping me. The best part was the sweeping view across the valley to a majestic church on a hillside and then behind it to the huge Anti-Lebanon Mountains topped with snow. The part that most contradicted my romantic image was the livelihood of the local men, many of whom were truckers transporting goods from Lebanon to the Gulf countries. There was hardly a moment when huge trucks were not roaring through the streets in preparation for departure or announcing the men's joyous returns, or sometimes just because sixteen-year-olds were ready to leave school and start their careers.

One reason for seeking out this quiet place was to finish a book I was writing on Egyptian family life. I knew it would keep me busy even if I didn't spend much time with the villagers. Fortunately I never needed Plan B. It took only one peddler calling out his wares the day I arrived to bring my neighbors and me together. His wares—olives—were heaped in great panniers on his donkey's back. "What do you do with them?" I asked my landlord's wife, Um Abdalla. It was complicated, and soon I was invited to join her and her sister in making the hard nubbins edible. It took days of slitting them and soaking them to remove the bitter taste, and then covering them with brine.

From that day on I was rarely alone, from 9:00 a.m. when the women finished cleaning their houses until 10:30 p.m. at night when they all went to bed. We cooked together, sewed together, ate together, helped the children finish their homework together, went visiting together, watched TV together, entertained guests together, did everything together except the early morning cleaning, which as a guest I wasn't allowed to do. As soon as the women finished cleaning, they sent the young children to fetch me. The first hint was giggling at my window, the scrape of a stool on the stone patio, and little eyes peering over the sill. Soon there was a knock at the door, "Jarti, sabah al-khair, dahli an ummi (Neighbor, good morning, come to mother)." And then, "Come have a cup of coffee." I would leave my writing and go to their cozy room next door.

It was not always easy in the village. I have never been as cold as I was when the wind howled across the valley and piled snow against my walls. The mice found a convenient refuge in my room, and it took only a day or two in Damascus for them to make a cozy nest from shreds they tore from my blankets. Each time I returned, I set out traps, but they still refused to give up the warmth of my blankets.

It was partly my fault I was so cold. Ten-year-old George, the family expert on kerosene heaters, came to install my stove one day. "Where do you want it?" he asked. "In the corner next to the exit hole," I answered, thinking it obvious. I soon learned that what provided warmth was the heat generated as the pipe crossed the room, and my request to mount the stove next to the exit hole gave the least heat possible. My shawls all bear scorch marks from huddling so close to the stove. Cold is not a condition that encourages writing when your hands can barely hold a pen, so I doubly enjoyed visiting my neighbors, where the heat blasting out of their stoves produced a virtual steam bath. Hot water was another problem too difficult to deal with. A bath required considerable preparation—firing up the water heater in my bathroom and then undressing in near freezing weather. Baths were so unappealing I stopped taking them until spring made it more tolerable.

Several things stand out from the time in the village. One was my disappointment at the way they always called me "Jarti" (neighbor), which seemed a particularly cold form of address. Egyptians called me "Um Dawud" (mother of David) or "Uxti" (sister) or at least "Khalti" (aunt, mother's sister). It was only later I read that the term "neighbor" in this part of the Arab world was a friendly way of addressing a person. Other words were also different in Syria, and sometimes when I walked down to the store to buy something for Um Abdalla, I simply conveyed her request to the grocer, "One kilo of yukhna, please," and only then would I know she wanted cabbage—a vegetable I already knew by three other Arabic names. Abu Abdalla, my landlord, was aware of my limitations and would start me nodding in agreement before taking me into unknown territory with words I didn't understand. In trying not to interrupt him, I imagined I knew his meaning until a twinkle in his eye revealed he had gotten the best of me. I was proud, however, when they asked me to translate words from the Egyptian TV soap operas. I knew for example that *shebka* was the gold jewelry the groom gives to his bride.

Another issue was that Um Abdalla's sister next door, Um Adil, never got over her suspicion that I was a foreign spy. I said I was interested in learning about ordinary life in Syria, but she couldn't understand why I would leave a husband in Damascus to pursue such an unworthy goal. Her main interest in life—surpassing all others—was competitive bargaining. We had interminable discussions about the cost of things where she always bested us at getting the lowest price. Um Abdalla did fairly well in the competition, but Um Adil would greet my efforts with scorn until I had no recourse but to lie. But even when I reduced the prices I paid to a fraction of their real cost, she was convinced I had no talent at all for this important part of life.

The good times in the village fortunately were more numerous than the bad. I especially enjoyed the children from both households. To them I was an oversized child who knew little about such grown-up things as cooking, cleaning, bargaining, and conversing properly. They loved sneaking over to "help" me do my dishes or to slosh soapy water over my floors. I had to stop them when they started organizing my writing papers. They sat next to me in the evenings and helped with the embroideries I worked on to keep from being the center of attention. In their own homes their mothers didn't let them do housework until they were old enough to do it right.

I sometimes listened to fifteen-year-old Liza striding up and down and reciting her homework. One evening she was reeling off a social studies lesson about the evils of America, when she stopped abruptly. "Jarti, why does everyone say America is the best country in the world? Which is better, Syria or America?" I tried to soften my answer by saying everyone likes his or her country best and that I knew at least one reason she would like Syria better than America. I described how my father lived hours away from me, that my children attended schools on two different coasts, and that my sister lived in the middle of the country. "We don't see each other very often." She agreed she wouldn't like to live in such a place and went back to her lesson. Somehow that encounter made me feel better about Syrian attacks against America.

I remember sitting with the women on the back patio late into the fall and in early spring when the sun streamed down on us as we prepared vegetables or sifted stones out of the rice. I still hear the tinkling bells of the goats returning each evening from the mountain slopes. I won't forget our trips on the tractor out to Abu Abdalla's chicken houses in the late afternoon and the warm reception of the Bedouin caretakers there. The ride home as the rich sunset streaked the sky with dark reds and purples gave me a deep sense of contentment. I loved seeing our house slippers lined up at the back door awaiting our return by the ever-considerate Liza. I also enjoyed the visits to the engaged daughter of Um Abdalla's friend and the local priest to commiserate with his recently returned brother who grumbled about missing American TV.

I liked standing in line at the village bakery and speculating on the missing episode of the soap opera the night before when the electricity failed. And even better I loved the moment when the baker tossed a stack of fragrant loaves into my sweater stretched out to receive them. I liked visiting the sympathetic Um Samir in whose parlor we shivered as the wind poured through the broken window that her constantly drunk husband never repaired. She wouldn't dream of dishonoring us by taking us into her cozy back room and made up for the cold by plying us with endless cups of hot tea. I won't forget the time we piled into our car and took the rutted road out to a saint's shrine on a cliff overlooking the valley. We stuck bits of paper in the saint's robes with our requests.

I put off the Egypt book at least partly because the village provided such a treasure trove of material on child rearing. It was soon taking every extra moment to record my notes and figure out how their practices fit together into some sort of consistent formula that made sense. Just as I had not thought much about my own child-rearing practices, Wusta parents acted with their own unerring sense of what parents should do. Watching them, I realized "my right way" wasn't necessarily theirs. It surprised me, for example, that Wusta parents never gave children free time to play. Even when neighbor boys came by for soccer, Abu Abdalla would decide it was time for cleaning the chicken sheds. I wanted to plead with him to let the boys have fun just this once. Or I wanted to point out the unfairness of interrupting the girls' homework to fetch water for their brothers just because it was a girl's job. I frowned upon mothers too busy to let little children help with baking or cleaning. The parents should know, I thought, that children needed to do these things. Soon I realized that whenever something felt wrong like this, there was something I should be figuring out if I wanted to understand parenting in Wusta. After a while, it was easier to slip into their mind-set and know why they behaved as they did. They were thinking in effect: "We are a family where everyone contributes according to the accepted rules of old, young, male and female. Life is a struggle that requires everyone to work all the time. As long as our family sticks together with all the talents of our children, we will enjoy a full and satisfying life."

This was the central theme, but there were corollaries. Parents encouraged each child's specific aptitudes—there was, for example, the child scholar, the skilled tea bringer, the mechanic, and the responsible chicken feeder. Each time these functions were needed, the especially skilled child performed the task. There was no need to teach every child every skill since in an ideal world they would all be together or at least close enough to help out. When the middle son, George, died of a brain tumor after I left the village, my first reaction was, "Who will install the stoves in the fall?" He would be missed for himself without a doubt but also for the mechanical skills he brought to the household.

When I finally wrote a book about the village, I tried to make it accessible to general readers. I wanted them to see how culture influences parenting, not only in the village, but in our own American homes. The everyday ways we have of dealing with our children have enormous consequences for the kinds of adults they become. One important difference, for example, was in how decisions were made. Each morning Um Abdalla set out white cheese, olives, bread, and tea, and the children ate. In my American family, the morning started with each child deciding what they wanted to eat—cereal, toast, eggs, and so on. As they grew older, my boys fixed their own breakfasts. In Syria the mother made choices for her children and prepared breakfast for everyone. The family accepted her choices. They learned that older people make decisions because they are wiser and more competent. Children may help prepare a meal under the supervision of a parent, but mothers put the ingredients together to produce the final perfect dish. We Americans, involve children in decisions about themselves all day long and let them perform tasks, however imperfectly, on their own.

Over time as these patterns are repeated again and again, the different behaviors create different kinds of people, ones who feel an integral part of the group in the Syrian case and ones who seek independence in the American one. It would be a mistake of course to conclude that all Syrians or all Americans conform exactly to these examples, but most approximate them in some way. For me this is what culture is all about—a way of seeing the world and acting upon one's perceptions.

⌇

As my notes developed into a study of child rearing in a Syrian family, I became concerned that I was only experiencing the lives of two families in a single village, and a Christian one at that. Were all parents like these, or would there be differences in Muslim families? I felt I needed to expand my experiences to include a Muslim village, and as often happens when a need arises, the perfect opportunity arose. A German archaeologist working on the site of a temple in a Muslim village near Damascus invited me to spend time with her, and I gladly accepted. I quickly got to know the men working on her site, and once they knew I could speak Arabic, they invited me to their homes to meet their wives. Almost immediately I was spending most of the day with the women. My friend's Syrian minder—a man supposedly from the Archaeology Department—soon became suspicious. Why wasn't I working on the site, and why would I, an educated Westerner, want to spend time with uneducated village women? He would follow me to the homes but couldn't enter when only women were present. Back at our house he questioned me at length about what I was doing and why. I told him I was trying to make Arab societies more understandable to Americans. This explanation only alarmed him.

One day I was invited to celebrate the first cutting of a little boy's hair. After his tears subsided, we sat talking and eating for the rest of the evening. My minder was back in Damascus and never discovered this suspicious activity. A young woman at the gathering insisted I visit her elderly mother who would be "so happy" to see me. So one afternoon she fetched me at a time when the minder was napping. I dressed in a long skirt and long-sleeved blouse with a scarf covering my hair and from a distance was not immediately recognizable as a foreigner. We were walking when suddenly I noticed we were passing a guard post and entering a large enclosure. The two sentries were asleep. "Where are we?" I asked, and my companion replied that it was a short cut to her mother's house. By now we were walking between rows of missiles on one side and tanks on the other. I pulled my scarf closely around my face and focused my eyes on the ground. What if they caught the wife of a U.S. diplomat walking through a military arsenal? Luckily there were no guards where we crawled through the fence. I had a nice visit with her mother, but later I insisted on taking the long way home. The minder said he had been looking for me. I explained I had gone for tea, and my companion confirmed it.

By that time the minder was truly exasperated, feeling that keeping track of me was preventing him from returning to Damascus and his family. The upshot of his complaint was that the Department of Archaeology issued a notice that no unauthorized persons could stay overnight on archaeological sites in Syria without permission. By that time I had completed my mission and was back in Damascus. Although my time in the Muslim village was short, I saw many of the same child-rearing practices: the emphasis on members contributing to family welfare, the decision-making hierarchy, and the way the day revolved around working together—in household chores, food preparation, and school homework. True, there were some differences, but they were more in form than function. The Muslim women dressed more conservatively and were poorer. The families were more protective of their women, and their household spaces were more rigidly sex segregated, especially where guests were concerned. Their households contained more children and unattached relatives—spinster aunts, divorced sisters, and widowed mothers—that made them livelier places to be. There was a more hospitable, generous, spontaneous, expressively loving feeling in these Muslim families, or so it seemed to me. But overall the same thinking guided the way they reacted to their children. This gave me the confidence to write about Wusta—not because every rural Syrian family is the same but because there are common threads in how they perceive child rearing, and these were noticeably different from our ways.

I would have been happy to stay longer in the village, but by late spring Israeli attacks on Lebanon were spilling over into our lives. The truckers of the village could no longer pick up fresh fruits and vegetables in Lebanon and continue on to the Gulf, and there was no way of knowing when trucking would resume again. Many of the men owed large amounts on their truck loans and were worried about paying them. It wasn't a good time for "an enemy of the state" to be ever present in the village or for my landlord to harbor a reminder of all they were suffering. I decided to return to Damascus.

The village helped me love rural Syria, but I had a long way to go before I would feel as comfortable in Damascus. There was something unmistakably and richly Syrian that took time to appreciate, but eventually I found it in the wonderful souks and residential areas surrounding the great Umayyad mosque. The visual excitement of masses of people and goods spilling out into the streets seemed staged against the darkened corridors of the covered markets. Dust-laden sunlight streamed theatrically through bullet holes in the arched ceilings of the Hamadiya souk. Stalls were piled high with goods in every imaginable color: sumptuous brocades, silver and gold embroidered tablecloths, silk gowns, inlaid mirrors and chests, and the rich blue, green, and brown wares of the glassmakers. Every side street promised more from the soft tapping of the leather-smiths to the harsher clang of the brass makers. And permeating the air wherever you went were the smells: pungent cumin and cinnamon from the spice stalls, the enticing odors of *kunafa* and *baklava* from pastry shops, and, blending with them all, incense chasing away the stale smells of overnight closings. Penetrating deeper into neighborhoods, you smelled the delightful aromas of frying onions and garlic, or in quieter alleyways, the sweet smell of laundry dripping down from overhead lines. Mixing with it all were the smells of sewage spewing into underground channels. In Cairo, people demand your attention; in Damascus, your senses are assaulted—with colors, smells, and tastes.

In 1981, in the name of security, the government tore down the old leather souk and cleared the shops huddled against the walls of the Umayyad mosque. The daughter of one shopkeeper told me that when the walls came down a large serpent slithered out. Since serpents are said to guard important treasures, the workers searched and found a chest of Russian gold coins. Perhaps the story was a metaphor suiting everyone's need to cry out against the destruction of the city's treasures.

The souk was a place where homes also leaned lazily against one another with their upper-story mashrabiya screens almost touching. From them, women dangled down baskets and, after disembodied negotiations with vendors, hauled up their purchases without leaving their homes. Scattered throughout the side streets were "Turkish baths" with doomed roofs embedded with colored glass "eyes of God" and towels hanging in doorways to dry. The special aura of Damascus was especially strong when you penetrate the larger homes in the old city. The rough walls outside—designed not to inspire envy—give no indication of the breathtaking beauty within. Step over the raised doorsill into a small entrance hall and you still don't know the surprises ahead until you pass through the doorway to the side and enter paradise. There in an open courtyard a large fountain splashes soothing background music. And scattered in large planters are tall orange and lemon trees and jasmine vines to perfume the air and flavor glasses of water drawn from the well. The courtyard has at least one deep niche in its walls where people sit on cushioned marble benches under a high arching roof to shelter from passing showers. Although the courtyards are small, their soaring walls give a sense of space, to set off the elements that indulge the senses—sight, sound, taste, smell, and even touch. Suddenly you have an urge for a cardamom-laced cup of Turkish coffee with its glass of cold water and floating jasmine. Your host within minutes satisfies your desire as if reading your thoughts.

But I still didn't feel the full effect of Damascus until I met the indomitable Siham Tergeman. I got to know her when I asked my Arabic tutor to find a more "friendly" book for my Arabic lessons. He chose Siham's book, *Treasure of Damascus* (*Yamal Es-Sham*), an autobiographical account of growing up in the inner city of Damascus in the 1940s. It added the human character to the physical beauties of the old city: the personalities, holiday rituals, family relations, tasty foods, proverbs, legends, and much more. I came away from class transported to a different world. I would hear my teacher chuckling, "My God, Siham, you are really something!"

One day my teacher arranged for me to have tea with Siham, who was enormously warm and welcoming. Before I knew it, I was agreeing to translate her book and find a publisher in the United States, neither of which tasks I was particularly qualified to perform. Two years later with the help of my teacher, the daughter of a friend, and nearly constant reference to a dictionary, I completed the work. Siham gives perhaps the best feeling for the sensuality that lurks behind the cookie-cutter people stalking the streets.

I did basically the same thing for another Syrian writer. Samir had been a soldier in the Golan Heights when he picked up a grenade thrown at his men, and it exploded. When I met him in the early 1980s he was blind, had lost the hearing in one ear, and was left with only stumps of arms below his elbows. I didn't want to do another time-consuming translation project, but his situation so touched me that I found myself offering to see what I could do. From relatives and merchants in Aleppo, Samir had been gathering two kinds of tales parents tell their children: full-scale stories, and short poems and aphorisms that keep children in line. This time I worked with a Lebanese friend who did the rough translations while Doug did beautiful block prints to illustrate each story.

In the late 1980s no one was much interested in a manuscript of this kind, but the very act of completing it added to my own appreciation of the richness of Syrian culture. One example I especially liked was when a busy mother tells a toddler to go tell his grandmother to "tie the goat," signifying that the grandmother should keep him busy and out of the way while his mother finishes her chores. The genres in the book include examples of most of the ones that constitute Syrian oral culture with the exception of some varieties of poetry and widely published romantic epics such as the stories of Antar and Abla.

By 2003 the world had changed, and when I tried again to publish the manuscript, the first publisher I asked snatched it up. The University of Texas Middle East Center Press gave me a lump sum for the work. I of course wanted Samir to have it, but there seemed no easy way of delivering the money to him. If I sent it through a bank, I would probably find myself on a U.S. terrorist watch list. And if I sent it another way his family would know—I felt it would better to deal directly with him. Bill and I decided the only answer was to go ourselves after our annual trip to Cairo. Samir had no idea he might receive money for the book. We spent two days in Aleppo with him and members of his family, and I managed to slip the cash unobserved into his pocket. My suspicions were confirmed that he preferred to keep the money secret. He said he would use it to publish some new books he was writing, and true to his word, later two much-torn packets of books arrived for me.

There was a grimmer side to Syria in the early 1980s that we also experienced. When the Lebanese forced the evacuation of Palestinian militias from their country, the men paraded through Damascus with guns blazing and soon took out their frustrations on the American Embassy. The embassy had erected a decorative wall of blocks to make the building "more secure," and the Palestinians used the wall to race to the roof, where fortunately they were unable to open a heavy metal door. The Americans inside, including Bill, called Syrian officials to send help, but none arrived until it was all over.

One day President Hafez al-Assad was suddenly taken to the hospital, and although bulletins downplayed his illness, everyone thought it was serious. His brother, Rifaat, moved his militia to the outskirts of the city, while the military loyal to Assad set up tanks near the presidential palace. Our apartment unfortunately was located between the palace and the parliament where the standoff was likely to take place. Fortunately Assad recovered and regained control, and Rifaat went into exile in Spain.

By then Bill had gotten to know Rifaat fairly well from his efforts to get American hostages released. Rifaat was known to be close to Hezbulla and Iran, and therefore might be useful in gaining their release. A black limousine would appear at our house, and Bill would be whisked away. At one point Bill complained to Rifaat about Syria's poor response during the embassy attack, and Rifaat with brotherly affection told him, "Don't worry Mr. William. If you are ever in danger, call this telephone number and say William is calling, and we will come get you." This "reassurance" implied that Rifaat's men always knew where Bill could be found. It showed however that continuing contact creates a bond of affection even between the most unlikely of people.

As regularly as clockwork for a while, a large bomb would go off each month somewhere in Damascus—at the Ministry of Defense, at the Ministry of Information, at major traffic circles or apartment blocks. No one could predict where or when the next one would come, yet we knew it would be places we passed. A few days before the International School opened in September, a bomb at the Ministry of Defense blew fragments of bodies over the playground wall. If it had been a week later, the children would have been playing in that grim location. The staff cleaned up the mess, but many parents felt it was the last straw and sent their children back to their home countries.

During this period, the Syrian authorities informed the embassy they had intercepted a man at the airport with plastic explosives in his suitcase and three addresses in his pocket, including our apartment building. Since we lived on the ground floor, we would have taken the brunt of any explosion.

I had my own run-in with the Syrian authorities one day when an anthro-pologist friend wanted to visit the area where colorful designs were painted on transport trucks. We hailed a cab and found the place on the outskirts of town. My friend began photographing trucks when a man appeared and asked what we were doing. My friend answered snippily in an Egyptian way used to intimidate "inferiors," but it infuriates people in Syria. "Where's your permit?" he answered frostily. My friend had submitted her permit for renewal and didn't have it with her. He pulled out his Baath Party credentials. "Let me see your passport." She showed it to him, and he kept it. He ushered us into our taxi, and we drove off toward town, stopping at a place where three men in plain clothes with Kalashnikovs were lounging on the sidewalk. We got out, and just as we were being taken off in another car, they looked at my diplomatic passport and released us, warning us against "taking any more pictures in an industrial zone."

While I was still in Wusta, tensions heated up between President Assad and Islamic radicals in Hama. Assad brutally retaliated by destroying a large part of the historic center of the town, where he suspected the radicals had a warren of escape routes. A few days later I was traveling on a bus from Aleppo to

Damascus, when we stopped in Hama and I got a firsthand view of the damage. The government was bulldozing away the last of the rubble, leaving little more than a large field. It was shocking to see an empty field where once had been an endless array of randomly scattered alleyways. The illusion that old quarters go on forever gives these cities their particular magic.

It was a disaster for the people of Hama who were used to coming out ahead in jokes they told about neighbors in Homs. A typical one was said to have taken place when the towns were quarreling over the use of water in a lake that separated them. Mediators erected markers halfway along the lakeshore, and both sides agreed to take water only from their half of the lake. The Hama people heard noises in the night and found the Homs people pouring water from the Hama side into their own side.

When we had time Bill and I would travel in our own small car (without guards and armor) to various parts of Syria, including the monastery near the great Crusader castle Krac des Chevaliers on the border with Lebanon. One day branching out from the monastery in search of encounters, we wandered into the beautiful little village of Husn al-Amar. We had walked the whole town and seen few people, but just as we were about to give up, a young man asked if we needed help. We said we were just out enjoying a walk. He suggested we have a cup of tea at his nearby house. After polite refusals we agreed and after that returned often to the village to enjoy his mother's picnics bundled onto a donkey's back and carried to a lovely spring up a mountain. Over the years we followed Riad as he decided to marry Izdihar, graduated from university in Damascus, went through training for a position in the church, had two children, and eventually rose up in the church hierarchy. When Doug visited, we spent an evening with other students playing music tapes and listening to Doug play his guitar.

One weekend we visited families in the Jebel Druze area in the south of Syria and were introduced to the shaikh of the Druze. We already had a soft spot for the Druze after knowing Aunt Belle's genial neighbor Shaikh Abu Shakib in Baysour. This secretive sect of Islam (some say it is not Islam) had especially well-manicured and clean villages, and the people wore distinctive costumes that made them easy to identify: the women in white veils with beautiful velvet gowns, and the men in baggy pants and white shirts and a fez-like hat. The shaikh of Jebel Druze often dropped by the embassy to see the ambassador or Bill, so it didn't seem strange to hear that he planned to come say farewell as we were about to leave Syria. Our household staff was off, but I thought I could manage myself. It was therefore a shock to see a large entourage filling our living room. After a reasonable period of pleasantries, the point of the visit became apparent. The shaikh had brought every constituent who might have the slightest interest in a visa to the United States, thinking there might be no one left once Bill was gone to help him obtain visas. His friend Mr. William directed him to the consul to start the normal ten-day process.

~~~

During our first year in Syria, we were particularly anxious about Doug. The previous summer he had graduated from Putney, where the wonderfully creative atmosphere suited his temperament perfectly. But one day after graduation he announced he was going off into the world. In late fall we began receiving letters forwarded through our last address in Cairo. He wrote that he had decided to go to art school, but it was too late to apply for the second semester. We suggested he stay with us while he waited. The day came when we drove to the airport to pick him up. The bodyguard and driver were in good spirits anticipating our joy at being reunited with our son, the first of the boys they would meet. They stood at attention when Doug came out of the VIP lounge accompanied by protocol officials, and then their mouths dropped. There was Doug with shoulder-length hair, a flapping sole hanging from his beat-up shoes, shrunken pants, and most apparent a sweater he knit for himself with leftover yarn a friend had given him. There were patches of red that continued with blue and then other colors in bits and pieces as each yarn remainder ran out. One sleeve was longer than the other and the neck was somewhat raggedy. The Syrians were shocked. Dress is important to them, and as with Egyptians, clothes indicate your class status as well as your respect for others. In this case I suppose it showed an extreme lack of respect for his parents. We felt silently amused at the reactions he was causing and just happy he seemed pleased to be home again. To be fair, he soon endeared himself to the staff with his quiet friendliness.

We tried to think of ways to amuse him—a weekend at the monastery where he and the young monks enjoyed one another, and drives through the mountains where we dropped in on my rural family. He was scornful of a village with so many mansions lining its entrance and houses like Abu Abdalla's made of concrete. One event brought us together, though for a brief moment. We were eating dinner one night when an enormous explosion rocked the room. From under the dining table Bill called the Marine who looked out his window and saw fireworks welcoming in the New Year. Doug went on to the Maryland School of Art and after other training became an accomplished artist.

~~~

One of Bill's jobs was to check on the welfare of the Jewish community. The community in Syria was engaged in the traditional brass industry, among other things, and so it was a pleasure to visit it in the souk. With the exception of a few minor problems, its leader always reported that the community was treated well. Complicit with the Syrian government, Jews were given preferential treatment when they applied for visas at the embassy. At a time when it was virtually impossible for young Syrian men to obtain visas, young Jewish men obtained them immediately. This created a problem after many men emigrated and there were not enough husbands for the remaining Jewish women. The community made arrangements with the embassy, and soon a number of eligible women traveled to the United States to marry the earlier emigrants. All this goodwill was shattered when a Jewish congressman from New York, needing publicity for a difficult election, decided to visit Syria. Bill accompanied him to the synagogue and visits with community members. When the man returned to the United States, he presented such a distorted view of what he had seen that it caused tensions between the community and Syrian officials who no longer gave visas for Americans to visit the community. The congressman said, for example, that Syrian troops surrounded the synagogue, implying that they somehow prevented access to the building when in fact they were protecting him.

Our three years in Syria went by quickly. Just before we left, embassy staff came to inventory our house and found that more than $1,000 worth of silverware was missing. That was a huge sum to repay, and I broke down in tears when I told the cook about the loss. Nothing had been missing a month before, and it seemed strange that suddenly so many pieces were gone. The cook acted surprised, too. But the next morning he told me the staff had simply counted wrong—not true, I had recounted the silver myself—and that when he counted again that morning everything was there. Somehow I felt betrayed by this old man whom I had respectfully called "Uncle" (as befits older men), and to me that was worse than the disappearance of the silverware. When I lost things in other posts, people told me I was to blame for leaving temptation in the way of poor people. Probably they were right, but it was a sad ending to our stay in Damascus.

13

ROADBLOCKS:
SANA, YEMEN (1984–1987)

A fairytale country sits at the southwestern corner of the Arabian Peninsula, a country where every person's home is a castle, where the clear mountain air moderates the climate, and where the tiny fruit and nuts are sweet beyond compare. This is a slight exaggeration but not much. There is also dire poverty, poor health care, much illiteracy, and high rates of fertility and infant and maternal mortality. The tribal structure is strong, which on one side means an ethic of solidarity and mutual support and on the other is a factionalism where people still settle conflicts with guns.

We were pleased when Bill was appointed ambassador to Yemen, "the Arab version of Afghanistan," as many described it. Yemen rarely appears in the Western press except when there's an incident such as the bombing of the USS *Cole* or tribesmen kidnap foreigners to express their complaints about not receiving enough of the oil wealth that flows from their lands. Haynes Mahoney, an American diplomat we knew, was kidnapped one day in Sana. He learned in security training that it's best to develop rapport with your abductors. Luckily he was fluent in Arabic and kept up a conversation out to the camp where they held him. The media reported the story extensively, and soon shaikhs from other tribal sections came to see the American hostage. According to custom, hosts must honor their guests with banquets worthy of their status, and Haynes's abductors soon found they were killing sheep at unsustainable rates. After a week or two, the chief freed Haynes to avoid bankruptcy. By that time they were good friends, and a few years later when Haynes returned to Yemen, he made a special trip to see his old friend, the shaikh.

Our embassy "fortress-house" was one of the best examples of Yemeni architecture in Sana, conveniently located within walking distance of the souk. You entered the ground floor through a heavy wooden door and climbed sixty stairs to the living quarters and then sixty mores to the *mafraj* (guest room) with views over the city. If Yemenis had been living in our house, the entire top floor would have been a magnificent mafraj accommodating 100 or so guests in cushioned comfort with views of the city from three sides. But our predecessors reduced the mafraj to an alcove, and although cozy and comfortable, it was not what it should have been.

The bottom floors were a warren of rooms where we stored foods we shipped with us. Although many of the items were available in the market, their exorbitant price was more than we could afford. Every month I checked the store with our houseman, Abdul Hamid. Once we noticed mice had gotten into the cereals, and I asked Abdul Hamid to buy something to get rid of them. When they were still there a few weeks later, the gentle Abdul Hamid explained, "But Madam, they eat so little."

To reach the upper floors, you took a central stone staircase, ducking your head under the heavy beams of the doorways at each level while stepping carefully over the high wooden sills. Abdul Hamid and Ali, our house help, raced up the stairs like gamboling goats, simultaneously ducking their heads and leaping over the sills without losing their stride. We foreigners labored upward in the high-altitude air and then whacked our heads or stumbled over the sills no matter how hard we concentrated.

Our tower-house was a unique work of art, starting with the carved wooden entry door and continuing with intricate patterns in the carved plaster of the interiors. Each room had white plaster window frames encasing panes of intense red, blue, and green glass that sent colors dancing across the walls by day and lighting the alleyways by night. The depth of color, size of the pieces, and intricacy of the design indicated the prominence of the owner. A sheet of alabaster behind the windows muted the sun's rays.

For a house located in the city, ours had unusually spacious grounds. On the Fourth of July, the Americans gathered to run relay races, compete in tugs-of-war, and eat traditional hot dogs and hamburgers. The evening before, the garden was transformed with strings of lights and tents for our "National Day." Ibrahim supervised an army of kitchen staff, and Abdul Hamid and Ali arranged the drink stands, while Bill and I took the congratulations of diplomats and Yemeni officials. At the post mortem the next day, the staff reviewed the lists of guests to see who had come—with possible implications for our relations with various countries and the Yemeni government.

The garden held several modest embassy buildings, including Bill's office and the home of the full-time caretaker, and a vegetable garden that provided us with fresh vegetables. Several months after we left someone would fire a missile into the ambassador's bathroom—seeming more of a joke than a serious attempt to target anyone. Near Bill's office was the embassy entrance, where visitors had to show IDs and have an appointment. On our first Friday in Yemen, Bill told his bodyguard, Ali, to take the day off since we had no appointments. It was a beautiful day, and we decided to go for a walk in the nearby souk. It seemed perfectly safe—we were new and it was unlikely anyone would recognize us—and besides, spontaneity was the best protection against problems. So we walked by the surprised guards and headed downtown. In the first shop, the storekeeper approached us, "Hello your Excellency. Please have a cup of tea." "How did you know?" "I saw you on television." We realized then that Sana was a small town where everyone knew what was going on.

In the beginning we were not unduly alarmed about security. As a "high-value" target, Bill was driven in an armored car by Abdul Wali, our young, dashing, and somewhat unreliable driver. Next to him was Bill's wonderful tribal bodyguard, Ali, always leaning forward intently. From time to time he instructed Abdul Wali to take another route or speed up around a parked car. He was courteous and competent and seemed to know every guard at every checkpoint on every road in Yemen. Under his seat was an Israeli Uzi that he undoubtedly knew how to use.

Ali knew all about desert plants and what they were used for. The little melon-like fruits, for example, could be applied to arthritic joints to relieve pain. Once I asked a Yemeni the name of a small tree, and he answered *khutib*. I discovered from Ali it meant firewood. On our way home from a Peace Corps village one day, Abdul Wali was looking tired. Ali told him to stop so he could gather a plant from the roadside that would keep him alert. Abdul Wali chewed the bitter stuff and within minutes was stopping every few miles with ferocious diarrhea—Ali's joke. By late afternoon most drivers were chewing *qat* (a mild narcotic plant) and throwing the tough leaves into the roadway—the mounds being a reliable indicator of the amounts of qat consumed in Yemen.

Once a week we joined the "Hash House Harriers," a group of expatriates who ran over trails set out by their colleagues. Ali insisted on running alongside Bill on the race. Lithe and small, he probably could have kept up were it not for his loose Bedouin sandals, flapping gown, and heavy gun. When he came in 100 yards behind Bill, it was Abdul Wali's turn to make fun of him. Once a year the group had its signature run, "The Highest Hash House Harrier Race in the World," up the 12,000-foot Jebel Nabi Shuaib. I walked the route, doubling back in time to reach the finish line at the same time as the runners. Once passing villagers still in a state of shock from seeing fifty or so "half-naked" men and women run by, I tried to explain the race, but concepts such as "exercise," "running up mountains," and "undressed men and women" were too much for them. Why their village, they asked, and what treasure were they looking for? When I couldn't answer satisfactorily, they moved on to other subjects. "How old are you?" one woman asked. "How old do you think I am?" "99?" Being fifty at the time, I was not flattered, since in comparison to a hardworking fifty-year-old Yemeni woman I thought I looked much younger. They said they heard foreigners lived longer than Yemenis and figured I must be old to look so "sick" (white faced) and "weak" (thin).

~~~~

Every embassy has "codels" that require a lot of extra work. A year after we arrived, we hosted a delegation with fifteen or so congressmen and staffers. They wanted to visit local officials to get a feel for the country. Plans flew back and forth, but nothing jelled until they touched down at the airport. The discussions with Yemeni officials went as scheduled, but there was a gap one afternoon when the Yemenis wanted to be chewing qat and not seeing American officials. Finally a Yemeni official invited them to a qat chew (this was before the United States classified qat as a banned substance). The congressmen looked at the schedule and demanded cars be ready to take them to their hotels if they became bored during the five hours scheduled for the chew.

Meanwhile, the women staffers asked me the usual question, "Isn't it difficult being a woman in an Arab country?" As usual I answered truthfully that it wasn't as difficult as they might think. With the permission of our host, I took the American women to visit the Yemeni women upstairs, telling the Americans they could ask the women themselves about their lives.

"Yes, we stay in our homes most of the time—why shouldn't we since the men do all the shopping." "No, we don't work—our husbands support us and there are children to look after and meals to prepare." "Yes, all the children go to school. Education illuminates the mind and makes the girls responsible mothers and wives." "Yes, we arrange marriages for our children. It's the parents' responsibility to find suitable mates."

After several minutes the Yemenis wanted to ask the Americans questions: "Are you married?" "Yes, most of us are married." "Where are your husbands?" "At home." "Why do they let you travel unprotected with so many men? Don't they care about you?" "Do you have children?" "No, we have to establish our careers first." "What happens if they divorce you?" "We would have to support ourselves." Most staffers said they worked ten- to fourteen-hour days and the Yemeni women expressed horror at the idea, "What's wrong with your men that they don't support you and make you work such long hours? Don't you know that children are the most important thing in life? Why do you care more about work than having children? Why doesn't someone support you if you're divorced? Why aren't your parents, brothers, and uncles demanding that you be better treated?"

The staffers joined the congressmen downstairs in a more sober mood, one commenting that it made her wonder if maybe her own priorities *were* mixed up. Some tried *qat* and felt little effect. All were surprised at how quickly the hours passed.

One of our visitors was Vice President Bush, who was traveling to several countries to polish his foreign policy credentials for the 1988 election. At the urging of his friend Ray Hunt, Bush decided Yemen would be a good stop since he could showcase several American projects, including laying the cornerstone for the new embassy and speaking at the opening of the new Hunt oil refinery. The Yemenis wanted to be sure the Bushes were properly welcomed. We spent days planning their schedules and dealing with Yemeni sensitivities over the preparations. What rankled most was the Secret Service's plan to fly in an armored car for Bush, as if "Yemen's plush limousine was not enough." We made trial runs between events with the Secret Service checking times to the second, including stops for photo-ops. Yemeni security staff commented that time didn't work like that in Yemen. The Secret Service said that it would!

I was working on Barbara Bush's schedule. I thought she would enjoy a traditional women's dancing party. These parties, as the qat parties, never lasted less than five hours. My request presented problems for the Yemenis who wanted to give her a Western-style reception. In the end they held two parties—one the dancing party, and the other a reception for mainly Westerners. Although pretty sterile, the reception went off well with everyone standing with glasses of fruit juice and eating from a buffet.

The second evening was the Yemeni party at the home of a high official. Mrs. Bush and I arrived punctually as mandated by the Secret Service. For half an hour we sat alone with our hostess who was still lighting incense burners. As each Yemeni guest arrived, she was introduced to Mrs. Bush who remained seated on the floor cushions. I tried to make up for this lapse in manners by jumping up Yemeni style as each guest arrived. As the room filled with perfume and incense, she asked how long she had to stay. I knew the Yemenis would be deeply disappointed if she left before the dancing started. She said she felt ill and a half hour more was all she could take. Meanwhile, the room was filling with women in their "princess outfits" of chiffons and silks, with high cone-shaped headdresses that draped material to the shoulders. To me the room was a fairy tale and would be even more beautiful when the dancing started.

We never reached that point, for suddenly Barbara Bush said she had to go, and we rushed to the door without acknowledging any of the guests. The hostess steered us through a hall full of food, insisting that she eat something. She took a small morsel and we headed for the car. The moment she was inside she vomited. I probably should have been more sympathetic, but I could think only of the trouble the Yemenis had gone through trying to please her, and knowing that no matter what we said they would think she didn't like their entertainment. In the car she mentioned for the first time that she suffered from altitude sickness, which she usually controlled with medicines. I felt she could have prevented the attack and should at least have warned us about the problem.

By the next day Barbara was recovered, and we all went to the opening of the refinery in Marib, thankfully at a lower altitude. George Bush, as usual, was unfailingly modest, polite, and interested, and conducted himself with dignity.

Barbara Bush seemed always calculating the effect of what she did. Instead of walking with the dignitaries, she hung back with the U.S. press corps, in a motherly way asking if they were being housed and fed properly. In the middle of the Yemeni president's speech, she suddenly waved to attract the attention of a redheaded press woman on the side. When the woman came closer Barbara Bush told her she would be burned if she didn't get out of the sun! By then she had managed to distract everyone from the Yemeni president's speech. Perhaps I was too sensitive to the dignity officials should show in their public roles, but I found her behavior very disrespectful.

We'd been in Yemen for several months, and I was becoming restless. It seemed impossible to know Yemenis with my "suspicious" links to the U.S. Embassy. Several friends in the United States had told me enthusiastically about the friendliness of the Yemenis and how easy it would be to get to know them, and sometimes I sensed Yemeni women wanted to know me but hesitated because of the situation. My friends who loved Yemen so much hadn't had to cope with a Yemeni government that played the Soviets and Americans against one another to get assistance from both sides. The Soviets gave military aid and thousands of scholarships to train (and indoctrinate) Yemeni security personnel in Russia, while the Americans provided large sums for military equipment but modest amounts to train Yemenis to operate them. The Yemenis trained abroad invariably developed sympathies for the country where they trained.

The Yemenis returning from Russia were highly suspicious of Americans, and since these Russian-trained Yemenis provided security for embassies, we were stuck with their heavy-handed methods. They kept detailed lists of Yemeni visitors and turned them in to security services. If a woman visited they insisted she take off her veil to see if she was who she said she was. No woman would submit to this indignity, and so it became nearly impossible for me to invite Yemeni women. Moreover, if we wanted to have a reception or dinner, we had to submit our invitations to the Foreign Office for approval.

Once when some American businessmen came to town, Bill thought he could get around security by inviting Yemenis to lunch at a hotel. But only one out of the twenty-five invited Yemeni guests appeared, and he reported that the hotel guards were turning the Yemenis away. After the lunch the brave guest was picked up and interrogated for hours, while his frantic wife called everywhere trying to find him.

As part of the U.S.-Russian competition every year, the Yemenis staged war games outside the city and invited foreign embassy officials to watch. I could imagine the pleasure the Yemenis felt in forcing these Cold War enemies to put on so public a display. We may not have won the battle for Yemeni minds, but each year we won the military exercises. The Russian- and American-trained Yemenis would charge up two sides of a hill in tanks, and the one that took the hill first was the winner. Invariably the American tanks reached the top first, leaving behind a hillside of broken-down Russian tanks. Then the air force would swoop down on the scene, dropping bombs to simulate a battlefield. One year a Russian plane dropped its bomb while it was too close to the ground and spectacularly blew itself up, the shrapnel just missing the dignitaries, including Bill.

These tensions were not getting me any closer to meeting people. Critics of embassies often say diplomats only "know" a country through their servants and high officials, and I was beginning to feel this statement was true. Bill was seeing the president and officials while I was home with the servants. I grew particularly fond of Abdul Hamid who, with his gentle ways, reminded me of Hamud in Saudi Arabia. Sometimes I would ask about his home near the border of South Yemen, which was still under communist rule in the late 1980s. When I asked if life had become better or worse under communism, he replied carefully that it was better for the poor who had opportunities to raise their standard of living but not good for richer families who were reduced to middle-class status. Everyone, he said, ended up at the same level.

I liked to consult Abdul Hamid about proverbs, since Yemenis, like other Arabs, have a rich knowledge of aphorisms and wise sayings. I had collected Egyptian, Omani, Qatari, and other proverbs and now had a collection of Yemeni proverbs compiled in two volumes by a well-known Yemeni judge. I worked for a while trying to translate them but had difficulty with the highly colloquial nature of the language. Even when I managed to understand individual words, the proverbs as a whole didn't make sense. One aphorism said simply, "Like a bull without a tail." Abdul Hamid immediately understood the meaning and explained it to me. It describes the difficulties a farmer would have plowing a field with a "tail-less" ox since he needs to twist its tail at the end of a furrow to turn it around. The saying describes a person who is uncontrollable.

Abdul Hamid saw his family only once a year on holiday. Each year when he returned, he would tell me about a new child born nine months after his last visit. One year a baby daughter was born with red marks on her face that the doctor told him would have to be surgically removed. Abdul Hamid was sad because disfigurement meant she probably couldn't marry. I told him to bring her to Sana to see what the embassy doctor recommended. Dr. Paul saw her and felt pretty sure they were only birthmarks and would go away by themselves, but to be certain he sent us to a specialist. I took the baby to the appointments because male doctors, even foreign ones, couldn't see the mother. Each time I unwrapped the swaddled child down to her soggy interior so the doctor could see her, and then awkwardly rewrapped her again with the fresh cloths the mother gave me. The final opinion confirmed the diagnosis, and I warned Abdul Hamid not to have them surgically removed or she might bleed to death.

Abdul Hamid's baby was saved but not so the children of Ibrahim. I knew he was excitedly awaiting the birth of a child shortly after we arrived in Yemen and hoped this baby would survive since none of his previous children had lived. The baby boy arrived, but a few weeks later Ibrahim reported that he had died. "What happened?" I asked. "It was God's Will," he answered. I assumed it was diarrhea or some illness related to poor sanitary conditions, so I asked whether his wife kept the baby's things clean. When I asked about flies, he answered, "Oh, Madam, don't worry. Every night when we put the babies to bed we sprayed the room with a poison that kills flies." He insisted it was God's Will, but the following year the next child lived.

The embassy gave me several opportunities to know Yemenis. The caretaker, Abdul Rahman, lived with his wife and daughters in a little house at the corner of our garden. One day I called on them, and although his wife was shy, she soon warmed up to my questions about the families whose houses overlooked our walls. I asked if I could call on them, and she agreed to take me to the ones she knew. We began a series of afternoon visits with the neighbors that I hoped would lead to more contact, but although they invited me to weddings and various other events, the visits didn't lead to a more intimate relationship. There was too wide a gap in our experiences to converse easily, and their dialect meant a schoolchild knowing Egyptian had to translate for me. I hoped my Egyptian dialect didn't connect me too closely with Egyptian teachers who had a reputation for harsh discipline and looking down on Yemenis. The visits at least meant I could put faces to the neighbors who I imagined looked down over our walls and knew more about us than we did about them.

Soon I met Sabourah whose royalist family left when Yemen became a republic. She lived several years in the United States, married a Yemeni-American professor, and after discrete inquiries came back to Yemen. Sabourah invited me to her teas where I met other Yemenis, including a cousin who had been a dental assistant in the United States and a full-fledged dentist in Yemen. I went to her with a complicated problem that she managed very well.

Sabourah lived not far from me, and we sometimes went to the souk together. We made an odd couple walking in the streets—I was tall and dressed in modest Western clothes and she was much shorter and completely covered in the black Yemeni *shirshaf* with black skirt, cape, and head and face veil. People usually turned to stare at foreigners, but this time it was Sabourah who made them take a second look. Wearing sneakers (instead of high heels) and walking with the sauntering gait of an American identified her as not the usual Yemeni woman. Sometimes her friends would stop us, and I realized that local women recognize each other as easily when fully veiled as when their faces are exposed.

Sabourah invited me to workshops she organized to train kindergarten teachers. For that job she brought in a Lebanese trainer, Dr. Mona Habib, who later became my friend and colleague on education projects in a number of countries.

Sabourah was Americanized enough to speak more candidly about her family than was usual for Yemenis. Once she told me she was four years old before she realized which of the four "mamas" in her father's household belonged specifically to her. The wives used to joke, she said, that her religious father treated them so equally that "he never showed affection to any of them." This may have been an unusual case since it was my sense that multiple wives rarely got along well, and indeed, the women's greatest fear was that their husbands would take other wives.

We made many visits out of town—our favorites being weekends with Peace Corps volunteers in their villages, where I was invariably sent off to the women's quarters to emerge a day or two later. Usually I got my hands hennaed and in the meantime had a wonderful time learning about their lives. We visited every town of any size in Yemen—the spectacular mountain-top town of Hajja where sons of chiefs were once held hostage to ensure their fathers kept their agreements, the dirty oil-soaked Red Sea coastal town of Hodeida, and the archaeological sights of Marib, including the remains of the ancient Marib dam whose collapse in the sixth century (said to be the day the Prophet Muhammad was born) sent Yemeni tribes spilling out across the Arabian Peninsula. Traveling through the mountains we saw tiny terraced fields cascading down the mountains and drove through groves of trees that once produced coffee. The cool uplands where coffee grows best, unfortunately, also is optimum for growing the now more profitable qat. The derelict port of Mocha from which coffees once sailed is testimony to its decline. We often visited the second most important city in Yemen, Taiz, where the town's reputation for "being modern" showed in the colorfully dressed market women and the form-fitting coats and head scarves (but no face veils) of the city women.

One weekend we descended the escarpment to the hot, humid coastal plain to visit an agriculture project. A woman came out of a grass hut and invited me to tea. I accepted immediately and spent time enjoying her company as "her clients" dropped in for dress fittings. I had previously seen the round African-like huts dotting the plain and wondered about the people who obviously had immigrated from Africa across the Red Sea. Another time, taking a little-used route from the highlands to the coast, we saw similar dark-skinned women gathering water at a well. The incongruous part was that they were naked from the waist up in a country where women in the towns were so totally covered.

I visited a hospital in the northern town of Saada that was a gift to the local tribes from the Saudis who that were more sympathetic to them than to the Yemeni government. The hospital was staffed by rotations of volunteer American doctors. They told me they saw childhood diseases that had been eliminated everywhere else by immunizations and surgical cases normally found only in war zones. The doctors were amazed at the toughness of Yemeni patients—giving the example of a patient who walked in carrying his intestines spilling out of a knife wound. "If they reach the clinic alive," one doctor said, "we can save them." A Yemeni custom to avoid bloodshed involved men throwing down their knives before starting an argument, so they wouldn't end up in knife fights. The staff told me the Saudis required them to separate male and female newborns in different nurseries and to inter unclaimed bodies in sex-separated cemeteries.

Some visits to Saada, as in Syria, were responses to requests for information about the Jewish community. Once we went to check on a Jewish silversmith whose shop had been closed "by the authorities." We made the long trip north and visited the silver shops where we learned the man in question had decided to close his shop because business wasn't very good. "We have no problems here," he assured us. Members of this community kept to themselves but didn't appear any poorer or more maligned than the rest of the population. The already existing tribal-trader divide would have made shopkeepers second-class citizens in any case, whether Jewish or not, at least in the eyes of the "noble" tribesmen. If Jews were being persecuted, we reasoned, why did they make their Jewishness so apparent, with long side curls, and going back further, why had they remained in 1949–1950 when most other Yemeni Jews left for Israel?

Several times we camped on the Red Sea coast with our "retinue" of Ali, Abdul Wali, and local guards and made use of their knowledge to buy at the most delicious *baladi* (popular) bakeries or eat at restaurants where fish, baked in clay ovens, are thrown on newspaper-covered tables with a side dish of hot sauce. We started the mornings with Arabic coffee prepared at camp and watched fishermen loading their nets and setting out to sea. Then we returned to town to "morning" baladi restaurants for beans cooked overnight, with grilled liver or an omelet.

We grew to love this baladi food: *halba* (a green frothing concoction that includes fenugreek) and the sweet, pancake-like *bint issahen* were unique to Yemen, as was the spiced drink made from coffee bean husks. Another favorite was a dish made of coarse wheat flour and meat broth that is stirred for hours. Like other cuisines in countries of the Arabian Peninsula, a complicated protocol of sweet and sour, and "hot" and "cold" dishes determines the order in which they are eaten. Many are cooked in the wonderful stone Yemeni casseroles and bean pots that keep food warm for hours.

Coming back from these trips around Yemen, we realized we were missing delicious foods by submitting to Ibrahim's ideas of what foreigners ate. Bill and I began sneaking out of the embassy early in the morning to the "hole-in-the-wall" restaurant around the corner where we could eat a good bean and liver breakfast. We told Ibrahim we would no longer eat tasteless "toast" bread and henceforth wanted only "army bread," the heavy multigrained dark bread the lucky army recruits ate. Abdul Wali would stop by a small grated window on a back alley where the bread was sold illegally.

The most memorable week I spent on embassy business was accompanying the consular officer and his Yemeni staff to the Governorate of Ibb. The purpose of our trip was to investigate visa and Social Security fraud. Many Yemenis lived and worked in the United States for years with the thought of retiring to Yemen and living comfortably on Social Security checks. The embassy had two issues: whether these retired men were actually producing new children every year, as they said, and whether Yemenis claiming to be relatives of American citizens to obtain visas were actually kin. The embassy required blood tests to prove kinship, but word spread that the tests might discover other fathers. Since semen moves in extraordinary ways in Yemen, through clothing or other contact, even innocent women were afraid of the tests. Some, such as women with babies born eighteen months after their fathers left for America (called "sleeping babies"), were probably even more worried. Many had doctor's notes sent to the embassy saying they were dead or too sick to travel to Sana. Our job was to see if they were truly dead or ailing, as they claimed.

The trip to the remote area where most cases resided took eight hours on a tortuous, unpaved track. Along the way we saw occasional farmers working their plots or shepherds with flocks of goats. It was hard to distinguish men from women—both wore turbans with long curls falling to their shoulders, the men with *futa* skirts wrapped around their waists and the women with long dresses. We stayed overnight in the home of the local shaikh, the men in the men's quarters and I in the women's quarters and

Early the next morning, I walked down the dim staircase into the brilliant sunshine where women were slapping loaves onto the walls of baking ovens. The smell of the burning wood and freshly baked bread was indescribably delicious. Down a path elderly women were patiently feeding their cows handfuls of alfalfa. When I asked if the cows could eat by themselves, they said no, they always had to be fed by hand.

We started out after breakfast and were soon questioning passersby. If they were women or children, I asked directions or showed them pictures of people we were seeking. The adults invariably didn't know anything even before looking at the pictures. If we persisted, they would offer to take us to the local chief. On the way, I would show the pictures to the children scampering beside us. Used to being obedient to adults, they would compete with one another to tell me the details, "Oh, yes, we know him. That was not the name you gave us. He is so and so whose father is so and so and his mother so and so." And then they would tell us, for example, where the mother or father was or whether the mother was dead or sick. The chief would say nothing or tell us the story the applicant wanted us to hear. By that time, word had spread that the "consul" was in the area.

In one village some women approached me and invited me to tea. After a half hour, when we had become "sisters," they told me the details of the cases they knew. I felt I was betraying them, but it was a matter of our newly formed sisterhood against the interests of the embassy. Fortunately it would be several months before the visa was denied or the increase in Social Security turned down. I imagined the villagers saying philosophically, "It's God's Will!" without connecting the information they gave us with the outcome. Of course, some cases came out well. In one village where adults weren't sure what story to tell, the children informed us that indeed Hamid had fourteen children, with one newborn even though he was an old man. Hamid got the increases he claimed.

Finally, one case remained, and we set off in the direction indicated by our map until we came to the edge of a precipice. A herder nearby pointed to a house on the other side of the ravine, less than a mile away as the crow flies. Three hours later after zigzagging down the side of one mountain, fording a stream, and zigzagging up the other, we reached a fortress-house with gun slits for windows. Anticipating that the men might be away, I went to bang on the door. A head heavy with curls and a turban peered out of a small opening, rifle protruding first. I quickly said we were from the American Embassy and looking for such and such person. A smile broke over his face as he said, "Honey, that's me. What can I do for you?" with the thickest Brooklyn accent I ever heard. Over a cup of coffee he told us about his life in America and the Yemeni civil war that had raged in his area. Luckily, he was an honest case, and we didn't have to abuse his hospitality.

~~~

Interesting as these glimpses of Yemeni life were, I still felt like a glorified tourist.

One day at a party, I met "Susie," a European woman, who told me about teaching in a Yemeni school while I described my proverb project and the difficulty in understanding their meanings. She knew a Yemeni who had studied abroad who might help. I could meet him at her house several blocks from the embassy. We started meeting two afternoons a week, "Ahmad" and I in her cozy mafraj, translating the proverbs and Susie bringing tea. Over the course of several weeks, I learned their story. Ahmad had been a scholarship student but found it difficult adjusting to a foreign country. Before long he developed a sympathetic relationship with Susie who was studying in the same school. Susie moved in with him and helped write his assignments and eventually his dissertation. The relationship didn't falter even when Ahmad's wife and four children arrived for a visit. When Ahmad returned to Yemen, they corresponded, but there were signs that Ahmad was no longer as interested in the relationship. In desperation Susie flew to Yemen. Once there, Ahmad was unable to help her financially, so Susie found a teaching job so she could rent the tiny apartment. She wanted Ahmad to marry her—even as a second wife. He seemed to agree, but there were always obstacles. The *Qadi* (judge) said she had to convert to Islam first, and more; I didn't think that was true from my rudimentary knowledge of Islamic law. Then Ahmad's wife got wind of Susie's presence and her family—Ahmad's paternal relatives—warned him not to insult his cousin by taking a foreign wife. He confided in me that the family would throw him out if he married her and wanted me to encourage her to leave the country.

Susie decided to win over Ahmad's mother and took me along to the village to breach the language gap, but as usual the village accent was more than I could handle except at a rudimentary level. Ahmad introduced Susie to his mother and then left. She pushed aside the present Susie brought, and all her questions were aimed at trying to find out when Susie was leaving Yemen. It was a distinctly unpleasant meeting for Susie.

Even though the proverbs had seemed a good way of learning more about Yemen, I hadn't bargained on becoming the indispensable part of Susie's plan to see Ahmad. Eventually I returned to the United States for summer holiday, and although I visited Susie when I returned I didn't renew the translation sessions.

Tensions grew noticeably during our three years in Yemen. A major cause was the ongoing problems between North and South Yemen. Following the overthrow of the Imam in 1962, President Nasser had sent troops to support the fledgling Republicans while Saudi troops and northern tribes supported the Royalists. After eight years and 200,000 deaths, the foreign troops left Yemen and a coalition government was formed of Royalists and Republicans in 1970. But although there was talk of unifying North and South Yemen, Russian support for the South meant it resisted unification. This was the situation while we were there, but shortly after we left, the Soviets in 1989 drastically reduced their support, and South Yemen in 1990 eventually unified with the North. With the exception of a short rebellion in 1994, the country remained unified.

One Sunday morning in our third year, we received a call saying an American communicator from the embassy had been shot. We rushed to the hospital to see what we could do. His car in the parking lot was riddled with bullets and spattered with blood. It seemed hard to believe he could still be alive. He had been returning home from an errand when a car followed him into a road that led to his house. As it came alongside, the occupants began firing. Somehow the bullets missed except one that scraped the side of his neck, just missing his artery, and took off a piece of his ear. He survived, and later we discovered the Libyans were behind the attack.

Soon afterward someone called the embassy and said something unfortunate would happen at 10:00 p.m. The American community was alerted and the guards were told not to let anyone in the embassy gates. Bill and I were watching a video that evening when at precisely 10:00 we heard a car moving slowly down the gravel road toward our building. From a window we could see it stop, and a dark figure emerged and bent down near a small electrical unit. Bill called the gate guards and asked if they had let anyone in. "No one," they said and sent someone to investigate. It was the caretaker, Abdul Rahman, just checking to make sure everything was all right.

Still, these events were a wake-up call for us. We had become accustomed to the gentle Yemenis who worked in our houses and reminded ourselves that most of the tensions were caused by the political difficulties between North and

South Yemen. Nevertheless, the State Department sent out people to make a security assessment. They decided two problems were urgent. The first was the diplomatic license plates that identified American Embassy cars on the road. We were given ambiguous plates. The second was the perimeter wall of the embassy that in the infrequent rainfalls actually melted in spots. Our landlord refused to let us replace the mud wall with a concrete one, so one day our enterprising admin officer arranged for an embassy truck to "accidentally" bump into the wall. She apologized profusely but rebuilt the wall in reinforced concrete.

Washington put us on the priority list to construct a new embassy. That meant acquiring a large piece of property, not an easy task in a country like Yemen where titles to properties are subject to multiple and conflicting claims. The admin officer, however, found a well-situated piece of land that most of the claimants agreed to sell. Washington hounded her to complete the transaction. But the lawyers kept stalling until one day in their office she broke down and sobbed. They were so dismayed they signed the papers. She was not the crying type but knew when an emergency required drastic action.

The next problem was to figure out how much land the embassy had acquired. Washington would cable, "We understand we now own x-number of *libnas*—but can you tell us how much a *libna* is?" The admin officer replied that it was the standard land measure in Yemen—the length from the fingertip to the elbow. But she was having difficulty finding out exactly how much it was. Eventually she found a local surveyor who, with his knotted leather strap, could measure the boundaries more precisely.

~~~

There were good experiences, despite the tensions. One of the most fortunate for me was a friendship I developed with another Mouna. Once flying back to Yemen, I sat across the aisle from a tall, beautiful young woman who struck me as possibly a Yemeni going the same place I was. Waiting for the next flight, I found out I was right. We must have talked for five hours or more. I learned she was brought up in Beirut and went to London before going to school in the United States. She was working on a Ph.D. in development planning and was on her way to Sana to work with a team evaluating USAID-funded water projects. She was to interview rural women to see how the project worked for them.

I was reluctant to tell her I was the wife of the American ambassador for fear she might not want to associate with me. But when I told her where I lived she knew. Coincidently her relatives lived only a block away. Several times we got together so I could hear more about the water project. She found that the proximity of the pumps near the women's homes made collecting water easier, but the runoff attracted flies and mosquitoes and created unsanitary conditions that led to more illness.

Mouna and I kept in touch over the years, and she became a regular visitor to Woods Hole in the summer, where her incredible culinary skills added wonderfully to our menus. She not only cooked Yemeni and European foods but had a delicate touch of her own that turned out exquisite dishes of unknown origin. "What shall we have today?" I would ask her, and she would reply, "Well today I am in the mood for X," and if her mood hadn't changed by dinner we would have the delicious X. She said once when she was jotting down a recipe for a traditional Arab dish, her mother left a wooden spoon in the pot, and Mouna asked innocently if the spoon was one of the ingredients. Her mother had the same problem I found everywhere in the Middle East—she couldn't give exact measures. When I tried to make a dish later with pinches of this and that, it never tasted the same.

Mouna was a good companion who loved long walks and talks about our mutual interest in education. She also loved Woods Hole and its pastimes: walking, jogging, and swimming. She proved a good friend to Doug when he needed a place to stay one summer in New York to work with a graphic artist and turned over her Greenwich Village apartment to him without hesitation. Another debt I owe Mouna was that in the midst of building a winterized addition on the Woods Hole house, she informed us we simply couldn't do it the way we planned. Our accommodating builder saw she was right, changed a few studs, and did it Mouna's way. In the end if I took nothing else from Yemen—and I took a lot—my friendship with Mouna would have been enough.

~~~

By the time we had been in Yemen two years, I had been invited to numerous qat chews, women's parties, engagements, weddings, births, and other events, but I felt embarrassed that almost no Yemenis had ever come to my house. I asked members of the American community if they would like to join me in putting on a dancing party for the Yemenis we knew. We booked the largest auditorium at the Sheraton and sent out 450 invitations. The Americans agreed to bring finger food, and the hotel provided drinks. We set a time in the afternoon when Yemeni husbands were usually off chewing qat.

Among the Americans we had North Carolina clog dancers, aerobic dancers, break-dancers, and a small group of square dancers, as well as guitar players and singers. My friend Leila Martin at the American Institute of Yemeni Studies would act as the mistress of ceremonies, explaining the context for the songs and dances. I memorized a welcoming speech in Arabic, saying that we Americans wanted to reciprocate in a modest way for the wonderful Yemeni hospitality we had enjoyed.

But would they come? I wasn't sure. I knew all the reasons they might not. Few Yemeni women go to public places like hotels because of the male staff there. Although the hotel gave me some female servers, the audio and lighting people were men. We invited women employees of female sections of government departments, many of whom I met from working on a USAID project. But a few days before the party, the government ordered these employees not to attend. The notice was the usual effort to prevent us from seeing Yemenis. I assumed the ministers' wives would also be included in the ban.

Two days before the party, on April 14, 1986, the United States bombed Libya to retaliate for an incident at a West Berlin discotheque that killed an American serviceman. The Yemenis were outraged at our air strike. The embassy's Yemeni staff thought the bombing was the fatal blow to the party—no Yemeni could possibly attend. The American security officer recommended I cancel the party since a large gathering was a perfect target for some form of retaliation. I told him I wanted to go ahead anyway.

On the day of the party, I arrived early. The staff was arranging tables in the anteroom and American women were covering them with finger foods. I had lingering qualms about whether Yemeni food might have been better rather than American food that they might not like. Everything was ready as the clock ticked toward the start of the party. Four o'clock came and the auditorium remained empty. About 4:15 p.m. a few women straggled in. I greeted them and led them to places near the stage. Soon others were coming, and with the help of our

Yemeni staff we identified and seated the VIP visitors at the front—not an easy task with their black coverings. By 4:30 p.m. the hall was full of black-shrouded women—not one removing her coverings.

I gave my welcoming speech and received a rousing ovation. Leila introduced the pieces, and at the end of each, there was thunderous applause. Everything was going well, and though the songs and dances were different from typical Yemeni dances, they seemed to be enjoying them. We came to the last two performances. The first was an American woman doing aerobic exercises. She walked onto the stage in a leotard that revealed every outline of her body—a gasp went up from the audience. They watched spellbound as she gracefully completed her routine. When she finished there was thunderous applause, catcalls, and feet stomping that shook the hall.

The last performance was a break-dance performed by a Yemeni student from the American school who happened to be the son of the governor of Ibb. He was a spectacular performer and aroused the same appreciation as the previous performer, this time because he was a Yemeni. Leila and I went on stage again to thank everyone for coming and offer them refreshments at the back. Some of the women rushed to the stage, turned on their cassette players, and started dancing Yemeni style. I watched for a few minutes and then went to the refreshment tables. By the time I arrived only crumbs were left—they had con-sumed it all!

As the women said good-bye, one minister's wife told me she ignored the government ban because "you visited me in the hospital after my car accident." She brought other ministers' wives with her. Although probably not all the government employees came, there were more than enough to make the party a success. Indeed, the entire 500–600-person hall was filled, meaning that more women came than had been invited. This was one of those times coverings were an advantage—no one knew who came or didn't come—neither the government nor us. Many years later a Yemeni woman told me the women were still talking about the party as one of the big events of their lives. I felt as if somehow together we had bucked the naysayers of both the Yemeni and U.S. governments and contributed to better understanding between our two countries.

14

BRIDGES: YEMEN (1987)
AND PAKISTAN (1987–1994)

Before we were assigned to Yemen, I was asked to join a team to assess Yemeni primary education. As in Egypt, the aim was to recommend how USAID funds should be invested in education. The team was a good one, comprised of several experienced educators and development specialists. We spent nearly a month talking to Yemeni officials, teachers, community leaders, parents, and students and analyzing textbooks, their production, and distribution. Although there were obvious problems, we were impressed with the occasional dedicated teacher (usually Yemeni) who managed to work around the obstacles. One issue was foreign teachers from the Sudan, Egypt, and Syria, some of whom were excellent, but others who used harsh discipline, taught poorly, and treated Yemenis as inferior. Training barely made a dent with their short tenures in the country.

Probably the most depressing aspect of the Yemeni system was the high rates of failure due to absenteeism, poor teaching, inadequate instructional materials, and exams designed to eliminate weaker children. Many dropped out before achieving functional literacy, and those who persisted by repeating grades clogged the system, preventing new students from entering. The per-student cost of graduates was high when these dropouts and repeaters were figured in. Parents also bore the high costs of "private tutoring" that had been established by some teachers (mostly Egyptians) to add to their incomes.

We recommended a mix of measures to increase enrollments, especially of rural children and girls; to improve program quality; and to build the capacity of education officials to make their own improvements. We also proposed studies of schools to identify what was likely to increase the ratios of students passing.

I was still in Yemen when Noel McGinn from the Harvard Institute for International Development (HIID) called and asked if I would work on a new project called "BRIDGES"[1] that was about to be funded by USAID. When I expressed an interest, he suggested I come to Cambridge, Massachusetts, to discuss the work. I made a quick trip to the United States and when the negotiations were complete I called my father in North Carolina to say gleefully, "Daddy, guess what? I just got a position at Harvard." "What," he sputtered. "Why ever would they hire you?" Such was his confidence in his daughter, but by that time I was only amused by his remarks. He had been a professor at several universities and then a dean at several more. For him Harvard was a pinnacle of intellectual aspiration, and here a daughter who was a "soft" scientist had been asked to join the staff.

Of the seven countries where BRIDGES conducted studies, Noel wanted me to be chief of party for Yemen. Noel came to Yemen to help me start the work. During one long morning, he tried to draw ideas out of our Yemeni counterparts, but they clearly didn't want to engage in a design that might prove unpopular with their bosses. It was frustrating, especially since our aim was to train Yemenis to carry out their own research.

The study would compare "high-performing" with "low-performing" primary schools to discover the elements that might prove effective if instituted in all schools. The sample of schools would be chosen on the basis of pass rates, an admittedly weak measure since even comparatively "good" schools had low pass rates. We agreed that I would return to Yemen in a few weeks to settle on a sample of schools. Meanwhile, clerks in the ministry would select a sample from the pass records. This job was part of their "training" and therefore a normal duty. But they refused to do it without compensation. We should have seen this as a red flag, but USAID approved the idea of modest overtime pay. The Yemenis estimated the work would take roughly five hours.

Several weeks later, I was presented with an enormous bill for overtime. Instead of one junior clerk being paid for five hours work, half a dozen officials appeared on the bill—the higher the official the more time he claimed to have put in. Altogether more than twenty hours of work were claimed. While Harvard

---

1. BRIDGES stands for Basic Research and Implementation in Developing Education Systems.

and USAID officials mulled over this problem, I decided to visit the selected schools.

My ministry counterpart and I set out in a rented car for Taiz. My first mistake was to give him his per diem for the trip, carefully explaining that the money was to pay for his food and hotel expenses along the way. We settled in a hotel from which we could take day trips to sample schools. The ministry official stayed out late each night and had trouble getting started in the morning. And we were delayed further by having to pick up a local education official each day. The first morning we made two quick visits to schools, and on the way to the third, we found our ministry official had directed the driver to the best restaurant in town. He ordered an entire leg of lamb for himself while the rest of us ordered something simple in order to get to other schools before they closed. The check for this was given to me, and I paid so as not to embarrass the local official.

On the third day as we were checking out of the hotel, my colleague brought me his bill. I told him he was to pay the bill with the money I gave him. He said it didn't cover his phone bills and his expenses for qat. "You can't expect me to come to an area where I know people and not bring them qat." I told him the money wasn't meant for qat or phone bills, and that it was quite sufficient for his hotel room. I reminded him that I had paid for his main meals both days, which was also something his per diem money should have covered. He fumed but paid the bill and got into the car. A few miles out of town, he told the driver to stop and got out on a lonely stretch of road. He said he wouldn't work with us because we didn't pay enough. He probably expected me to beg him to come back, but by that time I was fed up with the whole business and couldn't imagine continuing a project that would require constant fights over money.

It was obvious the project wasn't going anywhere. USAID wanted it, but there was too big a gap between their expectations and those of the Yemeni officials who seemed more interested in money than in education improvements. My colleagues at Harvard agreed and aborted the Yemeni part of the project. For me it was disappointing, but it was better to stop when we did than continue with so little likelihood of success.

After Yemen we were assigned back to the United States, this time with both of us looking forward to interesting jobs. Bill would be teaching at the

Fletcher School in Medford, Massachusetts, as "Diplomat in Residence," and I would be working at HIID on the Pakistan part of BRIDGES. Best of all the boys could visit us often at the wonderful old sea captain's house Tufts gave us—a house that inspired the rhyme, "Over the river and through the wood to Grandfather's house we go." It was the image of the verse.

The summer of 1987 was the year Ansaf visited Woods Hole, and the day our household effects arrived, she accompanied me to Medford to help unpack. But "mystery" boxes remained in the dining room to await our arrival in September. Ansaf wondered who would help me move all this stuff to its proper place. "No one but me," I answered. She was appalled that a "big person" would not have a bevy of helpers to settle in. She was seeing how difficult life in America could be. "Call your sons," she said. "It's their duty to help." I thought about David in California and Nick in North Carolina and wondered what they would think of such a request.

Meanwhile, Bill was finding academic work unpressured in comparison to embassy life, where crises and deadlines meant very long days. He worked hard preparing lectures and holding office hours but still felt the pace was relaxed. He especially enjoyed the rich class discussions stimulated by the many mid-career international students with multiple points of view. Two Arab students approached him once after a class "to apologize on behalf of the students who challenged what you said in the lecture." Bill explained that students were supposed to challenge their professors in America. We loved getting to know the students and helping them with problems they faced far from home.

~~~

When the Yemen part of BRIDGES collapsed, Noel asked me to supervise the qualitative study of classrooms in Pakistan. That work later led to work on the USAID-funded Pakistan Education Development Program as a Harvard consultant. The work kept me coming and going to Pakistan on six-week visits for seven years (1987–1994), first from the United States and then from our next overseas post.

Between assignments, I participated in BRIDGES activities at Harvard, getting to know my colleagues and attending conferences with other BRIDGES participants from subcontracted universities and organizations. The best minds in education for the developing world attended these meetings, and I learned a lot from them. I also attended the seminars Harvard graduate students organized on assistance to education and at their invitation talked on the "Cultural Determinants of Development," showing how people's cultural mind-sets affect the way they view development and the development process.

Some women colleagues made me aware of Harvard's reputation as a sexist institution, and it was not long before I experienced this problem. Males hired in the same capacity as I were automatically given offices in the main education building, while no one mentioned an office for me. When I asked, they grudgingly gave me a tiny office to share with a graduate student several blocks off campus. I also found that when the research staff met to share study designs, we two women came prepared with multiple copies of our designs while the male professors had "not had time" to prepare theirs. At one meeting with visiting Pakistanis, professor colleagues, graduate students, and others around the table, one professor slammed the other woman's design and then turned to mine. I had designed a qualitative study of classrooms with intensive observations. My sample included thirty-two Pakistani schools with equal numbers of urban and rural, and boys-only and girls-only schools. He aggressively challenged my sample as not representing the proportional numbers of these groups in the population. I countered that small qualitative studies are not expected to be statistically representative and that they represent categories not populations—a well-recognized way of doing qualitative sampling. Finally one graduate student bravely commented that in statistics class he learned that my approach was the correct one, and the professor subsided. But I was furious and went to the director to ask why he hadn't supported me and why he and the other male professor didn't have their designs ready. He had a lame excuse about being too busy and said my challenger was his friend, and therefore he couldn't embarrass him by saying he was wrong. There were other incidents like this, but fortunately most of my time was spent overseas and I didn't have to deal with Harvard sexism very often. In Pakistan, it seemed easier to deal with when no one gave lip service to anything else.

I started the study of classroom practices in the fall of 1967. My two Pakistani counterparts, "Dr. S."—my senior colleague—and his assistant, Mr.

Nawaz, were employees of an education research institute in Islamabad. Together we recruited four men and four women from the anthropology department at Pakistan's elite Quaid-i-Azam University to become our researchers. The study was designed to collect basic information for an impending U.S. government grant to Pakistan and build local research capacity.

By the time my Pakistani colleagues and I reached the data collection stage, we had overcome a number of intractable problems. In the time available, I simply could not train anthropology students to do qualitative observations in classrooms. It would have meant undoing years of their schooling where they memorized the ideal and considered everything else deviance. I wanted them to observe teaching carefully and record accurately what they were seeing. But they would come back from a day of observation saying, "Two children answered incorrectly and the teacher should have hit them with a ruler so they wouldn't make mistakes again." I gave up and created forms with blanks to fill in. Dr. S. and Mr. Nawaz were infinitely pleased with the structured formats.

Another intractable problem was the enormous ego of Dr. S., who felt too important to learn anything from our studies. When I asked how he produced the volume of studies published under his name, he explained that he analyzed existing data until he came to an answer. Then he produced the same report again and again, substituting rural for urban and girls for boys to come up with more specific reports. Curious to find out what an "American" field study might entail, however, he condescended to accompany us on a field test of the forms where, since we were interviewing education officials, he felt his seniority would be useful in getting "truthful" information. He explained that he already knew the answers to the questions, and I could save much time and effort if I simply interviewed him. In the district offices I had to prevent him from brushing aside the local officials and answering the questions himself "to make sure the information was correct." As the research wore on, I would find him filling in the questionnaires before we even started the interview. In response to my protests, he complained that little would come of the studies since we weren't consulting "experts." He cooperated, I felt, because he anticipated the large grant that was coming and saw the studies as a way of positioning himself for the future.

Compounding his sense of indignity was working with a woman who had the power to sign off on BRIDGES funds. He would have preferred sitting in Islamabad and collecting the money. At every opportunity, he made clear that he knew more than I did about research techniques. He knew, for example, that the forms were a better idea than free observation and was pleased to see my attempts fail. On my side I had trouble convincing my Harvard colleagues that our "qualitative" studies were really qualitative given their dependence on structured questions. I told them they would have to accept my compromises if they wanted these studies completed on time and within budget.

Perhaps the most intractable problem with Dr. S. was his insatiable interest in women. He revealed his colors in our first meeting. I had just arrived in my hotel when there was a knock on my door. Thinking it was a member of the hotel staff, I opened the door and in walked Dr. S. Being used to the propriety of Arab men, I was surprised at this rude act of entering my room while I was alone. Soon he was reclining on my bed and explaining that he couldn't sit on a chair because of his inflamed hemorrhoids. After relating the history of his affliction, he told me how much he was looking forward to our collaboration. I excused myself and telephoned my colleague to come "meet my counterpart from the Institute." Her arrival dampened his ardor, and he left. I never again opened my door without knowing who was on the other side, and when I knew he was coming, I preempted his intentions by meeting him in the lobby. My colleague faced the same problem with a relative of an employee at the institute who would show up at odd hours, asking what he could do for her. These men seemed to have illusions about the extracurricular benefits that might accompany the USAID grant.

But that was not the end of the problems with Dr. S. We needed equal numbers of male and female field researchers to work in the sex-segregated school system, and it was very difficult to find women whose parents would let them stay away from home overnight. I had to personally guarantee that I would ensure their safety. This seemed an easy promise to keep until, on the first night of our field trip, Dr. S. came knocking at the door of the women researchers. It was hard to see what he expected since the girls always slept four to a room even when some had to sleep on the floor. The next day the boys said I had to do something about Dr. S. They couldn't confront him as their senior but wanted to protect their "sisters" from his advances. I kept a vigilant eye on Dr. S. for the rest of the trip, and when we returned to Islamabad, I went to his boss and explained that I could not have him along on future trips. He understood immediately and gave Dr. S. an assignment that kept him in Islamabad for the rest of the fieldwork.

His deputy, Mr. Nawaz, took over as supervisor. He was a dour, serious man who saw religious outrages and violations in everything that happened. "Did you see that? She put money in my shirt pocket. She should be reprimanded." His hands were wet, and she was contributing her share of the food money, but her hand had brushed his shirt; therefore, she had committed a sexual provocation. He arranged separate rooms for the girls and boys to code their forms so there would be no chance of flirtation, but it only made it more inconvenient for me when I had to repeat instructions twice. At least once a day there was an outraged complaint related to sexual mores—for example, "He brushed against me." "She wasn't dressed properly." "He said something that wasn't proper." I was called on to mediate these complaints when often I didn't even know what the problem was.

On the initial field trip, I realized the long skirt I was wearing was not sufficient in Pakistan. Sometimes little boys threw themselves at my feet to see what was underneath. One of the researchers told me the director of education had spent more time looking at my exposed ankles than listening to our questions, and he respectfully suggested that I wear the Pakistani *shirwal khamis* of tunic and baggy pants. By the next trip a tailor had made me a wardrobe of Pakistani outfits that I wore for the next seven years in country.

Eventually the field trials were over, and we could set out on our formal data collection trips. I wanted to join the researchers on the first trip to establish the routines Nawaz would use in the three other provinces. Our sample gave us middle-of-the-road schools, neither the "best" the capital offered nor the "worst" that presumably existed in remote areas. I chose the most difficult of the provinces, Balochistan. The schools looked easily accessible from maps—and perhaps they might have been if the roads were asphalted or other conditions were more normal. Balochistan was the largest province of Pakistan with a terrain mostly of deserts and remotely scattered settlements. It was so large and the population so scattered the government couldn't control the lawless bands that smuggled goods from Karachi to Afghanistan. The researchers and I—both equally ignorant of conditions there—hadn't known our schools were in the heart of this lawless land.

The director of education in Quetta looked grim when I named the study sites. After several phone calls, he said it would take a few days to arrange our travel. The government didn't want to reveal its lack of control over a region whose low literacy rates made it a focus of the USAID project. Under normal circumstances, a request by a foreigner to travel there would have been turned down, but local authorities were aware the study was a preliminary to the untold U.S. millions that would pour into their country.

A few days later, the director informed us we could leave the next day for Sibi and Harnai on the train that visited those areas once a week. We couldn't believe our luck—traveling by train rather than bumping along rough roads for hours. Meanwhile, an expatriate had predicted the government would never let us go to those areas, as he put it, because "the tribe controlling the area—the Marri Baluch—were sympathetic to the communist regime in Kabul and were kidnapping foreigners for ransom." The ease with which we received permission made it seem he was overstating the case, especially given the fact that the Soviets were in the process of withdrawing from Afghanistan.

Early the next morning, we arrived at the dusty train station, one that more than fifty years before had been built by the British to move troops through the frontier regions. The miniature train chugged into the station looking every bit as decrepit as the station itself. We noticed a group of well-armed tribesmen in flowing gowns and large turbans also waiting for the train. They occupied one car and we another, and all the other passengers crammed into a third. The train chugged off down the narrow-gauge track at a pace hardly faster than a slow run. We soon got used to the drill. At prescribed points the train stopped, and the engineer climbed down to sign a register held out by a waiting man. The passengers piled out of the cars and took up places across the desert to relieve themselves and then, after the engineer finished his cigarette, returned to the train as it picked up speed. If the passengers had time, they gathered around our windows to stare. When they tired of me they focused on the female researchers who, being from Islamabad, quite casually let their *dupattas* (scarves) slide off their heads—an oversight that was akin to being naked to these onlookers. Thinking of Dr. S. back in Islamabad, I felt comforted by Nawaz fussing around the women and trying to shoo the men away.

Several hours into the trip and feeling stiff from the wooden seats, I got down from the car the next time the train stopped. By now we knew that the job of the keeper of the book was to alert the authorities if we didn't arrive at each spot on time. I proceeded with my short walk in the direction of the engine to avoid the peeing men who, although surprised to see me, were not surprised enough to stop in full stream. As I walked past the car with the armed tribesmen, they jumped out and formed a defensive circle around me, making me realize that their mission was to protect us through these dangerous areas. The engineer invited me to join him in the cab during the next stretch of track, and before long, I was doing "emergency brake duty." That meant peering down the track for explosives and pulling the emergency cord in time to stop before we collided with them. According to the engineer, this was not an infrequent occurrence.

We stayed several days at the train's final stop. Harnai still had a large woolen mill that once made materials for English customers. The looms no longer worked, but the warehouse contained bolts of fine tweeds and herringbone that the caretakers tried to sell us. In the outskirts of town in a grove of trees, we stayed in a quaint circuit house built for British officers riding inspection until the late 1940s. An ancient Pakistani caretaker, speaking very good English, was pleased to show us how everything was kept as it had been when the British turned them over to him—the faded chintz curtains; the solid, austere furnishings; the large bowls and pitchers for washing up; and a set of fine English china with only a few pieces missing. His pride in these items suggested that the glory days for him had been when the British enforced high standards. He was perhaps the most perfect relic of British efforts to bring "civilization" to Pakistan's frontier. He politely asked if we would like bed tea in the morning and warm water for washing up. Nawaz, as usual, organized the bedrooms into a women's room, a men's room, and a room for me. Our stalwart guards spread their cloaks on the ground outside.

The next few days we visited the sample schools and filled in forms. A local Sardar chief held a feast for us of *seji*—salted mutton buried in a bed of coals and cooked for hours—because as he said, he hoped our efforts would allow his intelligent daughter to continue her schooling. Through this Baluch Sardar, I learned about the difference between the two major ethnic groups in Baluchistan—the Baluch and the Pathans—not only in physical appearance but also in social organization. Later when we were working in government offices, these differences became important. The Baluch followed a vertical decision-making process where each layer only communicates with the next level up, and the top man ultimately made all the important decisions. If we went directly to him, decisions would be made quickly and authoritatively. But in a Pathan bureaucracy as in the North-West Frontier Province (NWFP), the egalitarian nature of tribalism meant everyone had to be consulted, and no one would take responsibility for actions that might be opposed by some.

We moved on to the bigger town of Sibi. There our accommodations were not so pleasant. Foreign aid experts once had the bright idea that building hostels for women teachers could solve the problem of finding female teachers for "far-flung areas." The idea seemed sensible in theory but didn't account for local custom that prevented women from spending nights away from home. Consequently, the hostels became guesthouses for local officials. They were in gross disrepair, the plumbing didn't work, and since male gate guards maintained them, the interiors looked as if they had never been cleaned. A thick layer of dust covered everything. After shaking out as much dust as possible, I slept in my clothes with a towel over the pillow.

We again divided the rooms into women's and men's rooms and a room in between for me. As the days wore on, the effort to separate males and females became more and more contentious. The morning started with the women breakfasting in their rooms to avoid being with the men. Then arguments began about where they would sit in the cars hired to take us to the schools. No female could sit next to any male, and if the numbers somehow didn't work out right, all the males had to take the gentlemanly course and sit in the far back, while the females sat in comfort in the wide seat behind the driver. The seat next to the driver was mine unless of course a male guide from an office accompanied us, and then as a female I had to sit with the women. As a last recourse, if the males didn't fit in back, I sat between the males and females on the middle seat—squeezed in against a male researcher. I was soon worn out from the "gender wars."

One day while we were interviewing a principal, a black Mercedes drove up and a distinguished man in tribal attire got out. The interviewing stopped as the principal offered the newcomer tea. After an hour or so, as he was leaving, he invited the researchers and me to an award ceremony that evening at 7:30 in the town auditorium. We mumbled, "God willing," and then forgot the invitation.

The researchers finished their coding late in the afternoon, and with time before our light dinner, the men went to the bazaar. The women, of course, could not go to such a public place. Around 8:00 p.m. there was a loud pounding at the outer door, and the gatekeeper announced that someone wanted to see me. I took Noor to translate and followed the gatekeeper to where I found the agitated driver of the tribesman we had met earlier in the day. Noor explained that half the population of Sibi had been waiting an hour for us to appear at the award ceremony. The shaikh insisted the ceremony could not take place without us. I consulted with the others who felt we would offend the shaikh if we didn't go. So we dressed quickly, covered our hair, and crammed into the Mercedes to drive to the ceremony. I told the guard to inform the male researchers where we had gone.

In the large hall overflowing with men, the shaikh and several male guests greeted us. As women, we of course didn't shake hands with them. The guests were well-known TV personalities from the capital there to honor the occasion. The shaikh gave us his position on the red velvet couch where we were well separated from his male guests in plush chairs on either side of us. The performance started with a schoolchild reciting the Koran, followed by the speeches of the movie stars. Suddenly Noor was nudging me and saying they had announced that their illustrious foreign guest would give a speech and hand out the awards. I tightened my headscarf and walked onto the stage in front of thousands of curious male eyes. There I gave what I hoped was a dignified ten-minute speech expressing my appreciation for the town's welcome, the cooperation we received in the two days we had been there, the beauty of the scenery, and when I ran out of ideas, about the importance of education for children. Since it was in English, I doubt that anyone but Noor understood a word I said. When I finished, the hall erupted into whistles of appreciation—the best-received speech I had ever made.

Then it was time for the awards ceremony. Each awardee mounted the stage, and the master of ceremonies described the important contribution he had made to the town. The awardee would answer with a speech and then approach me and bow his head, and I would hang a ribbon with a large medallion around his neck, being careful not to touch him. The awards went on and on until finally there was only one medallion left on the tray. No one came on the stage when the master of ceremonies gave his long speech about this last awardee, and I assumed he must be ill or deceased. But instead he took up the last award and hung it around my neck. I had been in Sibi a full day and a half and yet somehow my contribution to the town had been so significant that it warranted a ten-minute speech! I reciprocated with another speech that covered the same ground as my

Our house in Sana (1984)

Our *mafraj* with typical Yemeni window (1987)

Shop in the main souk of Sana (1986)

Andrea enjoying a Yemeni meal with villagers (1986)

Andrea interviewing women and children to confirm visa information (1986)

Taiz market women (1987)

Pakistan

Mona on a visit to Abu Dhabi
from Pakistan (1993)

Unknown novice
stuck on a pinnacle
while dune bashing
near Liwa in
Abu Dhabi (1992)

The favorite
Emirati sport of
falconry (1992)

Shaikh Zaid's *majlis* in
Abu Dhabi (1993)

Crown Prince Khalifa bin Zaid greeting Bill (1993)

Andrea and Bill waiting to
receive guests (1994)

Afghan supervisors and Andrea take time out on the way to refugee villages (2000)
Courtesy of John Gillies

"Light" lunch with Afghan male and female supervisors—carefully separated (2000)

Afghan boys diligently applying themselves in refugee schools in Balochistan (2000)
Courtesy of John Gillies

Trusted village man teaches a girls' class in a mixed school (2000)
Courtesy of John Gillies

Girls take our test to find out which refugee schools are most effective (2000)
Courtesy of John Gillies

Male supervisors express their joy at the end of our work with a traditional dance (2000)
Courtesy of John Gillies

first one. It was answered with a standing ovation as I picked my way back to my seat. There, little boys wanting my autograph mobbed me. We asked the shaikh for permission to leave and set off in a flurry of screeching tires and dust toward home.

A furious Nawaz was standing at the gate, demanding to know where we had been. "We left a message for you with the gate guard," we explained. He said, "He only said you'd been taken off by the Marri Baluch." Only then did I realize that the notorious Marri Baluch had been our hosts that evening and had indeed held us spectacularly captive for several hours. Perhaps they realized with the withdrawal of the Russians from Afghanistan that the wave of the future lay with the Americans.

~~~

We completed the research in due time with no major delays. But the data the institute staff entered during one of my absences was so riddled with mistakes that it took hours to correct the problems. The BRIDGES' director thought the participants might take research more seriously if they visited Harvard and cleaned the data with computer experts there. So I arranged for Dr. S. and Nawaz to visit Cambridge. By that time I recognized Nawaz as having the most potential for the project with USAID. I would have brought him alone to the United States, but Dr. S. felt it was his prerogative as a senior staff member to visit America. I met him at Logan Airport, and at his request we stopped at a drugstore on the way to his guesthouse to find the best hemorrhoid remedy available.

At the office Dr. S. spent little time on data cleaning—a task he felt beneath him—and soon was "making professional contacts." One such contact was an attractive graduate student whom Dr. S. invited to lunch "to talk about her research." She called later to ask if I would mind if she didn't accept a second invitation since she didn't have time for what she knew was a come-on. Then several secretaries asked if I had told Dr. S. he could requisition supplies from the storeroom. He had cleaned them out of pens, envelopes, and yellow pads by going to one after another with his requests.

On the first weekend Dr. S. and Nawaz both were in town, I invited them to spend several days in Woods Hole and introduced them to friends. One friend asked what their first impressions of America were—both good and bad.

They were positively impressed by the work ethic in America—the long hours Americans spent at their offices and their sincere interest in their work. As for the bad aspects of America, they felt it was disgraceful that women were made to dance topless in bars. How could Americans let their women do such immoral acts, and why would Americans even want to see such behavior? I was amazed they had located a topless bar in the first few days of their visit when it seemed I had to show them where everything else was.

One day while Dr. S. was too busy with his "contacts," I took Nawaz to visit an elementary school in Cambridge. The third grade children were completing projects on Egypt—one a poem about Cleopatra, one a pyramid, one a map, and one a play about Tutankhamen. There was a cheerful busyness in the room, and I was glad to show Nawaz an example of "creative" learning. But the scowl on his face alerted me to the fact that he might be seeing it otherwise. "You said this is a good school, but why aren't they drilling important facts about Egypt—its population, its geography, its resources? All they're doing is playing games. This is not the kind of learning we want for our schools!" Nawaz disapproved of the noise in the classroom, the way the children challenged the teacher, and their informality in interacting with her. As far as Nawaz was concerned, the children weren't learning what they needed to know.

This was an insightful moment for me, and I began to wonder if we would ever see eye to eye on reforms for Pakistani education. Indeed, when I thought about it, both sides were shaping children to their own expectations for educated adults. Americans liked children who could design projects, implement them, and learn from the process. Pakistanis liked disciplined children who could recite facts about matters the education system deemed important. The Pakistanis, in essence, were modeling their modern programs on Islamic theories of education that involved memorizing authoritative texts like the Koran (or a textbook of any kind) and learning the "correct" meaning from scholars. There was little room for independent analysis or creativity.

Nawaz was not without an element of adventure. On the weekend in Woods Hole, he said he would like to visit a church service, and I felt compelled to satisfy what seemed a laudable initiative on his part. I walked him to a nearby Catholic church and caught a couple on their way into the service. They were glad to let him accompany them and explain what was happening. I said I would be back in an hour to get him. When I returned, there was Nawaz clutching a Good Friday palm frond, and taking turns being photographed with various members of the congregation. He stood out with his Pakistani outfit and the frown every self-respecting Pakistani assumes when being photographed.

~~~

Nawaz endeared himself to me with his hard work, and I was ready to propose him for the USAID project. I suggested he write a paper on some of our study findings, thinking it might give him a boost with his career in the institute, and provide evidence of his abilities. Although I contributed substantially to the ideas and writing of the paper, I let it be published with his name first so he would get credit. He seemed pleased with the results. But several months later I learned that Dr. S. had been so angered by my attention to Nawaz that he arranged for him to be demoted after I left, and Nawaz resigned. This meant that no one remained who was trained sufficiently to do the work of the coming project. The rest of my colleagues from Harvard, with few exceptions, had virtually the same experience with their counterparts. Although I tried as much as anyone to involve my counterparts in the design and implementation of the studies, in the end I had no better success in developing their research capacities. We could not in good conscience recommend any of them for the USAID work. I know they were disappointed, but the efforts they made, with the exception of Nawaz's work, were superficial.

We had considerable data, however, both from my qualitative studies and the 500-school quantitative study my colleagues completed. There turned out to be few inputs that correlated significantly with student learning. That in itself was an important finding. One finding was that students of teachers with two years of training had no better exam results than students of untrained teachers, implying that teacher training programs were ineffective. Another was that students of teachers with longer academic study did better.

My qualitative study had identified a six-step protocol for more successful teaching—the more steps teachers used the better the student results. Since the steps were not taught in training, good teachers figured them out by themselves. The steps included: (1) statement of an overall goal for the lesson, (2) a clear presentation of the new concepts, (3) initial practice of the new concept under the guidance of the teacher, (4) independent practice in the new concept, and (5) assessment of whether the students learned the concept. Every few lessons the teacher would (6) review previously learned skills. This was not so earthshaking an idea, but in most classes, teachers only drilled memory work with the aim of having the students know the textbook by heart.

Several of us from BRIDGES made presentations at the provincial departments of education. Few officials turned up at the sessions, and no one seemed interested in the conclusions. A few months later, in disregard of our findings, the federal ministry decreed that candidates with two years of teacher training would be favored over candidates with longer academic training. By that time, I was pessimistic about having any impact on the quality of education programs in Pakistan. I wondered whether outsiders in any capacity could reform a system that didn't seem interested in change.

My pessimism lifted somewhat when USAID decided to take a new approach in Pakistan. The "program approach" (as opposed to a "project approach") was heavy on up-front collaborative planning and seemed to be trying to counteract problems in the Egypt project. USAID would invest enough to cover ten years of development rather than the usual two or three years. Although there was a brick-and-mortar component in girls' schools, funds would also be available to improve program quality. Finally and perhaps most important, a team of Pakistani and American educators would agree upon objectives and milestones before the work started so results could be measured and corrected along the way. As the relevant milestones were achieved each year, USAID would deliver a tranche of money for the next year's milestones. The idea was to push Pakistanis to streamline their bureaucracy to produce the agreed-upon results. Foreign consultants would work with local educators to help them meet the goals.

It was a novel idea that, on paper at least, was consistent with the worthy development goal of letting local people make their own decisions. The worrisome part in my mind was that after grant money was turned over to the Pakistanis each year, there was little oversight on how it would be spent. By now most of us who worked on BRIDGES were aware of the ingenious ways Pakistanis had for creating the appearance of results while subverting them in ways that satisfied their own interests. The "program approach" seemed a long shot, but maybe it would work.

Unfortunately my worst fears were realized before the program ended. Two examples are enough to show what happened. A major goal had been to increase the enrollment of girls. During planning the Pakistanis agreed that all new USAID-funded schools would be reserved for girls only. Most officials and parents, however, were more interested in educating boys. The officials announced that all rural schools in NWFP would become coed. USAID was delighted with this "breakthrough." However, as boys poured into the new schools, parents withdrew their daughters, and the new schools in practice became boys' schools. The officials, of course, blamed the conservative parents.

A second example was felt almost immediately. USAID funneled their moneys through the federal ministry in Islamabad. The ministry was then to distribute the funds as needed to the two low-literacy provinces where we worked. But the enterprising ministry officials discovered that the longer the money remained in the bank, the more interest it accrued. Consequently, we spent much of our time trying to extract our money from Islamabad, and when it came, it was only the budgeted amount without the interest.

15

ON THE ROAD TO REFORM: PAKISTAN (1990–1994)

I joined the design team for USAID's Pakistan Education Development Program (PED). Our task was to work with Pakistani educators to identify the objectives and annual milestones for the program in the North-West Frontier Province and Balochistan. At the first meeting in Peshawar, the all-male Pakistani group shook hands warmly with the American men but ignored me. Their leader asked them to join subgroups to tackle various education issues. They volunteered for all the groups but mine, where the topic was girls' enrollments. The leader finally assigned the most junior official to me while he put himself in the preferred group looking at schools, furnishings, and cars.

My counterpart and I started our deliberations—with him trying not to look at me. I pretended nothing was amiss, and after a few days he relaxed—telling me privately that he saw me as an older sister. I made sure he reported our conclusions to the larger group. Now that I was his "older sister," he came early each day to consult with me over his marital and other personal problems. After a month we drew up milestones more ambitious than anything the Pakistanis ever imagined, but they took their cues from us, and we knew USAID had high expectations for the program.

We moved on to Quetta in Balochistan. At the first meeting, our counterparts announced that they had prepared a paper listing the number of schools and other inputs they needed. "But what about quality?" we asked. "Don't worry. Our contractors build high-quality schools," they assured us. We realized the issue of quality in academic programs had never come up before. If teachers completed pro forma training and children memorized textbooks, the program by definition was high quality. It took a month of painstaking discussions to explain the other inputs USAID had in mind. In the end, though, the staff of the directorate in Balochistan proved easier to work with than their more intense colleagues in the NWFP were. The director was from an ethnic minority that presumably kept him immune from the pressures of the larger Pathan and Baloch tribes. From the evidence of his small office and modest home, his needs seemed to be simple.

The negotiations in both provinces had been difficult largely because the Pakistanis had little interest in anything but tangible commodities. We compromised on some issues, such as cars, recognizing that without them it would be impossible to supervise rural schools. But we managed to limit school furnishings. Teachers' tables and chairs and blackboards made sense, but student desks for all but older children just cluttered up classrooms and, once distributed, became an indelible part of school inventories whether usable or not. In some classrooms, broken desks were piled ceiling high to protect them from rain while children sat outside on the playground. It was a small matter but with important cost and organizational implications.

Another contentious issue was walls. Walls always surrounded school compounds so guards could control who entered the grounds. But the walls cost almost as much as buildings, and we argued that communities could build them or find alternatives. This continued to be an issue, especially at girls' schools. But given the limited budget for schools, we were loath to cut their numbers in half to satisfy a "nonessential" need.

There were of course many milestones related to administration, education components, supervision, and assessment, but these were largely beyond the imagination of our counterparts. We made placeholders for them and hoped over time they would come to see their importance. The design work was finally complete, and we had a set of milestones that over the next ten years would serve as the basis for improvements in Pakistani education and trigger the release of funds each year.

~~~

We kicked off the program with a workshop on the "Usefulness of Educational Research" in the mountain town of Abbottabad. I started the first day with a review of international findings on the education inputs that increased student learning and then summarized BRIDGES findings in Pakistan. The chief of party planned to ask the newly arrived American consultants to conduct the subsequent sessions, but since he neglected to tell them in advance, they refused. He disappeared on important "administrative" business, and at the end of the first day, I was left with the prospect of carrying out a five-day workshop alone with fifty Pakistani officials waiting to be "enlightened" by American experts. I should have refused but didn't want the program to fail before it started.

Somehow I got through three days and decided in the last two to have the participants conduct a small study that would get them into the schools. The study would look at the importance of instructional time in learning. We knew from BRIDGES studies that students from multigrade classes had lower exam scores than those in single-grade classes. One reason was probably a difference in the amount of instructional time. The participants prepared simple forms to measure engaged time and then scattered to schools with multigrade and single-grade classes to take sample measures.

I anxiously awaited the results, worrying that if they were ambiguous it might negate the whole point of the workshop. Thankfully, they found considerable more academically engaged time in single as opposed to multigrade classes, and some participants even got excited that this could be demonstrated so clearly. We spent the final day analyzing the results and discussing how teachers in multigrade classes might increase the instructional time of students. When the week ended, I was exhausted but relieved that the workshop, although not the best, had at least ended well.

~~~

Most of my consulting trips to Pakistan from 1990 to 1994 were to NWFP with an occasional trip to Balochistan. I worked with the Pakistanis on needs assessments and evaluating new components as they were developed. That meant collaborating closely with Mona who was overseeing the revision of textbooks and improvements in teacher training. Part of her responsibility was to revive the moribund supervisory system in the sixteen districts of NWFP and to motivate often reluctant district education officers to deliver innovations as they were developed. Luckily, Mona and I had the same goal—to refocus the system on learning. Most students were not learning the skills expected of primary school children, and the majority dropped out before they were literate, often because of failed exams or the harsh schooling environment.

When we started, there was almost no connection among the parts of the education program. The curriculum (textbooks) had no relation to the federally mandated learning objectives, teachers were trained theoretically in methods unrelated to the books, and exams were based on memory of book content ("Name the different types of clouds"). Mona had to effectively engage every official and get them to focus on learning.

Facing Mona was an entrenched system where the units responsible for curriculum and teacher training were oddly situated in distant Abbottabad and were fiercely protective of their independence. They refused to have anything to do with the directorate in Peshawar. Unable to move them, Mona decided to establish a small unit for curriculum development in the directorate office in Peshawar. The first issue was who would staff a unit that would be rewriting textbooks and installing them in schools. The lucrative task of textbook writing had previously been assigned to "subject experts"—senior professors who knew their subjects but had little firsthand knowledge of how children learned. The math book for early learners started "logically" with the concept "null" without any thought about the difficulty of teaching such an abstract concept. Addition and subtraction were taught as memorization exercises without any explanation of their relationship to one another or to multiplication and division. The situation was similar in language arts, where the first primer consisted of one page each for the alphabet letters in their three written and one capital-letter form (the equivalent of teaching printing and cursive at the same time), a word starting with that letter, and a picture of the object. The second book started with paragraphs of writing with no intervening instruction on putting letters together or decoding words. The textbook pages had to be completed by specified dates so teachers had no time to fill in the gaps. Memorization was the easiest way to deal with what children couldn't understand.

Mona wanted to circumvent the subject experts and build a cadre of writers who knew children. She persuaded the directorate to advertise for primary teachers with university degrees who might be interested in writing textbooks. The applicants assembled in a workshop, and at the end of a week she chose nine men and three women. The participants' reaction to one assignment hinted at the difficulties ahead. "What concrete examples would you give to explain the cardinal points to children?" Mona asked. They replied, "East is where the sun is." "Don't you mean where the sun comes up?" said Mona. "No, where the sun is." They continued to cling to the idea despite Mona showing them the sun's changing position, because "that's what we learned in school."

Mona was formidable. She managed to rent a building near the directorate office, and one day, frustrated by the wait for furniture, she walked into the office and commandeered what she needed. The startled officials stared as their "extra" furniture vanished out the door without the paper trail required to do anything in the directorate. Even the director gave up a table and chair "for the benefit of the children." The staff members shook their heads in amazement and waited for the explosion that never came.

Mona set to work with the "boys," a term we used privately to refer to the young men and women she recruited to the unit. We meant no disrespect to them; indeed, "boys" conveyed the sense of *shebab* from Arabic, meaning "youth" or "young people of both sexes." To us as middle-aged women, they *were* young people for whom we developed a great deal of affection as we watched them grow in the new environment. In the tradition of a British school marm, Mona set high standards—a fact made possible by their youth and diffidence toward people our age, as well as her Arab origins, which her seem closer to them than a WASP like me.

No sooner did the Instructional Material Development Cell open than new problems appeared. Everything from toilet paper to tea and sugar started disappearing, along with Mona's carefully gathered collection of resource materials. Our tea bearer, "peon" as he was called in the Pakistani bureaucracy, was swamped by continuous orders for tea. And soon we learned the staff expected a hot meal at noon. By the end of each day, the floor of the workroom was littered with leftover papers, tea bags, and trash, and both the girls' and boys' bathrooms were an unspeakable mess. Mona set about putting order into the unit—locking up stores and assigning responsibility to the office manager. Tea breaks were limited to twice a day. Upon being told they would have to do the cooking and cleaning, the boys argued that the girls should do these chores. Mona blew up, and soon there was a list of who would cook each day. The men brought scribbled recipes from their wives and soon became tolerable cooks. Everyone tidied up the workroom before leaving and kept the bathrooms in decent shape.

I still find it hard to understand why the "boys" stayed with us given these "demeaning" conditions. Some even commuted long distances to be there each day. My guess is that Mona afforded an endless source of entertainment for them, as she cajoled, praised, and rejected their work and stood up to high officials in ways they had never seen before. She worked on other aspects of their behavior, too. She made them all, including the man who was an imam, shake hands with us and look us in the eye; she restricted the time they took from work for prayers; and she demanded that they all send their daughters to school and asked for periodic reports on how the girls were doing. "We can't be promoting girls' education and have you keeping your daughters at home," she said. She took them on as individuals, tailoring her comments at a personal level, and demanding the best they could offer in their work and behavior. I suppose one might say she had no right to intrude so much in their lives, but they adored her—taking special pleasure both in her censure of their fellows and in her praise when after multiple revisions of the lessons, she finally approved their work. The atmosphere was a cross between a circus, chaos, and a theater, but work got done.

Mona's first task was to develop a curriculum framework for learning competencies, and she was pleased to find a set in the ministry in Islamabad. That meant she wouldn't be imposing her own standards on the Pakistanis. Ignoring the irrelevant ones ("expressing an idea over the telephone"—most villages didn't have telephones), Mona and the boys soon worked out a sequence of learning objectives and assigned them to the grade levels where they belonged. Then with Mona's help, the boys developed a format for the lessons. The format came from the six-step teaching process we identified in the BRIDGES' study of classrooms. The steps again were a product of Pakistan and not a foreign imposition. The boys filled in the steps as they wrote their lessons. Later the formats simplified training as teachers learned a pattern that applied to all lessons.

The boys started writing the textbooks for math and language. Mona focused on these core subjects as the basis for all learning. The other subjects, including history, social studies, religion, and science, were so culturally sensitive she feared they might put an end to our work entirely. To compensate for neglecting them, the boys included content from these subjects along with life skills (for example, first aid and health) in the language arts lessons. Ultimately four groups formed to write the core subjects in Pashto and Urdu. Although Urdu was the official language of instruction, Pashto was the main language of NWFP, and it didn't make sense to start children in a language they didn't know. Slowly lesson by lesson and grade by grade, the textbooks took shape.

Meanwhile, I was working with supervisors to collect basic data on the school system, and once again observation proved problematic—the supervisors described what teachers should be doing rather than what they actually did. Despite their limitations, the studies accomplished several goals. They gave district supervisors—many of whom had never been to a rural school—a role in identifying the problems that needed to be addressed. We hoped by seeing the problems, the supervisors would be easier to bring on board.

Another goal was to understand NWFP classrooms so the books could be shaped to real conditions. The studies showed enormous variations in class size from fifty or more students in the lower grades to only a handful in the upper grades. They showed a lack of instructional materials and how in most rural schools children only had slates and chalk to write with. We saw how children were so tightly squeezed together that some couldn't reach the blackboard to answer questions. Teachers used rote methods and often didn't know the subject content themselves. The textbooks would have to be self-evident and highly structured if frazzled teachers could be convinced to change their approaches.

Probably the most important revelation in our early studies was the *Kachi* problem. Every school had a *Kachi*, or preschool class, despite official claims that the class didn't exist. "It's just the kids of teachers," officials told us. The main problem was that it had no official resources and therefore siphoned off space and teachers from the rest of the school. On average, the class comprised one-quarter of a school's enrollments with large numbers of underage (three- to six-year-old) children. Despite the difficulties posed by the class, every teacher claimed the class was absolutely necessary. Why? First graders couldn't complete all the work required in that year, and it was therefore essential to have a preparatory year to learn the basic alphabet letters and numbers. Many schools made these skills a prerequisite for entering first grade. The second reason, according to teachers, was that children needed to learn to sit still and obey the teacher before they started the serious work of first grade. Unfortunately the harsh discipline and inactivity caused over half of them to drop out and never return. We brought our findings to officials, and after some pressure, they finally agreed to recognize the class with teachers and resources and set age limits for the children. Mona's group divided the first grade curriculum and prepared separate Kachi materials.

By the end of the first year, we were ready to start testing materials in schools. But first we had to introduce the books to local officials. We started in Swat District with a gathering of Pathan officials sitting around a long table. The boys presented the new approach—a phonetic one—enthusiastically. When they finished, the grim faces of the officials indicated something was wrong. Were the boys too young to be lecturing their seniors? Was it too "foreign" an approach? Finally the most senior man spoke: "We appreciate your work but we cannot accept these materials. You have started the primer with the letter 'meem'(m). We've always started our books with 'alef' (a) as the Koran does." We explained that phonetic approaches start with consonants because they have more consistent sounds. They still looked grim. Another said, "Children need to memorize lessons until the age of twelve which is the age when they begin to reason. Your system can't work." Others complained that teachers and students shouldn't be told learning objectives since it gave away what might appear on exams.

Somehow we got through their objections and were able to introduce the materials into the Swat schools. We gathered the district supervisors and explained their role in delivering the new books. They watched us train some teachers by explaining the lesson format and then asking them one by one to demonstrate a lesson following the format. The teachers were given textbooks and told to use them as instructed. We would return after six weeks and test the children to see if they learned the objectives in each lesson.

We returned in six weeks, tested the children, and found a good percentage of the students did well. Those teachers whose students performed poorly we retrained, and they usually did better the next time. In tune with the Pakistani "shame culture," we posted the results by teachers, schools, and district supervisors to create stronger motivation to improve the scores. It seemed harsh, but Mona understood intuitively that it was necessary to get things done. The "coddling" approach natural to most Americans we began calling "the touchy-feely approach." As usual Mona was idolized everywhere she went, with officials falling over one another to please her. Part of it, of course, was to avoid confrontations they knew they would lose. But officials found it hard to challenge the "outrageous" things she did when she was so clearly improving the children's education.

Every fall we introduced more materials into the schools, with supervisors gradually bearing more of the burden of training teachers and testing results. The boys appeared twice a year for random testing to make sure the exams weren't being rigged. Occasionally we took amazed officials to see that children were reading almost anything written on the blackboard. Eventually the data came pouring in from the more than 700 classes where Kachi through grade two textbooks were introduced. The children were finally learning the skills they needed. The moribund system was beginning to awaken.

~~~

But there were still obstacles. The two main ones were that teachers didn't know many of the concepts in the primary school curriculum and that class sizes were often so big teachers didn't have time to help weaker students. Every now and then we found teachers with creative ideas about managing large classes, and Mona would bring them down to Peshawar to explain their methods to the boys. Mona brought one teacher to demonstrate alphabet blocks he had made from scraps of wood and arranged with a plastics factory to make the blocks for all the NWFP schools (with him getting the royalties).

To address the two problems Mona set the boys to writing small pamphlets entitled *Math Concepts for the Primary School*, *Language Arts Concepts for Primary School*, and *Classroom Management*. The last booklet contained simple tips about arranging students to make their learning more effective. We distributed the pamphlets to in-service teachers but had no access to teachers in training institutes (TTIs).

The sixteen TTIs of NWFP came under a different authority from the directorate and, just as the curriculum unit in Abbottabad, had proved highly resistant to working with us. Without them, it would be difficult to make much progress on teacher skills. We visited the institutes and told them we observed that many teachers had not mastered the concepts of the primary level. "Impossible," they replied. "Teachers are either high school or university graduates. Of course they know primary concepts." We asked if we could give entering candidates the primary school leaving exam. We assured them it would not reflect on the TTIs because candidates were just entering those institutions. They agreed, and we tested the candidates, using trainers in the schools to correct the exams. They were shocked to find the candidates passed the exams at only a slightly higher rate than primary school students, a majority of whom failed. But still the trainers resisted the idea of teaching subject matter, because, they said, it was their job to teach methods. We offered them our subject matter pamphlets to distribute to the trainees, and told them we would return at the end of the school year to test the candidates again. We publicly posted the results, and by the next testing the teachers did much better. We planned to continue this cycle of pre- and post testing each year until it became a routine.

~~~

In our second year in Peshawar, the federal minister in Islamabad decided that all primary students had to learn English. The major dividing line between public and private school graduates, and rural and urban students, was their command of the English language. Jobs in the private sector and in almost every government department required English. So we did a quick study to see the possibilities of introducing a more effective program. We found teachers could only introduce the alphabet and a few words, and their accents were so poor they were not understandable: "Bird" came out "bir-dey."

The only solution seemed to be Radio English, a program that had been used successfully in Africa. I had been skeptical of an approach that used radio cues and drills until I saw how quickly students and teachers learned from our test tapes. We decided to start at grade three when students were old enough to follow the radio instructions. USAID sent a team to negotiate with Pakistan Radio and upgrade their studios, and then helped Pakistani actors produce the tapes. We would have liked to have used the Kenya tapes, but the Pakistanis insisted on Pakistani accents, not even American or British ones.

The program started in a matter of months. Mona distributed pamphlets with explanations about radio cues and definitions of new words in Urdu. The children were given workbooks to help with reading and writing, and each class received a battery radio to listen to the broadcasts several times a week. Where radio reception was poor, tapes were substituted. My monitoring team developed tests, and we were soon out in the field collecting data on how well the program worked. It was a thrill to come into remote villages and be met with "Good morning, teacher," and other English phrases from the lessons. The program was amazingly popular with everyone, and we were all very proud of it. But when a new minister was appointed in Islamabad and was asked to sign off on the program, he said, "What? Children can't learn language from a radio—they need teachers!" And he canceled the program. Such were the difficulties of sustaining programs in Pakistan where officials' opinions meant more than evidence on the ground.

⁓

As we crisscrossed the province, we found abuses everywhere. In one district alone, we discovered thirty supervisors who collected salaries but never appeared at work. We found "paper" schools with paid staff that had long been closed or didn't exist. The officials were so enmeshed in kickback schemes that no one was blameless. Our Harvard colleagues discovered that schools were being asked to submit more than twenty (as I remember it) overlapping data forms, some of them dating back to the British era. Forms were added but never withdrawn. The data were entered laboriously by hand into ledgers that were stacked in storage rooms and after a year were impossible to retrieve. No one seemed to know how many schools and teachers actually existed.

We found other problems, too. Attendance rules were so elastic that a teacher could be absent one-quarter of the time for sickness or personal business without penalty. There were no substitute teachers, and children simply sat doing nothing until their teacher returned. Once an illiterate gate guard was leading classes. "Where is the teacher?" "On maternity leave." "But our records show she's not married." "Well, yes, that's true." Another favorite ploy was to show foreign funders the same new building so each would think it was built with their funds. We were increasingly becoming a threat to these abuse systems, and it wasn't long before we were told we couldn't travel anywhere without the director's permission. These permissions took days to acquire. The letter had to be drafted by an official who was rarely in his office and typed by a secretary who retyped it numerous times because of mistakes. Then we had to wait for cars going in the right direction to deliver the letters. The letters started with, "I have been asked to inform you . . . ," so the civil servant could not be held responsible for the content because he was "asked to inform others." We gave up and sent our own messages and made our own arrangements and informed the director that we were going. By that time the district education officers knew us and generally welcomed our visits because we left their gas tanks full after using the cars to visit schools. Even as we were exasperating higher officials, we were winning the hearts of local teachers who had battled for years to make education better for village children. It was Mona's unswerving honesty, fairness, and perseverance and our obvious commitment to their children that won their hearts.

Each June, Mona and I took the boys to Chitral to deliver schoolbooks. I still see the first glistening sight of the Hindu Kush as we emerged from the dark pine forests of the foothills. We would have been traveling all day through the greening fields of Swat and the rose-encrusted highways of Dir. Late June was the time roads opened to Chitral—when the glaciers melted enough for vehicles to gain traction on the steep mountain roads, even as snowmelt collapsed the still glacier-covered tracks. The boys sang their mournful Pashtun songs of unrequited love under the Chinar tree. This stately tree was always featured in songs about star-crossed lovers. Once I composed a happy love song, and the district education officer—a poet— translated and set my words to music one evening on the lawns of Swat's Serena Hotel. It may be the only happy Pashtun ballad that exists.

The previous year we had left books, observation protocols, and assessment exams with the education officers and asked them to introduce two years of the books on their own. We planned to test the children to see how well the Chitralis had carried out their instructions. The results showed they did well, and where teachers needed help, we showed the officials what to do.

An aim of these trips was to acquaint the boys with new regions of NWFP so the textbooks would reflect the variety of the province. A unique feature of Chitral was the non-Muslim animists who lived there. Most of the boys were intensely religious and on certain days donned green head scarves and joined throngs of men listening to radicals preaching jihad. We wondered how it felt to listen to preachers' rantings about infidels and then have to work with us. When the imam on our staff challenged Mona, a Christian, with verses from the Koran, she recited Koranic verses back at him and always won the argument. We hoped experience with non-Muslims might expand their tolerance.

The Kalash live in a remote area over tracks that wind through mountainous canyons. They are reputed to be descendents of Alexander the Great, and although several clues suggest the truth of this claim, nobody has really proved it. Their skin is light, and many have blue eyes. Their dress is reminiscent of Greek folk, dress and the women decorate their headdresses with cowrie shells. Their young people are slowly being absorbed into Pakistani culture through the public schools, but older people still adhere to animist practices, seeing spirits in the natural objects around them, placing their dead in trees, and celebrating rites associated with the cycles of nature. Their homes, elevated on poles, are made entirely of natural materials, and they subsist entirely on the meat from the sheep they raise, the corn they grow, and the apricots and nuts from their orchards. We came across a colorfully costumed group of mothers and children picking flowers in a field who waved at us. When Mona asked later what the boys thought, one replied, "I wanted to kill them." Mona returned, "But why would God give them such an abundance of resources if there were not some good in them." They seemed to like that argument.

On our return to Peshawar, an incident reminded us that our "gentle" boys adhered to traditions we were not always aware of. The driver, Nader, stopped at an overlook for us to see a spectacular view. As we returned to the car, a small truck swerved close to Mona, and the driver smacked her on the back. When we were back in the car, Nader tore down the mountain and stopped his car in front of the offending driver. Nader and the boys yanked the man out of the truck and started hitting him. Soon nearby villagers joined in the fray. Such was the consequence of insulting women in the care of Pathans!

Nader always carried a gun and if in doubt of our safety, would sleep outside our door. One night in the wildest of districts, Kohistan, we retired to our rooms in the governor's rest house just as men were gathering downstairs for a party. Later when they were drunk, they tried to break down our doors. Nader was dis-mayed that he had slept elsewhere and hadn't protected us properly.

Mona had other experiences when I wasn't along. Once she fell into a mountain stream on her way to a school. Not able to pull herself out, she called the boys to help. But they were frozen into inaction by fear of touching a woman. She screamed at them to help, and finally the most gentle of the boys, more afraid of Mona than what others might think, took her hand and pulled her out. Each time she raised the subject, Muhammad blushed a deep red. She revived hand-shaking practice to avoid this happening again.

A more serious moment also happened in Kohistan. Everyone knows that when it rains in the mountains, you must speed out of the area. Along with rain, stones start falling until an avalanche blocks the way. We were caught in several rainstorms where we escaped, but one time Mona and the boys were caught between two avalanches and it took them several days to trek out. Mona called it "the time the mountains walked on us."

~~~

Each time I went to Pakistan I stayed with Mona in her big house in Peshawar. USAID rented the house in a safe area of town where military officers built homes and gave us twenty-four-hour guards for security. When Mona's elderly cook asked for a helper one day, a gate guard recommended his sixteen-year-old brother who had dropped out of school. The family barely survived on the guard's salary and the small earnings of the father. Mona agreed to try Fazli, and later when she fired her cook, Fazli became her major domo.

Our workdays started at six when Fazli remembered to set his alarm. The first hint of his presence was the shuffle of his slippers in the kitchen and then the slapping of his flip-flops on the stairs as he set the breakfast table on the second floor. Mona and I loved this morning spot, looking out over the garden wall to the irrigation ditches and fields beyond. As we watched, the community came alive—first with the bread man pushing his bicycle with stacks of fresh bread, then men on bicycles dangling children, fore and aft, and ducking between horse-drawn carriages with more children clinging to their seats—all headed toward school. Servants walked blue-uniformed children in groups of twos and threes, herding them around puddled ruts. The contrast between these neatly uniformed, shiny-clean children in the morning and their rumpled condition on their return was dramatic. We watched the miracle each morning as they emerged pristine again.

Mona's challenge was to teach Fazli to prepare our breakfast and set the table properly. In Fazli's village, breakfast consisted of bread and tea, consumed without benefit of utensils. Fazli laughed out loud when Mona explained about knives, forks, and spoons; what they were used for; and how they and the plates had to be arranged. He tried valiantly to remember the items, but each day something was missing, and our breakfast conversation was punctuated by crashes as he skipped stairs in pursuit of the missing items. One day he appeared with everything present and correctly in place. When we asked to what he owed his good memory, he stretched out his arm on which in indelible ink were listed, from palm to elbow, all the utensils and their places, as well as the food items. As the ink faded, items were again missing but never as many as before.

Fazli became a tolerable cook, thanks to recipes he jotted down before Mona fired the cook. But his repertoire never exceeded ten dishes including desserts. He set up a schedule of meals to coincide with cleaning chores. If it was Saturday it was stew and a clean reception room. Sunday was lasagna and the kitchen, Monday spaghetti and my bedroom, Tuesday eggplant casserole and the open area upstairs, Wednesday meatloaf and Mona's bedroom, and on Thursday our favorite—shepherd's pie. All swam in grease no matter how often we suggested he go easy on the oil. On Friday we ate leftovers, if there were any, but that was rarely the case with Fazli's hearty appetite.

Our faithful driver, Nader, was waiting at the door early and roughly an hour later we reached our office in Hayatabad. There we separated into our offices: Mona downstairs to guide the curriculum work and me upstairs to the research room where, with my smaller crew, we developed questionnaires and analyzed data from the latest field trips. By 2:30 p.m. government work hours were over. By then Mona and I were either wilted from the summer heat or were chilled to the bone from the winter cold. At home we ate Fazli's meal, took a short nap, and as the shadows lengthened, set out on long walks to erase the tensions of coping with office crises. Our favorite walk was along the fast-flowing irrigation canals near our house. We wore our conservative outfits with a shawl enveloping us but nonetheless attracted more attention than was comfortable. Bicyclists swooped by, diverting just long enough to hit one of us as they passed. We began holding stout sticks sideways to catch their spokes. We passed Afghan refugee villages where children threw stones at us until an adult stopped them.

We took detours through fields and met surprised farmers. They disapproved of our strolling alone with no male along.

One day walking along the canal, an American colleague remarked that he believed Pakistanis had no capacity for logical reasoning. I argued that this came from a teaching environment that stifled rational or creative thinking. As if to prove my point, a ball flew past and fell into the canal. A young boy ran to the bank and without a moment's hesitation tossed rocks into the current to deflect the ball to the nearest bank. "Isn't that logical thinking?" I asked. I was right, but the larger point was that public education walled off parts of students' lives where logical thinking didn't apply.

When we tired of the canal, we walked to an amusement park for children, where there were stores with high-priced goods intended for Pakistanis from more cosmopolitan cities. We exhausted the supply of videos from two stores. Their selections included *I Love Lucy* and *Lassie* all sanitized of any touching, kissing, or other sexually suggestive acts. Several nights a week we watched these mostly "D" grade films, with Fazli lingering in the doorway to watch. Ever mindful of potential problems, Mona forbade him from watching TV, and they had several confrontations when she found telltale signs of disarranged sofa pillows. Another fascination for Fazli was "helping" with our jigsaw puzzles. He kept up an irritating stream of useless suggestions and, when temptation was too much, tried to jam puzzle pieces into holes clearly not suited for them. It drove Mona crazy, having as she did a well-formed idea of how servants should behave, yet feeling torn by a sense of responsibility for this feckless young man.

For me evenings were a time to catch up on my reports for USAID, documenting my activities and showing study results. I couldn't wait until the last minute for fear of the almost daily brownouts and blackouts when the electrical current was not sufficient for my computer. Fazli sat cross-legged at my feet, trying to strike up a conversation, "Shall I bring you a cup of tea?" "No, Fazli, I don't drink tea in the evening." "Well, it's cold and I thought you might like some"—a sigh and a moment of silence. Then, "I wanted to ask what to do about my sister's poor grades in English?" "We can discuss it later, Fazli!" Once I let him write an autobiography on my computer, but he took so long finding the letters, I didn't let him do it again. But he was immensely pleased with his story, as if his life took on meaning when it appeared in print.

If he was lucky the electricity would go out, and I could no longer work. Then he would light a candle and start his stories. I remember his dark, earnest face with the long, curling eyelashes accentuated by the shadows of the candle. "Madam," he would start, "I can tell you an interesting story" and thus began a series of evenings with episode after episode of the story that had captured his imagination—the Three Musketeers. Fazli had come one year short of finishing high school, and surprisingly his school had had quite a good English program. He remembered every detail of the story, especially the parts that involved duels over honor and fighting for beautiful women. He described the heroine in loving terms, stopping every now and then to ask what I thought of some action or whether the characters were behaving correctly. That got us into subjects such as how his admired heroine could maintain her pristine reputation when she traveled alone with men and more abstractly whether individuals could resist temptations if society didn't exert controls over their behavior. It was a tale that appealed to Fazli's romantic, idealistic side, in rare moments when he departed from his macho male pose.

The candlelight sessions eventually exhausted his trove of stories, and he moved on to the love poetry he composed—most of it not bad, considering it was in English. Then he confessed his aspirations to become a movie star and described the Indian movies he saw in a local theater on his day off. In his movie star phase, he wore his best outfit and lounged in the garden with languid looks that impressed the gate guards. He never dared tell his plans to Mona, who would have stopped such discussions with retorts about finishing high school. Several afternoons a week, Mona paid for him to attend a program that would lead to a diploma and hopefully to university. But each time he failed the final by a few points. He eventually quit, saying he couldn't get a job anyway.

One evening Mona and I were invited to dinner in University Town and gave Fazli forty rupees to find us a taxi. He didn't return until two in the morning, disheveled and with bruises on his arms and face. The police noticed his new clothing (an outfit Mona bought him for the 'Iid holiday) as he stood talking to the cab driver and booked him on a charge of trying to steal the car. He didn't even know how to drive. The officers took his money and locked him up until he told them the addresses of Mona and his family. Then they let him go, thinking he would be too scared to report them.

Mona was outraged, and the next day we marched down to the police station to lodge a First Incident Report with the police commissioner. He replied that "your boy had lied" and questioned us in detail. We gave him the exact time, place, and even a description of the officer involved. The commissioner said he would look into it. Then began a harassment that went on for weeks, with police coming to our gate when we were out and asking for Fazli. We knew by then that police planted drugs on their victims so the threat of a long prison term would make them withdraw their complaints. In the end, officials from the American consulate intervened. Incidents like this gave us a depressing picture of the obstacles facing young Pakistanis. Even though Fazli and his siblings persisted beyond primary school, there were no opportunities once they graduated, even though officials blamed local problems on a lack of qualified graduates.

~~~

Mona had been boasting about a wonderful, handheld, Chinese sewing device she bought in the bazaar that was going to solve all her sewing problems, "even buttons." She described how the salesman pressed it like a stapler to make a seam. One evening she took out the marvelous gadget. After several tries we managed to thread the machine and finally got it to make loops. Mona got out her mending and began pressing the lever energetically while Fazli and I looked on with admiration. She held up the two pieces of material that should now have been united, and one piece fell to the floor. Fazli and I suppressed our snickers. Mona fiddled with the thing, and again the pieces fell apart. By then we were holding our sides with laughter. Fazli was sure he could fix it, despite being notorious for destroying appliances. He took it apart but never could reconstruct it. "Oh well," said Mona, "it was only three rupees." So uneventful were our evenings in Peshawar that we remember the episode of the sewing machine as a highlight of our time there.

~~~

I subsidized a computer course for Fazli's brother, Samir Khan, hoping it might lead to a better job. His ambition to become a math teacher was frustrated by the fact that he couldn't be appointed without paying a bribe equal to a year's salary. Mona, with all her connections, couldn't get him an appointment, and meanwhile others with no math skills were finding jobs. Once Samir Khan told me he had been in love with a girl from his village, but she didn't return his affection, he thought because of his poor wages. At one point he said he was thinking of shooting her so no one else could have her. Both he and Fazli had few prospects, but they loved to dramatize their positions to gain our sympathy.

By that time Fazli was earning more than Samir Khan, and no sooner would he receive his wages than his family would claim them. Mona started saving part of his salary, and evenings he would draw sketches of the house he would build—a rectangle around a courtyard with rooms for his brothers and their wives— when he received the entire sum. Just before Mona left Pakistan, Samir Khan convinced Fazli he should demand the wages she owed him. Mona gave it to him, and he left without saying good-bye. As a result he forfeited the bonus he would have received and help in finding a new job.

We worked hard on PED from 1990 to 1994, challenging many conventional ways of reforming basic education. We worked around some ineffectual American colleagues and even managed to gain the cooperation of officials in the Directorate of Education. We operated in the sensitive space between a results-oriented U.S. government that believed an effective school system could be established in record time and a reluctant Pakistani bureaucracy that dragged its feet. Civil servants were promoted through time in service, not merit, and so there was little incentive to do more than was necessary. When we arrived, teachers were leaving their classes in charge of stick-waving students leading choruses of "times tables." But our system of checking student progress made them responsible for students' learning, and some were even pleased to be recognized.

With six more years to go, we felt certain we could transform the primary program in NWFP. Already we had introduced new textbooks up to grade three and were putting systems into place to support them. We needed only the final years to complete the last few textbooks and make implementation of the program routine. We had instituted a Radio English program with lessons that were mostly complete for the primary level. The boys had become knowledgeable education experts who were received in the provinces with respect. They were dedicated to the program and capable of implementing it if given a chance. Increasingly people all over the province were becoming excited about the prospects of establishing a good primary system. An unintended consequence of distributing free trial books to the Kachi class had been that large numbers of schoolchildren suddenly poured into the system. We had broken through the resistance of teacher training institutes and now made sure teachers knew subject content for the primary years. Everything was looking good, and although there were still problems, we were removing some of the major obstacles to learning.

Then suddenly we received word that the politicians in the United States had decided to withdraw assistance to Pakistan. The Soviets had left Afghanistan, and the United States no longer felt the need to support Pakistan. American officials for the first time seemed to notice that Pakistan had a nuclear program and, using the excuse of the Pressler Amendment, which forbade assistance to Pakistan if it had nuclear weapons, suddenly stopped aid to Pakistan. In June 1994 PED ended, and in the space of a year everything was gone. The old textbooks—produced by the same people who had skimmed off royalties before were reinstated. The district staff, with no means of transport, reverted to ignoring rural schools. I was devastated, but Mona was more philosophical. "Just remember," she said, "we planted seeds in NWFP that someday will blossom, when or where we can't know."

In retrospect this decision was disastrous. A decade later, NWFP's government was taken over by conservative Islamists who established Sharia Islamic law in the province. When they later lost elections, they took over parts of the province by force, including villages in the beautiful Swat Valley. A radical madrasa system became more attractive to parents than the chaos of the public school system. It was not only free but also fed the children and taught them to be good Muslims, while the public system cost money and taught little. While improvements in the school system might not perhaps have changed all these events, they certainly would have helped assuage the frustrations of parents and children who for a brief time were feeling pride in the accomplishments of learning. In 2008 USAID started all over again with a new program to improve education, this time coordinated out of Islamabad since the safety of foreigners in NWFP and especially Peshawar couldn't be guaranteed.

16

NEW WORLDS:
ABU DHABI, UNITED ARAB EMIRATES
(1992–1995)

In 1992 Bill became ambassador to the United Arab Emirates (UAE). We were excited about going to a part of the Middle East we knew little about but also ambivalent about the wealth and sophistication of one of the richest countries in the world.

Most Americans know little about the UAE even though they should. The country has four times the oil reserves of North America, is located near the strategically important shipping lanes of the Straits of Hormuz, and has a peaceful federated government that could be a model for other countries of the region. The country was established in 1971 when the British withdrew from the Gulf and the seven emirates, each governed by a ruling family, formed a federation under the leadership of the wise Shaikh Zaid, ruler of Abu Dhabi. Previous to that time the area was known as the "Trucial States," and in little more than thirty years the largest emirate, Abu Dhabi, grew from a settlement of brush huts to a prosperous state-of-the-art metropolis.

When we were settled, I began thinking about the role I would play as ambassador's wife. The 1970s' rules saying spouses should not be treated as unpaid civil servants had finally taken hold in the 1990s as many old-timers retired. Most spouses were young enough now to take their independence for granted. The embassy had a community liaison officer to see to the needs of families, so I no longer had a defined role. Others could organize functions in my home, and I didn't even need to attend. The theory was good, but its practice was unworkable in a country where hospitality was an art. Besides, it was hard to explain our non-roles to wives in other embassies where the rules hadn't changed.

I decided to take diplomatic life seriously while in Abu Dhabi and escape frequently to my work in Pakistan. People greeted me on my return with, "We missed you at this year's bazaar (or Marine Ball, or whatever)," and being a spouse of the old school, I felt guilty at being away so often. To establish a presence, I decided to revive the custom of formal calls on ambassadors' wives. At the time, diplomatic wives in Abu Dhabi mainly called on counterparts in their regions— the Europeans on one another, and the Arabs on Arab wives. I set out to visit every spouse, except, of course, the Palestinian whom I could greet at parties but not spend time with. Bill's social secretary made the appointments but found some wives weren't quite sure how to handle a visit from the American ambassador's wife. One African said she couldn't receive me because she didn't speak English. The secretary assured her that it was only a short visit to pay my respects. She agreed, and when I arrived, her eight children were there to act as interpreters. After asking their names, ages, and grades, I exhausted their English, and luckily the time allotted for the visit. The ambassador's wife begged me to stay.

A visit of another kind was to a European wife. When I arrived, she was still in her bath and only appeared ten minutes before I was due at the next appointment. She greeted me coldly, and our conversation went nowhere. Thereafter, she studiously avoided me at receptions. Once at the palace of the ruler's wife, she arrived with two guests and said to them, "Let me introduce you," and turning to me, "Oh dear, I seem to have forgotten your name." Since we were often introduced as "the wife of Ambassador X," it was not a credible lapse. I ignored the sleight, having figured out that her coldness came from my being an American right after the first Gulf War when we enjoyed the warm appreciation of Gulf Arabs, and she and her husband resented the attention we received.

Clothing was one of the significant burdens of diplomatic life. Most diplomatic wives knew all the names of designers and dressed accordingly. I hoped my tendency to dress simply would be enough. One exception was at Abu Dhabi's National Day when we paid our respects to the ruler's wife. Knowing dress was viewed locally as a way of respecting the hostess, I dressed several notches above what I would normally wear. It probably looked odd to the foreigners in fashionably rumpled linens, but I hoped the royal family appreciated my dress with its pearl-accented hemline.

In a city of extravagant wealth, it is impossible to avoid moments when American simplicity becomes embarrassing. Once I timed my return from Pakistan so Bill could pick me up in Dubai in our personal car—as embassy rules required. He was immediately recognized at the airport and ushered into the VIP lounge, and immaculately gowned protocol officers were sent to intercept me. I emerged from the plane's tourist exit along with scores of male Pakistani passengers coming to work in the emirates. The protocol people, seeing me still dressed in my shirwal khamis, brusquely pushed me toward the economy bus. One man on his cell phone, however, suddenly realized that being the only woman on the plane I had to be the American ambassador's wife, and they apologetically extracted me from the bus. In the VIP lounge, we drank cool drinks until my baggage arrived. The chief of protocol suggested Bill call his driver—"No driver. How did you get here, sir?" "I drove," said Bill. We followed the smartly stepping honor guard to our small Volkswagen. "This is it?" the chief's eyes widened. We loaded the baggage into the back while the honor guard looked on. The chief leaned in the window, and said, "Sir, a follow car at the exit will escort you to the border of Abu Dhabi." And then as an afterthought he said, "Perhaps you'd better identify yourself, sir." We kept straight faces until we rounded the corner and burst out laughing.

Even though I could now choose my role, choices are never free. If anything, life was more difficult caught between the expectations of the international and American communities. The first challenge came when some Emirati women and Arab diplomatic wives decided to hold a bazaar to benefit earthquake victims in Egypt. I felt I had to take part because of my friendship with the Egyptian diplomats. But when I sent a note to the American wives asking if they wanted to be involved, I found little interest. Somewhat incongruously, I decided to sell embroideries from a project for poor Afghan women, thinking I could kill two birds with one stone. Unfortunately local women were more interested in expensive clothes and jewelry and bought few of my goods. But being the only Western ambassador's wife to join the bazaar, I received lots of media attention.

One couldn't help but enjoy the pleasures of this amazing city. Cooks from around the world catered to the tastes of foreigners and Emiratis alike, so it was almost impossible to find a bad meal anywhere—in homes, restaurants, or palaces. On the weekend Bill and I walked a few blocks to wonderful Lebanese restaurants to eat roasted chicken with a thick garlic sauce or *fetteh*—meat and garlic poured over crisp pieces of pita bread. Another favorite spot was a fish restaurant in a boat moored at the end of a point where boatbuilders still constructed traditional Gulf dhows.

On free afternoons a friend picked me up to go swimming in the clear waters of the Gulf, or we would walk to the end of a man-made peninsula past the colored sands Shaikh Zaid imported to beautify the beach. We mingled with black-clad women walking arm in arm and some actually meeting young men in a perfect place for mild flirtations. I learned here that cell phones aimed at one another could transmit phone numbers.

Another favorite spot was the dock where Iranian smugglers set up their wares—brooms, glasses, artificial flowers, furniture—at incredibly cheap prices. The liberal policies of the Emiratis encouraged a free market economy to flourish. Further north, Iranians brought cheap goods to Musandem in boats designed to evade Iranian customs and returned with ludicrously large appliances that threatened to swamp their small boats.

On Friday a ferry took passengers out to Shaikh Zaid's nature reserve on Das Island, where he collected every kind of animal—oryx, mountain sheep, baboons, monkeys, gazelles, and more—that tolerated the environmental conditions. He experimented with growing plants they liked and created sheltered bays to attract migrating birds. Shaikh Zaid was an environmentalist before the term was fashionable. He created mangrove swamps along the shores of Abu Dhabi Island to attract fish and other sea life. He funded breeding projects to bring back native animals of the Peninsula and created protection programs for bustards and falcons. One of the great pleasures of an Abu Dhabi afternoon was watching a show of falconry—with handlers tossing out meat and the falcons deftly swooping down to catch their "prey."

The University of Al-Ain propagated millions of palm trees and other indigenous trees and bushes that were planted along the main highways toward Dubai and the oases of Al-Ain. In the town of Abu Dhabi itself, more than 800 gardeners changed the flowers seasonally along the roads and down the median divides. Great flower globes hung from stands at street corners, and sloping gardens with planted words proclaimed the airport and other spots around town. Shaikh Zaid established gardens where foreign workers and Emiratis could enjoy picnics on the weekend, and people said he drove around town checking to make sure these attractions were the way he wanted them. At one point he decided the corniche would look nicer if it undulated more along the coast, and for several months the whole area was torn up and reworked with an offshore palm tree island enlivening the horizon. Near my house was a women's garden I liked to visit to watch the Emirati women and their children enjoy themselves in privacy. Shaikha Fatima, Shaikh Zaid's wife, also organized a beach club for women where signs warned boaters not to come too near. Abu Dhabi was a paradise in the making, without the frenetic quality of Dubai, where everything was bigger and better than anywhere else.

We often joined regular weekend campers. Almost any place was good to go, but the preferred place was the desert near Liwa, where huge dunes were perfect for "dune bashing." The object of the sport was to race your car up a dune and then topple over the edge and slide down the other side. If the car wasn't pointed straight, it could roll to the bottom. Several times we suffered the fate of novices—balanced on a dune with wheels spinning uselessly. After experiencing the thrill once, I found it more fun to tumble to the bottom on my own. Careening across the desert with a good driver in itself was exhilarating without the danger, and it seemed enough for the elderly Dr. Ruth, the famous sexologist, who joined us once, clinging to her seat and whooping for joy.

We used to skip New Year's Eve parties and camp with friends on the desert. There is no more beautiful way to start the year than under an expanse of desert sky with stars so close you feel you can touch them. One night after dinner a great white ghost entered the light of our campfire and headed toward a bowl of salad. He seemed friendly, so we crowned his head with a "Happy New Year" sign, and sent the camel on his way.

Like all foreigners, we took sides about whether Abu Dhabi or Dubai was the more livable city. Perhaps because we lived there, we found Abu Dhabi more peaceful than chaotic Dubai. Others felt the opposite, that Dubai was better because of its many malls and entertainments. Each emirate had its distinct characteristics—Abu Dhabi clung to tribal traditions and showed a disdain for crass commercialism while Dubai aggressively built amenities to attract businessmen from around the world. While Abu Dhabi was proof of its ruler's love for the environment, Dubai's ruler was reported to have said, "What profit is there in a tree?" Dubai's ruling family loved sporting contests and cutting-edge modernity and brought the best of the world to its citizens. Abu Dhabi held sporting contests too—but with traditional racing sculls—and built a Heritage Village to remind people how their grandparents lived in the not-so-distant past. In truth, both cities had much to offer for anyone lucky enough to live there, and both were a testament to their rulers' visions for bringing the best of amenities to their people.

People sometimes asked if it was difficult to make the transition from work in poor Pakistani villages to diplomatic life in such an extravagantly wealthy country. There were differences, of course, but they had more to do with behavior than with degrees of wealth or sophistication. In conservative Pakistan, I had to remember that men rarely shook hands with women or looked me in the eye and that I needed to wear Pakistani dress to be taken seriously. But I also knew men would get used to working with me if I didn't challenge them too aggressively. In Abu Dhabi, men shook my hand and looked me in the eye and accepted the way I dressed if it was appropriate in my own culture, which they know well. In the egalitarian tribal way, they sought me out to talk to, just as they did Bill. But even though they behaved so naturally with me, I knew they wouldn't bring their wives to my house when other Emiratis were present and wouldn't introduce me to them if I didn't ask to visit. In the end, switching contexts probably wasn't any more difficult than switching languages for a multilingual person.

When I looked around Abu Dhabi with its walled compounds and rare sightings of women, I wondered how I would ever meet local women. Foreigners told me how easy it had been in the 1960s and 1970s, and I regretted not being there when, as one American described it, she rode her horse up to the door of prominent families where she would be welcomed without formality. Now most Emiratis lived in guarded compounds or well-fortified palaces, where it was necessary to have an appointment to enter. Too many foreigners had attempted to insinuate themselves into the company of the shaikhas to make open majlises possible. One group I sometimes saw were Arab women from other countries whose husbands owned shops and wanted to sell goods to the palace-bound shaikhas. But it clearly wasn't appropriate for me to hang around them in the same way.

Furthermore, I knew hospitality was a one-way street with the shaikhas. They might occasionally invite foreigners to their parties but wouldn't make return visits. This was because of the unspoken rules of hospitality. Hosts "control" guests, putting them in the position of being "forced" to accept what is offered. Royal family members don't put themselves in this "client-like" relationship. Only once did members of the royal family come to our house, and that was when we invited them to dinner with former president Carter. His stature and their wish to honor him meant they could come. These customs seem even more engrained with the increasing formality and wealth of the society. The days of open majlises are truly gone, except at certain times and under certain conditions.

Experience told me it would take persistence to break down the walls that separated the Emirati women and me. I started by never refusing invitations from local women—royal or non-royal—unless it was absolutely unavoidable. The first local event I attended was Independence Day where by special invitation every woman, foreign or local, offered congratulations to the ruler's wife. But what I hoped would be a chance to meet local women turned out quite differently. The foreigners, recognizable in their Western clothes, congregated on one side of the hall, and the hundreds of local women, covered in black, on the other. I couldn't begin to distinguish one local woman from another and certainly couldn't communicate with them in their undifferentiated "blackness." I assumed the woman at the center of the semicircle of chairs was Shaikha Fatima but only knew for sure when her attendant brought me to sit next to her. This was her way of recognizing me as a new arrival. We conversed in Arabic until I was escorted back to my seat. The honor substituted for a formal call, so I felt unable to ask for a visit later on. In the old days, I heard, Shaikha Fatima would gather up the diplomatic wives in her jeep and take them for a spin across the desert, but those days were long gone.

Over time, I came to know some local women fairly well and at large gatherings grew to recognize them under their veils—by their shapes, postures, and gaits. Because I accepted invitations, I became "a usual" when local women held parties. At one party, after she knew me well, a shaikha pointed out her husband's mistress whom she said she invited rather than alienating her. Sometimes foreign or nonlocal Arab women would also take me along when they visited shaikhas, until gradually I was invited on my own.

I used the excuse of "obligatory" visits—to offer congratulations for the birth of a new baby, or offer condolences, or congratulate someone on the 'Iid holidays. One shaikh sent us "announcements" he designed himself when his son and daughter were born. For the son, it was a prancing horse made of wood and decorated with brass saddles and harness. The daughter's announcement was a wooden decorated carriage. I called on his wife. I accepted every wedding invitation I received and tried to figure out the genealogies of bride and groom to settle them into their tribal contexts. At one wedding I saw some unusual dancers supplementing the normal women's band and singers. I couldn't figure out why they seemed so strange until half way through their performance I realized from their outsized shoulders and small hips that they were men dressed as women. This tradition of "special" men being accepted in the women's world is more familiar to Oman, where these men are called "xanu." Many later revert to male status, marry, and have children. I also attended condolences where women read chapters of the Koran simultaneously to complete the book in a single visit.

I particularly enjoyed visits to the wives of Shaikha Fatima's sons, whom I found amazingly talented not only in the daunting task of decorating their magnificent palaces and managing their staff, but also in taking a deep interest in the development and schooling of their children. I brought Mona with me to discuss the new school one shaikha was organizing. She was well read on the subject of education, and we tried to help her make the connections between her goals and their implications. The shaikha said that one of her main interests was to teach tolerance but later was aghast when Mona suggested that one way to do it would be to enroll a diverse student body. "Oh, no," she said, "this school is only for children of elites." Her husband eventually took over the establishment of the school, and from our perspective he succumbed to the grandiose schemes of a non-Emirati Arab. Foreigners were always ready to offer bad advice that filled their pockets.

Ramadan evenings were a good time to visit Emiratis, although Bill had an advantage over me. Women's visiting hours were often late, and the women were exhausted from supervising the huge feasts for drop-in guests. Bill followed local convention and drove around checking cars lined up outside the shaikhs' majlises to see who was breaking the fast with them. If the cars had royal license plates, then it could be an interesting crowd. If there were only scruffy flip-flops at the door, the visitors were foreign construction workers taking advantage of Ramadan open houses to have a good meal. Some shaikhs erected tents outside their palaces to receive Ramadan guests.

One of the shaikhs Bill visited during the year was the very effective minister of higher education, Shaikh Nahyan, from the powerful Bani Muhammad branch of the Abu Dhabi ruling family. Shaikh Nahyan's father had been a minister in the cabinet until he suffered injuries in a car crash in London. Each day Shaikh Nahyan returned home from work in the late afternoon to sit with his severely handicapped father and help the old man receive his friends. Bill was touched by the tenderness with which Shaikh Nahyan attended his father and liked to show his respect to them by visiting often.

Most of the shaikhas spent their summers abroad in Europe with a coterie of women friends and staff, collecting artwork, buying clothes and jewelry, or finding items to complete the continuing renovations of their palaces. They were evasive in talking about what they did there with the usual reserve women have for revealing their personal lives. A nonlocal Arab woman who was the household manager of one shaikha swore me to secrecy before telling me that the shaikha spent most of her time—always escorted, of course—in a children's bookstore searching out educational materials for her children. How that activity could compromise her reputation was hard to see, but it showed how carefully women guarded the news circulating about them.

I learned early in my days in the Arab world how important it was to compartmentalize information. I learned, for example, not to say anything that might be construed as negative about anyone because of the devastating consequences it might have for a person's reputation. It was also better not to mention one person in front of another at all. It might lead to problems, for example, if you told Person A that you knew Person B, that you visited her, or what was said or done while you were there. You might inadvertently be revealing personal information, or your hostess might simply be jealous of your spending more time with someone else. Local people were often careful when talking in front of foreigners, knowing they were "loose talkers" who couldn't always be trusted to keep confidences. One reason was that Americans filled silences with talk, while Arab women were comfortable saying nothing.

I was realizing that even when I spent time with women I had little context in which to place them or their conversations. So I decided to study their history and tribal genealogies. Abu Dhabi has a Documentation Center with a wonderful collection of papers on the Trucial States gathered from Europe, India, and other countries that once had contacts with the region. The richest materials were the almost daily accounts by British Political Residents and their Agents from the nineteenth century until the British left the Gulf. The director of the center gave me permission to use the archives, and soon I was a frequent visitor at the center. Up until the 1960s, this modest fort served as the seat of the Abu Dhabi government, and it seemed appropriate to look at documents in a building that was part of history itself.

When the materials I was studying disappeared for photocopying, I moved to the Higher Colleges of Technology (girls' branch) where the same documents were available. During breaks I joined the young women in the cushioned spaces where they relaxed between classes. One day I asked a student how her studying was going, and she burst into tears. She explained that she had been married for two years and recently had a baby. Her husband supported her studies, but her family wanted her to stop. She said sadly, "Neither my mother nor my mother-in-law were educated and don't know how much studying it takes. They say I don't make calls or receive guests or care for my husband and child as I should. I want to finish school but don't know if I can take the pressure." I commiserated, realizing she needed a mentor who understood her difficulties.

The center's documents were so compelling that I reconstructed the histories of the emirates and later published them in a book entitled *The Political Culture of Leadership in the United Arab Emirates*. I described how governance worked when it was based on personal networks and relationships rather than permanent institutions and charter documents. A large part of it was the important role women played with their networks of information and links through marriage. Their very "invisibility" made them the unknown extra resource in tribal conflicts and reconciliations. The more I added the names of women to the official family trees (where only males appear), the more exciting my visits to the women became. It didn't take much prompting for them to tell stories about their mothers and grandmothers and the part they played in UAE history. In one gathering I heard how Zaid I, grandfather of Shaikh Zaid of Abu Dhabi, had once gone to his allies the Manasir to chastise them for not supporting him in a battle. He found the men gone from camp, except for one young man who came forward and answered his complaint with, "Would a wolf eat its own paws?" meaning, "Would Zaid punish those whose loyalty made them an inseparable part of him?" He learned the young "man" was the daughter, dressed in men's clothing, of the Manasir chief. Zaid so admired her courage that he married her. She changed the course of history by discouraging her son and grandson from becoming rulers because of her dismay at the many assassinated chiefs.

One thing I particularly noticed was the difference between generations in the households. In one family of three generations, a spry grandmother talked about the days when she and her family trekked across the desert from Buraimi to Abu Dhabi with their camels, a journey each way of more than a week. She told me to punch her stomach so I could see how muscular she was. She kept goats in a corner of the garden and made her own yogurt every day in a goatskin bag. Her daughter was a massively overweight woman who never stirred from her chair. She complained of a host of medical problems, including diabetes and high blood pressure. The grandmother scornfully noted that her daughter was of the generation that moved into palaces where servants did all the work. Finally there were younger women who had married recently or were still in university. They knew foreign languages well, while their grandmother was illiterate, and their mother read a little Koran. The girls were obsessed with their weight and only ate small amounts of food from the table. They teased a girl with a new baby, saying she would never be thin again, and soon she left for the gym. They were avid readers of women's magazines that, like Western ones, focused on weight loss, skin care, and beauty.

I visited other families whose names I no longer remember but where I still have clear memories of what happened. One day I was sitting with some women when a ripple of excitement spread through the room, and the women quickly straightened their veils. The oldest woman moved toward the entrance door, where roughly fifteen men had formed a line from eldest to youngest. Each greeted her with a gesture—from rubbing noses, to kissing her shoulders, to kissing her hands, to stooping to kiss the hem of her gown. She reciprocated in most cases by kissing the top of their heads or their shoulders as they bent to greet her. I was lost in trying to figure out the protocols that distinguished the gestures of respect. She was clearly the most prominent person in the room, and it was inspirational to see each male using the proper greeting based on his age and relation to her, right down to the toddler brought in by his young father.

In several houses, older women would rub noses with me in greeting, and I found at the end of the visit that my face was covered in purple smudges from the indigo dye of their masks. These masks, the first item of clothing foreigners notice, were made of a stiff material with a flap down the front along the nose line. They varied from skimpy ones that barely covered the main part of the face to ones that covered almost everything but the eyes. One could see a rough correlation with age—the more the mask covered the face the older the person was likely to be. Those with masks also kept them on indoors, even with other women. Traditionally they cut their masks to accentuate their best features while covering less favorable ones. While there was an element of modesty involved the women talked more about masks as an adornment. Once in Musandam, village women tried various masks on me until they found one they said made me look very beautiful. Since it covered most of my face, I could easily have felt insulted. Younger women tend to wear veils in public, so they can see out but others can't see in, instead of these traditional masks. In the northern emirates, many leave their faces uncovered altogether.

By the time I arrived in Abu Dhabi, members of the ruling family were building bigger and more impressive palaces, and it was even becoming commonplace for royal couples to build two palaces, one for the women and one for the men, so the sexes could move freely in their own spaces. Shaikh Zaid with his simple tastes preferred a smaller palace where his children and grandchildren all lunched with him on Fridays. I was told that while his family ate the elaborate food normal in palaces, Shaikh Zaid preferred simple Bedouin fare. Many of the Abu Dhabi shaikhs also had palaces in Al-Ain, an inland oasis two hours from Abu Dhabi. These were the equivalent of vacation homes, where families spent weekends and school holidays away from the oppressive humidity of Abu Dhabi. Naturally all the buildings were comfortably air conditioned. So spoiled had the younger generations become that some grumbled about the hardship of joining

Shaikh Zaid on his annual hunting expeditions to Pakistan, where they had to endure living in a tent with few amenities. But no one, of course, dared refuse his invitations.

We frequently visited Al-Ain where the main UAE university was located, and got to know several of the Emirati professors. They asked Bill to give some lectures, and once going around the class, he asked the students what their career plans were. One student replied that he thought he would go into government, and the class laughed. Later Bill learned it was one of the younger sons of the ruler. In Al-Ain I was invited to visit Shaikha Hissa, the senior wife of Shaikh Zaid and the mother of Shaikh Khalifa who was crown prince at the time. I had heard a lot about Shaikha Hissa, or "Mama Hissa," as many called her. We talked about inconsequential matters—including that she exercised every day by walking the length of the wall of her son's palace. Since the wall was quite long and because exercise was usually an activity of younger women, I was impressed. It showed how much she kept up with the times. After a while, two old men hobbled into the room and joined us—the first time I had seen men attending a women's majlis. She told me they had grown up and studied together as children in the Koranic school in Al-Ain and remained good friends ever since.

One special pleasure in Al-Ain was to visit the Oasis Hospital where American missionaries starting in the 1960s provided medical care for local families. Most of the children and grandchildren of the royal family were born in the "Kennedy" hospital and felt a strong affection for the Americans there. The staff told me that when the Kennedys first arrived, many of the women were dying in childbirth because of the practice of packing the vagina with salt after a birth to prevent infection and tighten up the birth canal. The salt caused scarring that made subsequent births more difficult.

Once I drove to Al-Ain to accompany the staff on their inoculation rounds to villages. At the last minute the activity had to be canceled, and we decided to drop in on the wife of a prominent local man instead. I knew my Pakistani outfit was more suited to the village visits but couldn't go back to Abu Dhabi to change. Our hostess greeted my outfit of light tunic and pants with obvious disapproval. The outfit to her was something appropriate for a servant, not a person of my standing. After a period of disgruntled silence, she beckoned me into her bedroom with the rest of the women and rummaged through her cupboard for something more suitable. Unfortunately her floor-length dresses came to just below my knees, and she finally compromised by giving me a length of material that I "should have a tailor make up" so I could dress more suitably next time.

Bill presented an award to Dr. Kennedy who had been one of the first doctors at the Oasis Hospital. UAE Independence Day was scheduled during his visit, and Bill took him to pay his respects to Shaikh Zaid, whom he hadn't seen for years. In the receiving line Shaikh Zaid paused for a minute and then said, "O Kennedy, Saar aguz (you have become old). Dr. Kennedy answered, "You too, O Zaid, and they both chuckled.

One privilege I enjoyed as ambassador's wife was to request audiences with the ruler's wives through the Protocol Office in the Ministry of Foreign Affairs. I arranged the visits to coincide with Bill's calls on the rulers, and only the Dubai women did not respond. Perhaps they were too wrapped up in commercial ventures to maintain old forms of hospitality. Certainly the ruler's mother and grandmother had been respected businesswomen, and it was possible the younger generation of women were also.

I visited the other wives several times and was always warmly and generously received. Each emirate was unique both in terms of local scenery and the personalities of its ruling families. I came away with strongly positive views of all of them—feeling even in my short visits their strong sense of responsibility toward their citizens and the model way they conducted themselves. The Emirate of Fujaira on the Gulf of Oman was the farthest away from Abu Dhabi and the most recent to become a full-fledged state. Throughout history Fujaira had been relatively difficult to access because of mountains separating it from the emirates on the Arabian Gulf. Several emirates had small enclaves carved out of Fujaira that changed hands frequently because they were so distant and difficult to defend. When the British drew up boundaries in the 1950s and 1960s, they asked the loyalties of local tribes and then assigned them to relevant emirates, leaving these strange little isolated pieces of other emirates in the midst of Fujaira.

With the establishment of the UAE in 1971, an asphalted road was built that now makes Fujaira and the eastern coast more accessible. The single-minded interest of the Fujairan chiefs in the nineteenth and early twentieth century in independence finally paid off in 1952 when Britain recognized Fujaira as the seventh and last emirate and its chief as a full-fledged ruler. Fujaira is the only emirate with substantial agricultural production, and one reason rulers from other emirates owned holiday properties and gardens there was to escape the austerity of the desert landscapes in much of the region. The mother of the present ruler of Fujaira came from Ajman where he grew up, and his wife is from a Dubai family. It was through these women that he gained firsthand knowledge of the other coast and maintained a presence near the seat of power. This was yet another way that "invisible" women exerted political power.

The shaikha of Fujaira held her afternoon audiences in a modest palace. I remember her sunken sitting area that gave an intimacy to gatherings that was not the same in the vast halls of other palaces. Her majlis appeared to be a favorite congregating place for local Emirati and foreign Arab women. The latter included schoolteachers and the wives of other Arabs working in the emirate. Each time I visited, numerous guests dropped by at the conventional late-afternoon "tea-time." At some point during the visit, the shaikha's children would appear and before being whisked off would liven up the gathering with their antics. The friendliness and informality of the gatherings confirmed my impression of the ruler and his wife, that they were warm people in touch with what was going on in their small emirate. When we visited other Fujairans, our hosts always wanted to take us to visit the palace as a special treat.

Ras al-Khaima (RAK) and Um al-Qaiwain (UAQ) were small emirates even though the Qawasim rulers of RAK had once been a major power in the Gulf. I thought of the rulers' wives as a pair, since both came from the same Dubai business family. The first time I visited the UAQ wife, she scolded me for visiting her "sister" the previous day and not coming to her first. She had a lively wit that perhaps was responsible for the whimsical animal-shaped bushes lining the drive to the palace. Certainly her wit kept our conversations light and fun. When my companion mentioned I had written books on the Middle East, she immediately wanted me to write one on UAQ. I said I needed to know them better before writing about them, and she promptly invited me to stay as long as I liked. I always regretted not accepting the invitation.

In RAK, the shaikha was a gracious, dignified presence. Usually several of her daughters sat with her—they were all well educated, with the youngest still in high school. The latest small grandchildren would be brought for a moment before they were removed, and I was always careful to say my mashallas to guard against any evil my compliments might bring. Once when I visited the shaikha, we had such a good time that the leisurely pace of refreshments took longer than usual. Several times her telephone rang, and she adamantly refused a request at the other end. Finally after all the phases of the entertaining were over, she told me the ruler had been calling for some time to say that he and Bill had finished their appointment. The car picked me up from the shaikha's palace and drove the short distance to the ruler's palace. I intended to stay in the car, but Bill beckoned me to meet the kindly old shaikh standing at the top of the stairs. He took me by the arm and brought me back into his audience room to sit next to him and talk for a while. Finally, he got up and with a twinkle in his eye said, "I just wanted to see why my wife was so fascinated by you that she kept us waiting so long." The shaikha agreed to receive me another time, but when I arrived at the palace, she was too ill to see me. I spent the day at the shaikh's palace where Bill and I had lunch with his sons and other family members, and I was very much included in the discussions even though I was the only woman present. The sons, according to convention, remained respectfully silent in the presence of their father except when he spoke directly to them. The shaikha died not long thereafter, and I felt sad that such a lovely woman was gone.

Ajman and Sharja were two emirates that also are linked in my mind, though more because of their geography. Ajman is the smallest of the emirates with a ruling family from the Nuaimi tribe that is also prevalent in Buraimi. On the map, the emirate looks like a bite taken out of Sharja, and when you pass from one emirate to the other, there is no visible way of knowing. The shaikha of Ajman is a young woman who was married to the shaikh after his first wife died. She is from the branch of the Abu Dhabi ruling family that has been socially isolated ever since her grandfather assassinated the father of Abu Dhabi's Shaikh Zaid. She is well mannered, beautiful, and well educated and speaks English fluently. She is very interested in child psychology and development, and our conversation mostly revolved around those subjects.

The shaikha in Sharja is a cousin of the ruler and a very dynamic person in her own right. Her interests lie in establishing services for women, including a large center where women go to use gym facilities, swim, and socialize. She told me that when foreign Arab women were encouraging too Islamicist an atmosphere in the club, she closed it down "for repairs." Her husband is a true scholar with broad-ranging interests. He has a doctorate from Oxford, has written books refuting the characterization of his ancestors as "pirates," and is a collector of old maps. He is credited with bringing libraries, international schools, and first-class museums to his tiny emirate.

I had one problem with these visits to the rulers' wives. Several of the shaikhas insisted on giving me expensive gifts. I wanted to visit them often but feared they might think I came for the gifts. The truth was that I was required to turn the gifts in to the State Department. I explained my predicament to the Emirati protocol officer whom I'd grown to like and suggested she inform the shaikhas that they shouldn't give me gifts—because in any case I couldn't keep them. She was aghast at the implication and assured me the gifts weren't meant to influence me. I told her that of course I knew that was true. The gifts still seemed a problem, however, for even though I agreed with the rule, the manner of handling them didn't address the problem. I couldn't refuse a gift outright or I would have insulted the shaikhas, but since I quietly accepted them, the givers couldn't possibly know I didn't keep them. The price limit of $250 was an annoyance, too, for it meant the embassy had to assess each item. One time Shaikha Fatima sent me a huge tray of chocolates when I broke my arm in a bicycle accident, and the admin officer was at a loss what to do. He decided if I distributed the candy to embassy children, I would have satisfied my obligation to turn the gift in. Several years later it felt like a betrayal when President Clinton took state gifts as he left the White House! The gift I most regretted turning in was a set of Bedouin earrings like those a shaikha's daughter wore at her wedding.

The protocol officer either didn't tell the rulers' wives or they couldn't bring themselves to discontinue the gifts. So I felt obliged to bring gifts to them to make our relationship more reciprocal. But it was hard to think of anything worthy of their status that I could afford. I found some beautifully embroidered white prayer shawls from Pakistan to present to them, hoping the personal nature of the gift made up for its lack of material worth. That worked for one visit, and after that, I resorted to flowers or candy, even though their palaces were equipped with such extravagant bunches of flowers and trays of sweets that my offerings seemed embarrassingly meager. Nevertheless, despite these small problems, I always went away buoyed by the warm hospitality of these women, their daughters, and the grandchildren gathered around them.

⁓

In the spring of 1995, just short of three years after our arrival in Abu Dhabi, Bill resigned from the Foreign Service. He had been offered a position as president of AMIDEAST, an educational and training nongovernmental organization working in the Middle East. His tenure was nearing an end as ambassador, and AMIDEAST with its twenty offices in seven different countries seemed an ideal way to keep in touch with the Arab world.

17

ULTIMATE DESTINATION: AFGHANISTAN UNDER THE TALIBAN (1998, 2000)

fghanistan, the dream destination of my childhood, still remained elusive. During the early years when we might have traveled there, the children were too young. And when it had become easier to travel, Americans were no longer very welcome—during the Soviet occupation from 1979 through the Afghan communist government in 1989, in the early 1990s when Afghan warlords battled each other in Kabul, and after 1996 when the Taliban took control of large swathes of the country.

It was 1998 before the opportunity arrived. The United Nations Children's Fund (UNICEF) education officer for Afghanistan called from Pakistan to say they needed help with Afghan education. By that time the Taliban had consolidated control over all but the northern areas of Afghanistan where the Northern Alliance still held out. The Taliban, as their name "students" implied, were students who had studied in the religious schools of a radical Islamic splinter group called the "Deobandi" that originated in India. Their surprising successes in wresting control from local warlords attracted the interest of the Pakistani secret service whose material support—much of it provided by the CIA—increasingly sustained their activities. It was a complicated time to be going to Afghanistan ,but I didn't hesitate.

The UNICEF officer, Ellen, was calling about the thorny issue of girls' education. One of the Taliban's first actions in 1996 had been to ban girls and female teachers from public schools. In response, many international agencies suspended their education programs, hoping to force the Taliban to retract their ban. Two years later, with no sign they would change their minds, twenty-four organizations involved in Afghan education joined forces to see if they could restart primary education. Ellen wanted me to attend their meeting in Islamabad and, depending on the outcome, identify options that would help them move forward. The organizations included among others DIFED (the British USAID), Ockenden International, Save the Children, and Swedish Afghan Assistance (a group that continued to support 500 or more schools under the Taliban), and a number of Afghan groups that delivered programs inside the country.

The Islamabad meeting ended with three requests. The groups wanted an education project that would coordinate their efforts, that would be accessible to all children, and that would be a solid investment no matter what happened in Afghanistan. I remember the sinking feeling in my stomach as I realized they were looking for a miracle to solve their problems. But I couldn't refuse an opportunity to make a real contribution.

The next few days I interviewed staff of participating organizations in Islamabad and Peshawar to see what they thought could happen and visited refugee schools to learn about internationally supported programs for Afghan children. Simultaneously, I surveyed the participating groups to find out what capacities they had that might be available for a new program. An assistant given to me by a nongovernmental organization (NGO) followed up with an inventory of the organizations' skills. I was struck with the fact that the staff of these organizations seemed strong in adventuresome spirit but weak in any expertise about education. They were mostly young people, effective at getting around obstacles but less interested in discussions about education quality. By that time, I felt strongly that any future program must have as its goal instilling at least a minimum of academic skills.

Ellen and I took the UN plane to Kabul, where we stayed at a Save the Children compound. Within the walls, several small mud-brick and stone buildings were connected with walkways gracefully winding through carefully tended gardens of flowers and fruit trees. The furnishings of the whitewashed rooms were simple and without frills—touching my soul in a very elemental way. We started with a security briefing to teach us to differentiate incoming and outgoing rockets by their whooshing sound. Presumably the sandbags piled near the buildings would protect us from any but direct hits. The shelling luckily remained too far away to differentiate the whooshes. Every morning a lull signaled the time for the UN plane to take off from the airport.

I began interviews with staffs of organizations based in Kabul, including the International Committee of the Red Cross (ICRC), which had continued to support a number of small, privately funded schools. My most important meeting in Kabul was with a group of Afghan and foreign educators at the Afghan Coordinating Body for Afghan Relief (ACBAR). When I asked for advice on understanding education, they told me to do two things—first, to visit the secret girls' schools that Afghan women operated in their homes, and second, to talk to Taliban officials to see what their plans for education were. They warned me my presence in the Afghan homes could endanger the schools and teachers, if known, and added that they weren't sure I could get into the ministry.

That evening I prepared to visit the home schools by trying on blue chadors (the full-body covering women wear) that would be my means of concealment. None of the chadors the Afghans had collected were long enough so they sent out for a longer one that would cover my ankles. When it came, it had the smoky smell of a wood-burning stove. The Afghans explained that I shouldn't don this disguise until I arrived at my destination, since Afghan women were not allowed in international cars.

The next morning a taxi pulled out of a side street, and my car followed. I was dressed as a foreigner with hair covered but face open. We took a circuitous route through Kabul until the taxi stopped and let its passenger out. Our car drove on and after ensuring that no one was watching, circled back to the corner where the woman was waiting. My Afghan helper threw the chador over my head, and I stepped out. Although I could see straight ahead, the light blue silk floated up around me so it was impossible to see my feet. I quickly extracted a hand through a side hole and pressed the folds of silk to my chest. The woman emerged from a doorway without a word, and I walked silently behind her for a few blocks before we ducked into a private home.

For two days I followed the woman from house to house. On the second day, a man escorted me to an apartment block occupied by the Taliban after Soviet officials vacated it. He walked Afghan-style several paces in front of me to show me the correct apartment. Once he hissed at me to watch out and caught me gracefully before I fell over a pole in the pathway. I mentally chalked one up to Afghans for being able to touch a woman in an emergency, unlike the Pakistanis when Mona fell in the river.

The teachers and students in the home schools welcomed me warmly. Most students were young girls, but there was also a sprinkling of small boys. The women seemed to be teaching more effectively than in the usual public schools where memorization was the exclusive means of learning. Indeed, I was told these schools were better in a number of ways. The teachers received supplies and were trained quietly by groups like the ICRC, while in public schools the Taliban neglected to pay teachers' salaries or provide textbooks, and most teachers and students saw no point in attending. The Taliban claimed they were using government resources to win the war in the north and couldn't support education. In any case, they preferred that boys attend religious schools where after graduation they could be recruited to jihad and martyrdom.

The Taliban tolerated the home schools but felt strongly about girls not attending beyond the third grade (or the age of puberty). Girls who were physically small sometimes attended unnoticed, but it was dangerous for taller girls to be seen walking to school. Fourth grade, in any case, was the time when the Afghan curriculum expanded to seven subjects with several requiring trained specialists. The teachers would take a cohort of children through the third grade and then start over with a new group of children. Some older girls simply started over again with the new class. Because children often waited several years before enrolling, they only had a year or two before they reached the Taliban's age limit. It was difficult under these conditions to develop functional literacy.

Something else that attracted my attention was the almost indelible impact of training on teachers. If the trainers—many of them foreign—said a technique was correct, the conscientious Afghan women implemented it whether it made sense or not. A trainer at some point must have told the teachers that students should practice adding numbers both horizontally and vertically. In every math class, teachers wrote problems horizontally and vertically with one number in common to connect the two methods. Children copied their problems in this cumbersome way and never got the point that horizontal was equal to vertical and that both didn't need to be written each time. Teachers would have been more effective if given a list of competencies and told to figure out how to teach them to their own students. I mentioned this to them, but they believed firmly that everything had a right and a wrong way and only experts knew the right way.

I found in these home schools what was true elsewhere in the region, that if I asked children to read sentences from a lesson they hadn't learned yet or to write simple sentences or to do math problems presented in story form, most could not do it. Occasionally when they responded correctly, their teachers were just as surprised as they were. Said one teacher, "Oh, is that what we're supposed to teach?" They were so focused on method, they couldn't see what it was they were trying to accomplish.

My meeting with Taliban ministry officials was more difficult to arrange. An official in the Ministry of Foreign Affairs informed me that the deputy education minister "never sees women." Fortunately a new head of Norwegian Aid had just arrived in Kabul and already had an appointment to present his respects to the minister. He invited me to come along as "his delegation." Perhaps he was too new to know what he was doing.

The crowd of men at the ministry entrance went silent when I trailed in behind the large Norwegian and his Afghan translator. Too late, the gate man saw me and started shouting and waving his hands, but Islamic taboos prevented him from touching me. The minister's secretary also complained, but our translator prevailed on him to remember Afghan hospitality, and he finally let me sit at the far back of the minister's office.

As if prompted by my presence, the minister launched into a discussion of girls' education. He said the Taliban were not against girls' schooling but planned to establish proper sex-segregated education once they had conquered the north. He noted ominously that "nothing was invisible to the Taliban," implying that they were aware of the secret home schools. As long as girls didn't go beyond third grade, he said, the Taliban wouldn't interfere. Several weeks later the foreign press announced that the home schools were closed, but they failed to note that the schools opened again a few weeks later.

I sat listening to the minister's remarks feeling strangely sympathetic. He looked to be in his late twenties—the age of my sons—and was struggling to appear dignified and say weighty things. He was dressed in Taliban dress but the cloth seemed finer than most, and he had an impressively large turban of subdued colors. I felt he was observing me through his opaque sunglasses. One funny episode occurred when a servant brought a platter of fruit for us. He set it down in front of me with a knife, expecting me to peel the apples for the men. I said I didn't care for any fruit—making it a breach of decorum that he had offered me hospitality before the men. Since women normally don't eat with men, I was not amiss in refusing. The men were embarrassingly left to peel their own apples.

After Kabul, Ellen and I traveled on the rough road to Jalalabad, a journey that once took less than two hours but now took eight. We traveled according to UN regulations in two vehicles with an Afghan staff member radioing our office in Kabul every half hour. We had been warned that there would be no bathroom stops along the way because of land mines dotting the sides of the road. Splashes of red paint on rocks, seemingly everywhere, indicated where mines still existed. Several Afghans a day died from explosions, and one of Save the Children's most creative projects was to establish safe playgrounds around Kabul for children. Along the road were remains of tanks and whole villages destroyed in retaliation for attacks on the Soviet military.

Before going to Islamabad, I had read as much as I could about education in Afghanistan. I knew that modern education, as opposed to Koranic education, was started in the mid-nineteenth century (1868) by Amir Sher Ali who was also founder of the nation-state of Afghanistan. The system grew under his successors until it reached its peak during the reign of Amanullah, who became emir in 1919. This colorful gentleman set up eight foreign language schools, including three for girls, where elite urban students studied. He was such an admirer of the West that he insisted upon Afghan tribal leaders wearing top hats and tails during their *loya jirga* meetings. He was assassinated in 1929 largely because of his pro-Western reforms. Girls' schools closed and modern education declined while the parallel religious system flourished.

Over the next decades, there was an increasing involvement of pro-communist Afghans until, in 1979, the Soviets finally occupied the country. By that time, Afghanistan had one of the lowest literacy rates in the world with few rural residents able to read or write, although many attended religious schools where they memorized the Koran in the foreign language of Arabic. Modern schooling opportunities, including institutions of higher learning, were only available for elites in the main cities.

When the Soviets arrived, they reserved special privileges for the ethnic groups they considered natural allies. In the north, they stressed the commonality of cultures bordering nations in Soviet Central Asia. In the resistant southeastern Pathan areas, they sought to depopulate the land by destroying irrigation systems, bombing villages, and creating a kind of random terror. These were the areas that later spawned the Taliban, and once they were victorious, where they found sympathy for their activities. The oppressive tactics of the Soviets intensified in the mid-1980s when they started thinking about withdrawing. To increase their control, they forced rural villagers to move to cities by withholding services and randomly bombing their villages.

Schools were a major instrument of Soviet policy. The Russians rewrote schoolbooks to include pro-communist content and required students to take special courses in Soviet ideology. Although they didn't ban religion, they discouraged it. Whereas Dari had been the language of instruction before, the Russians printed schoolbooks in Dari, Pashto, Usbek, Turkic, and Baluch as a means of intensifying the divisions among ethnic communities. Dari remained the lingua franca in the north and Russian replaced all foreign languages. Pedagogically the schoolbooks may not have been so bad, but their ideological content made some parents reluctant to send children to school.

When Afghans resisted these changes, the Soviets established a program to educate children in boarding schools in the Soviet Union where they could be fully immersed in Soviet ideology and culture. Between 1980 and 1985, more than 50,000 Afghan students were sent—many forcibly—to the Soviet Union, and 20,000 of these children were between the ages of four and eight. They were expected to return to Afghanistan as indoctrinated adults to implement communist practice, but many were never seen again. During the Soviet era, the total number of primary schools decreased 82 percent to only 210 schools. In 1978 there had been 1,400 schools in rural areas, but by 1984 there were no schools located outside cities (data from 1978 to 1984). A similar decline was found in middle, high, technical, and teacher training schools. So many male teachers were jailed, killed, or fled to avoid conscription and so many boys abducted, that for a time the upper grades held mainly girl students and female teachers.

Eventually we reached Jalalabad and spent several days looking at schools. One was a tent school for refugees where again I had the impression that although the school was extremely well organized, the program lacked a focus on academic skills. The students were eager and the teachers motivated, but the content of their programs left much to be desired. When I pointed out the discrepancies between the declared intent of teaching and the result of these programs, it left little impression on their thinking, so entrenched was the fixation on rote methods and the authority of the printed word.

In Jalalabad, we spent a day with an Afghan family with ties to the UN. They gave us insights into how educated Afghans coped under Taliban rule. Two daughters in the family had been in medical school and close to graduating when the Taliban banned girls from continuing. Now they stayed at home watching TV programs brought to them by an illegal satellite dish hidden in the garden, and video movies passed clandestinely from family to family. The father gave us a tour of Jalalabad, pointing out a place where the week before, the Taliban had arrested a group of men for not wearing the skullcaps that were decreed a necessary part of male attire. He pointed out men peddling vegetables and other goods who, he said, were university professors trying to earn money to keep their families alive. We stopped at an outdoor market where families with no other income were similarly selling beautiful antiques and textiles for almost nothing.

The next day I drove the length of Kunar Province, one of the areas where Usama Bin Laden was later said to have taken refuge. Accompanying me was an elderly government official who had been appointed by the Taliban for his experience in education. We passed through rich agricultural valleys contained by craggy cliffs and mountain ranges where gun emplacements indicated the true nature of the activity in the hills. Guerrillas were said to fire down on these roads and kidnap local Taliban officials. We stopped at schools supported by German assistance money where the curriculum and teaching were much better than in other programs, although it still required considerable ongoing training in "modern methods of instruction." Again it seemed there must be an easier way to establish programs in remote regions that didn't depend so much on training. The idea of developing self-evident textbooks that explicitly taught basic skills seemed the best option for these conditions. Further on we stopped at a community school and were minimally welcomed since we had interrupted the religious lessons that were the mainstay of the school. They weren't quite sure what to do about me but fell back on the default mode of offering Afghan hospitality. Further on in Assadabad, we saw a compound surrounding a small field where the Soviets one day gathered the men of the town and gunned them down. Tragedies like this seem too much to even comprehend.

The elderly Afghan official who had avoided any contact with me up until then kindly asked me to join the men for lunch on the floor of an office space. I accepted, knowing it was a generous offer that could compromise him in front of his men. He unwrapped a newspaper full of hot fried fish that hit the spot in the cold mountain air.

In the lush agricultural areas near Jalalabad, the farmers were harvesting their crops, and at each farm an armed Taliban soldier waited to take a tenth as the Taliban's share. A pro-Western Afghan who pointed this out to me accompanied me at this point. I asked him if I could exchange a dollar for Afghan coins for my coin-collecting postmaster back home. He reached into his pocket and handed me a thick wad of bills for my dollar, explaining that people rarely used coins since they were worthless.

The next day, our UN vehicles deposited us at the border, where with our UN credentials we easily moved into the Khyber Pass and down to Peshawar. The trip, although short, had in every way been satisfying—meeting my expectations for scenery, professional interest, and the opportunity to meet interesting Afghans. All the Afghans I met were correct with me, including Taliban officials, and sometimes even friendly. Back in our guesthouse, Ellen and I talked until late at night about what I had seen, with Ellen adding details I might have missed. I began formulating ideas for the report, and she helped me see where I was on solid ground or asking too much of the assistance groups. We shared a passion for getting it right, and our long friendship allowed us to talk freely.

Despite the obstacles created by the Taliban, there was one decided advantage of working in Afghanistan—we didn't have to deal with the bureaucratic hurdles that were a major difficulty of working in much of the developing world. The Taliban generally ignored the projects of international groups, especially those of the UN, knowing that without their services the civilian population might become restive. As one Afghan put it, "If you ask the Taliban, they will say no. If you don't, you can do almost anything." Certainly the Taliban and their sympathizers were everywhere and knew what was going on. An Afghan I dropped in on in his UN office in Peshawar quizzed me about my ideas on education before I went to Kabul. On my last day, he said, "The Taliban would have no problems with your approach. I'll tell them so they won't bother you in Kabul."

The trip was over. The pleasures of moving through the various landscapes —the bleak mountains in Kabul, the rugged mountain passes down to Jalalabad, the lush-well-watered valleys of Kunar—remain a vivid memory. I felt exhilarated by the chance to help Afghans improve their education program. Surprising as it might seem, there was every reason to believe at the time that with the funding of foreign organizations, we could produce a first-rate primary system even under a Taliban regime. It took several years for this hope to die as a result of American politics.

The briefing on my conclusions went well in Islamabad. The hall was filled with members of the organizations present in the initial meeting, as well as others who traveled from Peshawar and Kabul. I explained, using PowerPoint slides, what I had found out in my interviews and observations and showed them charts prepared by my assistant of the capacities of the existing organizations. I ended with the options I believed met the requirements they had charged me with.

Although there were several options, the most compelling was also quite simple—a program based entirely on children's textbooks that could be delivered anywhere children wanted to learn and a literate person was available to teach. The books would include instructions for teachers and lesson formats similar to those that had proven effective in rural areas of Pakistan. A major focus was delivery—how to get the books to where they were needed and how to use them effectively once there. The delivery systems would address the special conditions of Afghanistan: the remote villages, the absence of school buildings, teachers with only minimal education who could not travel for training, and supervisors who only rarely visited schools. Competency exams would make it possible for children to receive credit equal to the grade levels in a formal system.

All this was put in a written report along with other alternatives including ways to increase enrollments or build the capacity of Afghans to make their own reforms. Ellen took the options to the Afghans at the Peshawar branch of ACBAR and asked them to decide. They chose improving the quality of the program and basically incorporating everything we suggested—training, skill competencies, and assessment—into textbooks that could be delivered anywhere in Afghanistan. Many wanted the "quality option" because they were unhappy with the books being used in Afghan classrooms. These books had been developed in the 1980s under a USAID contract to the Afghan Center at the University of Nebraska at Omaha (UNO). The main aim of the books was to support the *muja-hidiin* (warlord) leaders in their efforts to repulse the Soviets from Afghanistan.

Consequently, they were designed not as effective teaching tools but as propaganda weapons. Almost every page was filled with militaristic images and examples (five Kalashnikovs plus two Klashnikovs equal seven Kalasnikovs) and encouragements to perform jihad against the Soviet oppressors. The primary books included several exclusively devoted to Muslim religious practices (even though U.S. law prohibits taxpayers' moneys from paying for such materials). Supporters of the books argued that the aim of repelling the Soviets justified the violent, religious nature of their content.

I often watched teachers using the books in classrooms and—putting aside their content—was dismayed at how little they taught children. Nebraska officials claimed it was just a matter of training to make the books more effective, but experience showed that teachers couldn't compensate for all their defects. One measure of the books was that the Taliban approved them for their schools once pictures of humans were deleted.

Over the next several years, UNICEF followed up by funding an international specialist on curriculum development—my friend Mona. She conducted a series of workshops where seventy Afghan educators prepared a curriculum framework and wrote the core books for primary math and language arts. The language arts materials included content on Afghan history, culture, science, and life skills. The Afghans wanted to add religious content, but Mona refused, feeling there were enough primary books on religion.

The Afghans working on the project proved exceptionally dedicated, but two women deserve special attention. Ellen sent letters out across Afghanistan for Afghans experienced in education to work on primary materials, but on the day Mona's workshop opened neither she nor Ellen knew how many would show up. At the hotel the first day in Peshawar, one recruit was patiently waiting in the lobby. She was carrying a baby and was accompanied by her eleven-year-old nephew. Halima had taken a bus from Mazar-al-Sharif, around 300 miles away, down to the Pakistani border, walked over the mountains because she had no passport, and continued by bus the rest of the way. Her husband had died shortly before, and she had left four other children with relatives. Her nephew served as her male escort (as the Taliban required), and while she was working, he cared for the baby. She turned out to be one of the best writers in the workshop.

The second woman, Razia, had the same kind of determination. She was a refugee living in Peshawar. There, she had managed to finish high school, teach herself English, and learn computer skills. Her father was dead, and her mother was determined to preserve Razia's reputation so she could marry respectably. Razia was a quiet, unassuming leader in any group she joined, even while respectfully giving credit to the mostly older males. When the workshop moved to distant Islamabad, her mother said Razia could no longer attend because she would have to stay overnight. Razia negotiated a compromise whereby she would return home each night. She left the house in the morning in time to take the three-hour bus ride to Islamabad and returned on the bus in time to reach home before dark. Again she proved a quiet leader in the work and was acknowledged as such by all the men. Several years later she was offered a scholarship to go to a U.S. college, but again her mother refused, until she married a cousin and the two went together to the United States. I lost track of her but always hoped it worked out well for her.

Razia and Halima were no more dedicated than the men on the project, but the obstacles they overcame were greater. I was touched by these Afghans who wanted so much to contribute to their country and have never been able to reconcile the harsh media images of Afghans with the gentle, scholarly Afghans that made up our group.

During my Afghan trip in 1998, an NGO asked if I would evaluate the education programs for Afghan girls in refugee villages of Balochistan. In 2000 I traveled to Quetta to spend a few days learning about the home-based girls' program. In the NGO office, I sought out the respected senior Afghan adviser and asked him to describe the program. Dr. A. and I spent a day looking over the materials and procedures used in running the schools. One procedure involved testing teacher candidates to decide who should be hired. In the chaos of the previous decades, many Afghan teachers had lost the documents that proved their academic and professional training, and the organization had to develop its own methods of assessing their capabilities. The tests for language arts included the usual memory items, including one I remember that asked for the birth date of the Virgin Mary! The math tests were the tricky kind with multiple parts—if the answer was wrong it was not possible to know whether the teacher didn't know the concept or had simply made a computational error. The teachers with the least poor grades were hired anyway.

These exams were similar to those given students. Since tests drive teaching and learning, they are crucial in shaping education programs. Their emphasis on memorized facts was doing nothing to encourage the teaching of basic skills. Dr. A., in creating them, was just following the accepted pattern. "Experts" reinforced this problem by ignoring instructional materials and exams and stressing teacher training in "touchy-feely approaches"—the child-centered methods popular in the United States but impossible to implement in the different circumstances of Afghanistan. The teacher-directed approaches of the Afghans were not necessarily bad and, with some modification, could have been effective.

One afternoon I gave a "seminar" for the female Afghan supervisors. I asked them to write a list of the characteristics of a good teacher. The list included characteristics like "follows training by developing lesson plans and using materials as told, checks attendance, has a polite demeanor, is neat in appearance, keeps a clean classroom, and disciplines the class." When I asked if student performance should be used to evaluate a teacher, they said, "No. If teachers possess these characteristics they are bound to be good." This answer paralleled foreign experts' views that if "enlightened" methods were used, students would learn. No one looked empirically at whether or not this was true.

I asked them if they had two teachers, one with all the characteristics they mentioned but whose students did poorly on exams, and another who had none of these good qualities but whose students did well on exams which they would judge the better teacher. They preferred the teacher with the proper characteristics but noted that such a case was impossible. Although I didn't convince them then, the lesson apparently sank in because on one school visit they teased me when I praised a teacher whose students performed well, saying, "Yes, we know the most important point is student learning."

We decided to visit schools in four of the seven refugee villages. There were two types of school—formal refugee schools and home-based girls' schools. Everyone believed the home-based schools were inferior. The classes were held in the homes of female teachers who usually did not meet the academic qualifications required of teachers in formal schools. Most also did not meet professional training standards. Most had been homeschooled, which meant they had no diplomas to document their schooling. Their salaries, based on qualifications, were considerably lower. This might have been a savings to the program were it not for the costly supervision program that supported them. The school day was also an hour shorter than in the formal schools, and the academic year extended over ten instead of eleven months. These characteristics, like those of the "ideal teacher," were assumed to produce inferior teaching. I too was expecting less diligence from students and teachers working in the informality of private homes.

It was therefore a pleasant surprise to find an atmosphere of great industry when I made surprise visits to the classrooms. In each school roughly twenty-five girls sat on plastic mats with the teacher sitting among them or standing by a blackboard to demonstrate a concept. Each child worked on a slate with chalk. Most of the teachers were well organized, and there was less rote learning than I had seen in other schools. The congenial atmosphere and the intent focus of the children impressed me. A telltale sign was that they barely looked up when I entered the room. During breaks, several told me proudly that they were the first in their families to learn to read and write and that their families called on them frequently to read medicine bottles or religious pamphlets. One could imagine how satisfying that might be to a little girl. They all claimed to want to become doctors and teachers. There was an informal atmosphere with teachers and students working together to solve problems in their books, and a few times I even saw a student correct a teacher who didn't seem to mind the challenge.

One teacher pointed out a ten-year-old girl who had been married the previous week to a blind man. The old man needed someone to care for him, and the girls' family was so poor that for the cost of a dowry they gave her to him. She missed a couple of classes but was now back in school. Her eyes were alive with the excitement of learning, but otherwise she showed nothing of what must have been a traumatic week for her.

The home schools offered the community several advantages even before considering their quality. They provided virtually the only salaried employment for women in the chronically low-income families and the only "role model" of working women for girls. Home schools were fairly invisible in times of turmoil, while the formal schools attracted the negative attention of the increasingly Talibanized villagers. We saw two cases where family feuds closed formal schools for several days while home schools in the same villages remained open with girls from both factions attending.

There was also the fact that home schools provided the only chance of schooling for many girls. Some were too old to enter the formal school, or the formal school was too distant, or there were male teachers, or parents feared they might be "annoyed" by boys on their way to school. A substantial number of parents simply didn't believe in schooling for girls, but they might succumb to the overtures of a kindly woman neighbor who promised to take care of the girls. That their fears were not exaggerated was brought home to me in one village when people told me about a girl and boy who had been noticed looking at each other from a distance and perhaps even exchanging a note as they walked home from school. The bodies of the two had been found a week earlier, and no one dared object because of the growing influence of the Taliban.

There were, of course, also disadvantages to home schools. With only one teacher carrying the class through the grades, she had to be strong academically or the girls would suffer. The program had not been implemented long enough to know what would happen at grade four when more difficult subject specialties would need to be taught.

I returned to Quetta and briefed the staff on my findings. I told them I was impressed by the comfortable little schools and their dedicated teachers and students, but that I couldn't definitively say whether they were better in terms of learning than formal schools because I had no data to compare them. I recommended not waiting to open more home schools because the girls were clearly benefitting. I suggested a few obvious ways to improve quality including that supervisors look more at learning results than ticking off whether teachers were neat, polite, or properly distributing supplies. Finally, I made the strong recommendation that a study be made using learning as a measure to assess how well the refugee schools were doing. The staff of the organization was pleased with the report and accepted the idea of doing a quantitative study of student learning.

I had not intended to be the one to do the next study, which would require someone with more skills in data processing. But soon another consultant, John, and I were asked to compare the results of student learning in three types of refugee schools: home schools, co-ed formal schools, and girls-only formal schools. While the supervisors administered tests and John supervised data entry, I visited classrooms to identify the three kinds of "classroom cultures."

With the observations of home schools fresh in my mind, it was easy to see what might prove a weakness in the formal schools. I discussed these points with the supervisors, and soon they too were picking up possible problems. There were "blind spots" where teachers rarely called upon students either because they didn't notice them—the children didn't raise their hands—or they knew they generally answered questions incorrectly and the teacher didn't want to "waste time" with them. The blind spots tended to be in the back of the room, the front row below the teachers' eye level, or, in a mixed class, where girls congregated. There were other problems, too, when teachers called on students in a predictable pattern, or certain classes were shortchanged by always being scheduled after lunch break.

John came to me with the results of the testing, and I was pleased to see the homeschool students doing consistently and significantly better than those in the formal schools. Teachers' formal qualifications—academic and professional—had no significant influence on student results as I predicted. Obviously something in the "culture of home schools" was working and producing better results than in the formal schools.

The visits left me with a strong feeling of sympathy for Afghans in the refugee villages of Balochistan. At that time in 2000, many were considering going back to Afghanistan because life in the villages was proving so difficult. Although the United Nations High Commissioner for Refugees provided health clinics and schools, families needed to support themselves, and in these remote areas few jobs were available. Most of the inhabitants had previously been farmers, but here the soil was too arid, and even drinking water had to be brought in by truck. The men either worked in distant cities in manual jobs or smuggled commodities and drugs by truck between Pakistan and Afghanistan. There were few alternatives. A woman whose home I visited lamented the many adolescent boys becoming drug addicted with so little to do.

They were vulnerable in other ways too. One teacher told me sadly that his most brilliant student had gone home one day with a fever and within twenty-four hours was dead. The clinic was too far, and his parents had decided too late that he needed a doctor. "What illness took him?" I asked. "It was God's Will," the teacher answered. As we traveled from one school to another, we heard about an Ebola outbreak killing people in the villages we visited. "Shouldn't we find out where it is?" I asked nervously. "Everything is up to God," they answered, and we went on. Another day we went to see why a crowd was gathering near the school. A truck had accidentally struck the house next door, collapsing a wall and killing the child of the driver. Dreadful things happened all the time in these villages, and there seemed little anyone could do about them.

Still, there were moments of great caring I won't forget. Our driver disappeared after work one day and drove back to a school we had visited earlier so he could take the caretaker's wife—a complete stranger—to a clinic because she was bleeding from a pregnancy gone wrong. He stayed with her until she was finished, paid the expenses, and then took her home. I often saw this almost feminine quality in Afghan men whose hearts seemed very close to their sleeves in their empathy for others.

I still retain a memory of the almost childlike exuberance of the staff after we completed our study and were on our way home. "Stop," commanded one as we passed a lush orchard. He said, "Put on the cassette," and they—the men, that is—were soon dancing in a slow circle with their shawls spinning in the air. I found this trip to be one of those magical consultancies with hard work, a significant problem to solve, good discussions, a spectacular venue, and, best of all, good companions.

18

FINISH LINE:
AFGHANISTAN AFTER THE INVASION
(2001–2002)

Ireturned home thinking it was my last chance to work in Afghanistan. But it was spring 2001, and unbeknownst to me, a storm was brewing more powerful than anything anyone had imagined. When it struck on that memorable September 11, the lives of Americans changed forever. Although no Afghans had been aboard the planes that slammed into the World Trade Center, they were soon at the center of world attention. Most of the hijackers turned out to be Saudis, supported by another Saudi, Usama Bin Laden, the leader of al-Qaeda. For some time, Bin Laden had threatened Arab regimes that he felt were not Islamic enough and the United States for supporting them. When he was expelled from the Sudan for plotting terrorist acts, the Taliban welcomed him to Afghanistan where he previously played a role in ousting the Russians. Bin Laden and the Taliban shared many of the same radical views, and it didn't hurt that he brought a multimillion-dollar fortune with him.

During 2000 and early 2001, international staff had seen al-Qaeda's influence in Afghanistan growing. The Taliban showed more rigid and consistent oversight of their work and insisted that all UN female Muslim staff, even if foreign, be accompanied by a *mehram* (a male family member). Girls' schools that were tolerated before were suddenly shut down, and this time the decision was not reversed.

After 9/11 the Taliban refused to surrender their al-Qaeda "guests" in what locals viewed as a natural adherence to Pushtunwali codes of hospitality and protection. The Americans, with the help of the Northern Alliance, reacted

281

by striking the Taliban. In a matter of days, the Taliban and al-Qaeda fled to Pakistan, and a new Afghan Interim Government was established in Kabul. At this moment, Ellen called again to say UNICEF was gearing up for the post-Taliban era and asked if I could help. I was only too willing to return. I had good reports from Mona about the curriculum workshops and hoped we could introduce the new materials into the Afghan schools when they reopened. Perhaps a high-quality education program was indeed within sight.

During the fall of 2001, the drafts of the new textbooks were still being edited in one of the organizations that had supported their development. Ellen went to see why, after six months, the books were not ready and found that a Western staff member had rewritten much of the math books to, as she said, "make them consistent." But not only had she changed the format and the sequence of objectives Mona and the Afghans had so carefully worked out, but she had also substituted her own math problems with answers that in some cases were computed incorrectly! We felt lucky she didn't know Pashto or Dari and therefore had left the editing of the language arts books to her Afghan staff.

Still, we had a crisis on our hands. The Afghans were proud of their work, and Mona had promised that their names would appear on the covers of the books. When they learned the math books were barely recognizable, they were furious and no longer wanted to be associated with them. For us it was a huge disappointment in what had been a carefully worked-out effort to put Afghans in charge of the work. Soon Mona found a copy of the originals, and the Afghans managed to restore them to their earlier form.

The books were ready to publish just as I arrived to help with post-Taliban planning in November 2001. In quieter times we had planned a period of testing, but the sudden need for the already delayed books left us no time. We were fairly confident they would work because of the similar books we had tested in 700 classes of NWFP in the early 1990s under similar conditions. And the teaching approach had been identified through BRIDGES studies of Pakistani classrooms, also under much the same conditions.

First, though, we were occupied with more immediate needs. To prepare for the post-Taliban period, UNICEF convened Afghan experts in education, health, women's issues, and child protection. Notes of their brainstorming were kept in English, and I, among others helped them prepare drafts of "vision" papers for their sectors. When the drafts were completed, we reconvened the groups to refine and finalize the reports. One of the most interesting was "The Framework for the Role of Women." The paper stressed the importance for Afghan women of education opportunities, health services, and legal protections, and pleaded with the international community not to impose Western models of gender roles upon Afghans. The Afghans felt these models would only solidify the resistance of traditionalists in Afghan society. Change, they said, would come about once the population was educated. As one put it, "If you send illiterate women to work they'll end up doing unskilled jobs, like construction, on top of everything else they do."

The education "vision" paper was endorsed unanimously by ACBAR, including parts that called for using the Basic Competency (BC) books Mona and her group had prepared. The World Bank (WB), the Asian Development Bank (ADB), and the United Nations Development Program (UNDP) in meetings on reconstruction also endorsed the paper. The paper was similarly circulated at subsequent Bonn, Berlin, and Brussels conferences on Afghanistan where again it was well received. Several recommendations, including the one about the Afghan BC materials, became part of the WB/ADB/UNDP preliminary needs assessment presented at the Tokyo meetings on Afghanistan. No objection was encountered on any front to the new materials, and most in the assistance community felt certain they would become the core textbooks for Afghan schools until the Ministry of Education established its long-term needs.

The immediate reason to prepare the papers was for Afghans to have something to present at the first international conference on Afghanistan held in Islamabad in December 2001. Ellen protested that only a handful of Afghans had been invited to the meeting to plan the future of their own country, and in the end, the roughly fifty Afghan invitees were inundated by more than 250 foreign experts. A well-known Afghan radio broadcaster, Shirazuddin Siddiqi, presented the education paper eloquently, stressing the importance of Afghans being involved in the planning. An Afghan woman presented the paper on "Women" and was cheered by the audience as if an Afghan woman appearing in public were something special. We had seen so many competent Afghan women working in NGOs during the Taliban period that it seemed patronizing to lionize this one woman, but it showed Westerners' stereotypic images of Muslim women.

The frameworks were soon forgotten despite their warm reception at all the planning conferences. We didn't realize at the time that we were seeing the self-interest of countries and organizations that would overcome any effort to plan rationally for Afghanistan's future. The real issues on the table were: who would control what happened in Afghanistan and how could the agenda be shaped to ensure roles for the countries in attendance. The participants had little interest in the substance of reform, although they listened politely to earnest papers like ours that assumed development was the main issue. They might still have supported the education vision the Afghans presented had not the United States intervened in its own interest.

Several Afghans asked Ellen for information on how other countries addressed the education problems they knew they would face in the post-Taliban period. So I wrote a paper for UNICEF taking education issues one by one and summarizing various options that had been used to address them, and suggesting the ones that might be most useful in the Afghan context. Looking back at that booklet, entitled *Models, Policy Options, and Strategies: A Discussion Paper in Support of Afghan Education*, I see how little of what I recommended was ever implemented. Again it was a matter of assistance agencies looking not at what made sense for Afghanistan but at what would give their organizations and countries recognition in international circles.

The Afghans found little response to their requests as well. Afghan delegates stressed the importance of creating a general fund that could be used to rebuild infrastructure and pay the administrative costs of establishing a government. Again the foreigners listened politely but were not interested in funds they would not control. They wanted visible contributions and, more important, they wanted their contributions repatriated in contracts for consultants and commodities from their own countries. Merging their moneys with funds from other countries would subvert these goals.

In my opinion, it was the failure to implement three commonsense recommendations described in the *Models* paper that prevented the development of an effective education program in Afghanistan. The first mistake was to stress, as USAID did, school construction over academic programs. Children were forced to wait for school buildings before a government program would be provided, and consequently, some would never enroll. Furthermore, new schools were built in heavily populated areas, where they aggravated the already large urban-rural disparities. The second mistake was the failure to coordinate the components of education—including books, training, and assessment—in a way that produced academic competencies. They were instead farmed out piecemeal to different countries and organizations. The third mistake was the emphasis on formal government programs at the expense of informal programs and, with it, the destruction of considerable existing community capacity. Rural teachers returned to their salaried positions in urban areas, and informal community schools went unrecognized by the government. At far less cost, there could have been a more inclusive and better education program if these mistakes had been avoided.

A trickle of refugees began returning to Afghanistan in the late 1990s and increased to a flood after 2001. Many returned with literacy skills to villages that had never seen schooling before. With modest support, these returnees could easily have started education programs, but instead the government set rigid qualifications for teachers that most could not meet. Also if a system had existed to give academic credit to students completing various grades, parents would have had an incentive to continue financing community schools. Literacy was important at one level, but students needed diplomas to qualify for the secondary and university training that led to jobs. By the time a credit system was devised for an accelerated program, the effort was too late and too little. These were just some of the frustrations in the effort to develop Afghan education.

~~~~

Meanwhile, a political storm was brewing that would ultimately affect the Afghan materials. When I returned to Washington in December 2001, I briefed USAID's Afghanistan Task Force on the new materials and UNICEF's efforts to incorporate them into the post-Taliban education system. USAID had previously refused all invitations ACBAR extended to coordinate plans for Afghan education, and we were afraid USAID might act unilaterally. What surprised me at the briefing was the spirited defense by some USAID officers of the University of Nebraska's work of almost twenty years before. I made clear that although there might have been some excuse for the politicized Nebraska textbooks in the 1980s when the aim was to oust the Soviets, it was time to change the books since they contained violent and inflammatory content and, moreover, were ineffective in teaching children. One officer said, "Well, Nebraska always completed their contracts on time and within budget." This was so off-track I was speechless. The issue was not whether Nebraska fulfilled contracts years ago, but whether Afghan children would have a first-class education now that quality materials were available. The fact that the new Afghan materials addressed the unique needs of Afghanistan, were gender balanced, and included life skills content—all features USAID professed to promote worldwide—didn't seem to matter. Their resistance left me feeling there was an agenda I was not aware of.

Looking back, I believe that the effort to control Afghan education was part of a larger U.S. scheme in which Nebraska was a small but important player. The United States had made overtures to Taliban leaders to build a pipeline through Afghanistan that would carry oil more cheaply to Western consumers. In a goodwill measure, the United States (through an American oil company) supported an office for the University of Nebraska group in Peshawar and staffed it with a skeleton group of Afghans. Nebraska's connections with the oil company and powerful politicians in Washington almost certainly affected how USAID perceived Afghan education in the early days after U.S. occupation.

In early January, UNICEF proposed a Back-to-School (BTS) initiative to the minister of education in the Afghan Interim Government, saying UNICEF would provide the materials and supplies for all teachers and students when the new school year started on March 23—the opening day for cold areas of Afghanistan. On January 9, UNICEF met again with the minister to get final approval for the initiative. The plan was to use the Afghan Basic Competency materials for math and language arts in grades one through six, and Nebraska materials in subjects where no BC materials were available—religion in grades one through three and five additional subject specialties in grades four through six. The deputy minister gave oral permission to UNICEF to begin printing enough books for the 1.75 million children expected to enroll on the first day of school, telling UNICEF that he would send an official letter the next day confirming the agreement. On the basis of this oral agreement and because time was short, UNICEF contracted virtually all the printing capacity of Pakistan, and a large UNICEF logistics team flew in to rent warehouses and contract planes, trucks, and even donkeys for the operation to distribute materials.

The letter from the minister, however, did not arrive for more than a month, on February 19, after it was too late to stop printing the materials. Contrary to his oral agreement with UNICEF, the minister now said the Nebraska materials must be used as the main textbooks in Afghan schools and UNICEF was only authorized to supply non-textbook materials. UNICEF complained to USAID that there would be a duplication of effort if Nebraska books were also provided and reiterated that the Nebraska books were pedagogically poor and had objectionable content.

Ellen and I attended a meeting of ACBAR on February 7 to describe the UNICEF BTS plans. We learned at that meeting that USAID had approached members of ACBAR to review and delete politically objectionable content from the Nebraska materials. So far the member groups had refused because of their commitment to the BC materials. Most felt the problems with the Nebraska materials couldn't be corrected, and in any case there was no point since the much better BC materials were now available. We realized with a sinking feeling that it was only a matter of time before one of the chronically underfunded Afghan groups would agree to the editing. There was also the point that although ACBAR was the generally recognized clearinghouse for activities related to Afghan education, USAID staff who had never attended its meetings were unlikely to seek its approval or feel constrained by its wishes, no matter how many international or Afghan organizations disagreed with them. And that indeed is what happened—just one more example of American hubris and the penchant for acting unilaterally without regard for others' opinions.

USAID's sudden interest in the objectionable content of the Nebraska materials undoubtedly was linked to a photo in the U.S. newspapers showing Laura Bush standing in front of a display of Nebraska books, announcing that USAID would pay for textbooks for the children of Afghanistan. Once the president's wife was involved, USAID couldn't take chances that criticism of the content might become public. They sent an official, Chris, out to expedite the matter and gave him the authority to make decisions about the materials. In our initial meetings in Islamabad, he seemed to agree that the new textbooks should be used for language arts and math, and Nebraska books for other subjects. He showed us a Nebraska wall chart with Islamic slogans that he said was not suitable for children. We agreed to meet him in Peshawar a week later, after he visited the Nebraska Center there. We discovered in the meantime, however, that he had contracted an Afghan group to expunge the objectionable parts of the Nebraska materials. When we arrived for the meeting in Peshawar, we found Afghans busy deleting inappropriate parts of the books—"sections related to violence, critical of other countries such as the Soviet Union, and demeaning to women." The Afghans told us that most pages in the language arts textbooks had to have portions deleted. The math books were easier to repair because balls could replace guns. But substitutions were not possible in the language arts materials, which were already of dubious pedagogical quality and only became worse when large sections were inked out.

USAID and UNICEF met with the minister in Kabul the following week. UNICEF asked Chris to propose the compromise he had suggested earlier of not duplicating materials, but he refused. It soon became clear that USAID planned to print all the Nebraska materials. The minister decided that both sets of materials would go to the schools at the same time and warned UNICEF not to send its materials in advance of the Nebraska materials. Nebraska didn't have the capacity to distribute its materials so the minister insisted that UNICEF distribute the Nebraska materials as well. This was adding insult to injury for us, and although UNICEF felt forced to agree, we were afraid Nebraska materials wouldn't be ready in time for the opening of schools.

Nebraska had a long-standing arrangement that its materials could only be printed in its own small press in Peshawar, and therefore it seemed impossible that such a large order could be ready on time. Its monopoly on the printing of the books meant it also profited from them. When another contractor later published the books in more durable versions, the costs turned out to be only a fraction of what Nebraska had been charging USAID. Now Nebraska had to produce enough books for more than 1.5 million children with multiple books for each child (eighteen titles for grades one through three and forty-two titles for grades four through six). By the end of February Nebraska announced it could only produce 100,000 copies of each title—a small fraction of the number needed. Meanwhile USAID realized that several of the Nebraska books were Islamic books and asked UNICEF to pay for them to avoid the potential scandal of it becoming known that U.S. taxpayer money was being spent on religious books. UNICEF refused. It had spent a great deal of money printing Nebraska titles that had to be discarded because they were no longer the approved versions. At the last minute, USAID funded the Islamic books to avoid angering the Afghans. During this time, UNICEF tried to schedule meetings with the minister to clarify issues related to the BTS program, but he was never available because, as we were told, he was in Peshawar with his friend, the previous deputy director of the Nebraska Center, working on the printing of the Nebraska books. In my view, the whole thing seemed unbelievably unsavory, but the worst part was the callous disregard for the needs of Afghan children.

In the midst of these distractions, I continued working on the teacher orientation for the BC books, which was the main reason for my coming to Afghanistan in February 2002. In Peshawar, I worked with the Afghan authors of the books to devise a concise orientation that could be completed in one day or less. It would consist of a short presentation of the goals of the program, a description of how to use the lesson formats, and then teacher practice using the formats. The training would be conducted locally so women who couldn't travel would become familiar with the materials.

In Islamabad, Ellen assigned an assistant to me, a capable young Nepalese UNICEF staff member who was to implement the orientation after I left. We planned to use master trainers to train provincial officers, who would then train the next level, and so on until the training reached the schools. Pressed for time, my assistant began agitating for me to put the plan on paper. But up until now we had always worked collaboratively with the Afghans, and I wanted the director of teacher training to see it as his plan so he would help implement it in the field. The training would give him an excuse to mobilize officials in the province, and when future training needs arose, he would have a ready-made network of trainers. Small amounts of funding were available so he could pay employees who had not received salaries for some time. It should have worked this way, but of course it didn't.

I expressed all this in my first meeting with the director, an Afghan brought in from years in exile. He was a pleasant enough man but one whose replies soon showed he had no long-term interest in developing his department. And he was "too busy to work on any plan." I asked if he could assign a group of ministry people to formulate a plan. Yes, that he could do, and I should return the next day to meet the committee. Then he left the room for "a meeting with the minister." The next day I returned with my assistant and our Afghan colleague. No committee was present, but the director said that on the next day he "would surely have them there." After a few minutes he left for another meeting, but not before inquiring about my attractive assistant: Did she like Kabul? What was her job? Where was she living? Would she be coming to live in Kabul? Exasperated, I said what I very much regretted later, "Her coming to work in Kabul depends on our getting the plan under way." She was rightly furious with me for using her as bait, and I apologized but the damage was done. I told him that since time was short, we would write out a plan to discuss with the committee the next day. We wrote a one-page summary of a training plan and described how it could be implemented through the ministry's provincial units with support from trainers we would recruit from the writers in Mona's workshops.

The next day the director had rounded up several people to constitute a committee. No one looked younger than the age of retirement, and some could barely walk. Our idea of building ministry capacity faded. The director was about to leave for a meeting when I stopped him and appealed to his ego: "Sir, you speak such good English, I wonder if you could summarize this one-page plan for the committee so they know what we're proposing." He agreed and read it for the first time himself. Then he got up to leave, saying as he did, "By the way I approve it." He signed the plan, and we drank tea, exchanged smiles with the committee, and left. I still don't know why he accepted the plan so suddenly. Perhaps he had given up on receiving any personal benefit from us, or he felt UNICEF's delivery the day before of cars, computers, and other supplies for the ministry was some sort of quid pro quo. I don't know, but from then on we were on our own—not what we wanted but with deadlines pressing we had no choice.

UNICEF called together provincial education officers from all over Afghanistan to explain the logistics of distributing school supplies, and we took the opportunity of their presence in Kabul to give them an orientation in the new books. Many of the officials had walked for days to reach the meeting and were clad in thin clothing that seemed inadequate against the cold outside. I have a vivid memory of sitting in a large room in the ministry building, listening to our Afghan coordinator explain the new system of instruction and showing them examples of the materials. The windows of the room were broken, and it was freezing. I was wearing all the clothes I had brought with me and still felt chilly. Despite the cold, the attention of the audience never wavered. After a few questions from the audience, an older man stood up and speaking for the rest said simply, "We are satisfied with the arrangements." At that moment, I was looking out over the bleak, snowy mountains that surround Kabul, and in the midst of an expanse of monochromatic grays and black, I noticed distant spots of red, blue, and green soaring into the sky. It felt like an omen of our high hopes for Afghanistan at that moment. The kites banned during the Taliban's time were flying again across the city—a tribute to the indomitable spirit of the Afghan people! We broke for lunch to a mound of kabobs we had belatedly remembered to send someone to buy. The trays were empty in an instant.

Fortunately for the training, we could recruit Afghans as master trainers who had worked on the BC materials in most of the major cities. Indeed, through them we had better capacity to work in these areas than the ministry itself did. It was early enough in the post-Taliban era that regional officials were willing to cooperate with outsiders in hopes that the education system would soon be back on track and they would again be receiving salaries. As it turned out, the government never controlled more than Kabul and its surrounding areas, and an opportunity was lost to develop a cadre of educators sympathetic to Kabul.

Our experiences in the ministry typify the difficulties of working with Afghan officials in the aftermath of the war. Some of those brought out of exile to run the government were extremely effective, but others saw their tenures as an opportunity to enrich themselves before elections brought new officials to run their offices. To be fair, they were inundated with foreigners proposing often useless projects that were hard to refuse in the cash-starved economy. One country, for example, offered to provide desks and chairs for "all the schools" in a country where schoolchildren traditionally sat on small stools or mats.

At the time, officials in the ministry were refusing to meet with representatives from international NGOs, even though many of them had long-term experience in Afghan education. The NGOs tried to get UNICEF to intercede for them, but there was little UNICEF could do. Afghan officials had grown suspicious of the NGOs, believing they might be spies (the Northern Alliance commander had been killed by "journalists" coming with a recommendation from an NGO). The officials were also wary of their local influence and resentful of the comparatively high salaries their Afghan and foreign staff members earned. As we climbed the stairs to appointments in ministry offices, we saw foreigners from the NGOs dejectedly roaming the halls, hoping for a break in the formidable resistance. Some with on-going education projects wanted only to know whether they could continue their projects and, if so, whether they would be subject to the new rules about instructional materials. Some had already printed their own books for the coming semester.

~~~~

In terms of our personal comfort in Kabul, we arrived at the right time. By February, UNICEF had organized better accommodations for its staff, many of whom had been sleeping in their offices. Indeed, coming to the offices in the morning we found still unrolled sleeping bags and other signs of nighttime activity. Ellen and I as "senior" people were assigned beds in a "luxurious" room of enough cots to accommodate several people, with one bathroom attached. I tried to take a shower once but the water was cold, and it was not until I was almost done that it became lukewarm. The rooms were heated with kerosene stoves that were difficult to regulate. They either got too hot or barely heated the room, and by morning most had gone out, leaving the rooms freezing cold and the air heavy with smoke. Going to bed at night we left most of our clothes on and in the morning added more.

Electricity was run by generators that were cut off at 9:00 p.m. to conserve fuel, and in any case we were subject to an evening curfew. All the staff converged on our building for dinner at 5:30 p.m. and then those sleeping in other buildings left. By around 7:00 p.m. the UNICEF cars had to be back at the motor pool. We ate around long tables in the common room and lingered afterward over tea to compare notes with colleagues in other sectors. The air was electric with the excitement of being on the ground at a historic time. Many of the staff had been in Kosovo and saw Afghanistan as the next crisis in a career of following crises. I remember a competent, young, blond woman in tight jeans who organized the distribution of supplies through local institutions that would later support an administrative system. Effective as she was, Afghans were not ready for such novelties—the clothes, her youthfulness, being a woman, and traveling alone—and eventually she was replaced.

The food was wonderful in our "dormitory"—Afghan *pilaus* and other hearty fare were made by excellent Afghan cooks who had once served embassies in the capital. They cheerfully accommodated everyone's needs, even holding back food for latecomers. In the evenings we received security briefings, and newcomers were informed of regulations: we should only use UN vehicles, always carry walkie-talkies, and not walk on public streets. We routinely violated all these rules. One night after dinner we walked to UN headquarters a few blocks away, where we could get a drink, play pool, and watch TV.

Cars were a major frustration for everyone—there were too few available for the many who needed them. Shuttles went between the UNICEF dorms and office buildings in the morning and before dinner, but the rest of the day you had to order cars in advance if you wanted to see government officials. Telephones barely worked, if at all, and it was impossible to make appointments. We would order a car, hoping for the best, and tell the driver to come back in two hours. If the official wasn't there, it was a long two-hour wait in the unheated ministry building until the car returned. If the meeting took three hours instead of two, the car was long gone by the time we emerged. We could then request a car on our walkie-talkies, but reception was poor and more often than not a car was not available. Several times, my Afghan colleague and I simply hopped into a taxi and returned to the office. Things were so chaotic at the time no one noticed.

When I arrived back in Islamabad, Ellen had one more assignment for me before I went back to the United States. An assessment team, sponsored by the WB, ADB, and UNDP, was forming to look into the postwar needs of Afghanistan. Ellen wanted me to work on the education part—in particular, the issue of girls' education. I agreed to attend the meetings in Islamabad before the team went to Kabul and wrote a short piece on the needs I saw for education in the new era. The group of almost all foreigners, many of them economists and financial experts, had already assembled when I arrived, and the chair introduced me. To my surprise they gave me a standing ovation, perhaps because of the *Models* paper or some short policy statements I had written for the Afghan finance minister. It was the first (and I'm sure the last) time in my life that I received this kind of attention. But after a few days I realized the group's agenda was different from mine. They were trying to identify small projects that could be funded individually by countries that wanted to participate but didn't want to invest a lot. To me that was not the way to assess a country's needs—schools here, training there, teachers' colleges here, books there. A main problem was already the lack of coordination among education components. If Afghan needs had been properly identified, the Afghans might have been able to establish a leaner, more affordable administration. In the end, the assessment report read like a list of projects with price tags attached. I wrote my piece and left for the United States, adding another disappointment to my mounting sense of disillusionment with the assistance process.

~~~

The tragedy of the Afghan story was the enormous sums of money that were wasted in the education sector—by a duplication of instructional materials and projects that were not essential—money that was sorely needed to rebuild the country. I talked to a *Washington Post* reporter back in the United States who wrote a front-page story entitled "The ABCs of Jihad." The article covered part of the problem but not what bothered me most—the terrible price Afghan children would pay in poor-quality education over the next several years. The reporter focused on what he could actually substantiate—the illegality of using U.S. taxpayer money to print religious books for Afghan children. The story had a one-day stand and was soon forgotten. The same *Post* writer later won a prize for investigative reporting into the failure of the USAID school construction project in Afghanistan. Not only did it not produce the number of schools that were promised, but the ones they built came at a higher cost and were of poorer quality. I of course had wished they had spent the money on working out ways to deliver good programs to every single Afghan schoolchild. It would have been possible if they had gone about it in a more thoughtful way.

Compounding my disappointment was that none of the twenty-four organizations initially supporting the BC materials stood up for them, undoubtedly because many received funding either directly or indirectly from the U.S. government. One Afghan woman summed up the sorry mess when she told the USAID official working on the Nebraska materials, "How is it possible that the rest of the world can have good textbooks for their children when they're denied to us? All we want is a decent education for our children." In the end, my country let down the hard-working Afghans who had had such high hopes for the materials, and I could not make the error right. The BC books subsequently were dropped from the Afghan public schools and have since been used only in informal accelerated courses alongside Nebraska books. When I read media accounts about the great strides Afghan education has taken since the American occupation—referring to the increased numbers of children in school—I wish I could draw attention to the fact that their education is still inferior to what should be expected of any normal program. For a long time I felt the pain of these events so acutely that it was similar to recovering from a devastating physical illness. I felt obligated to tell the story in as many venues as possible—in UN support groups and before community groups. But ultimately my accounts had no effect, and I decided it was time to move on.

In March 2002 when I returned from Afghanistan, I became acutely aware of how much the world had changed for Americans. There was a somber sense of foreboding everywhere. My six-year-old grandson, Thomas, summed it up when he wrote in an email, "Dear Grandma, I just want to know if the world is a safe place. Love Thomas."

19

REFLECTIONS

Thinking back to those lazy afternoons of my childhood leafing through the *National Geographics*, I am grateful they set me off on the course I took. The dreams, of course, didn't materialize as I had imagined them—exotic scenes to be passively enjoyed. Focusing on the exotic distanced me from people I wanted to know, and I soon turned to looking for culture in ordinary personal interactions and events. It takes time and effort to learn about other cultures, and in the end, I realized I learned as much about my own culture as I did about Middle Eastern ones.

Along the way, I lost many ideas that shaped my consciousness. I no longer see the "romantic" quality in poor people and their "picturesque" possessions—their donkeys and dilapidated dwellings being images outsiders photograph. Long ago I stopped taking pictures except when they reminded me of people I care about or scenes that bring back a rush of emotion for a place I once knew. Five years of almost daily contact with the people of Bulaq made it impossible to see them only as objects in a study.

Similarly I lost my awe of the super-wealthy and their vast palaces, even though the palaces took my breath away at first. The UAE shaikhas turned out to be as genuinely kind and simple as the super-poor of Bulaq. Um Abdalla's gift of my favorite village bread was as generous as the gifts of gold jewelry the shaikhas gave me. And although I enjoyed the challenge of understanding their messages, I no longer see traditional beliefs, dress, or practices as invariably to be preserved. Too often they provide an excuse for rejecting change. Yet radically changing them also won't necessarily solve modern problems and may even remove the scaffolding that provides stability in a turbulent world.

In the Syrian village, I learned that it is the small gestures and events that become compellingly important—whether Mona passed her exam, whether we had *kishk* or *farikhe* for dinner, or finding that the children had turned our shoes around so we might slip into them more easily at the door. I came to appreciate small acts of kindness and intimacy from breakfasting with Rima in Riyadh or in following Ansaf through the daily crises in Bulaq. I learned them working on education projects in Pakistan, Afghanistan, and elsewhere. Although the small gestures took time from our daily tasks, each had its own lessons in humanity and humility. Anthony Shadid, in his book *Night Draws Near*, captures their significance when he says he's drawn by the civilized propriety of the Middle East, whether it be the traditions of hospitality or respect, generosity or decency. It is those small, easy-to-ignore gestures, he says, that add texture and create familiarity in the Arab world. I found it a small price for comfortable admission into this world to learn to greet people properly, to dress respectably, and to learn the simple acts of propriety that make relationships flow more easily.

I spent too much time in a "childlike" state of learning to claim a monopoly on truth or correctness or even "right" values. We Americans have much to learn from peoples in even the remotest regions of the world. I would take from the people of the Middle East their understanding of the psychological complexity of personal relations, which they've raised to an art form. I would learn from the Afghans their intense sympathy for one another in the face of unspeakable tragedy. Who could claim moral superiority knowing people like Rima, who makes it her everyday practice to follow deeply held religious beliefs without any special ostentation, or like Ansaf, who day after day with the simplest of resources does what she can for the poor of Bulaq? I would learn generosity from the farmers on the banks of the Nile who don't hesitate to share the little they have with complete strangers. I have learned from Nayra to expand enjoyment of the sentient and creative—in writing, eating, decorating, and just living—and from Mouna what it takes to have a meaningful friendship wrapped in the pleasures of small things, such as shared daily walks or a cup of mint tea after dinner. From the other Mona I learned about accountability and holding others to the highest professional standards, and that there are times to be gracious and times to express anger. I have known some extraordinary people in the Middle East—individuals who have dissolved any residual barriers between "them" and "me."

Human potential is the same everywhere, or at least more similar than different, even though we tend, and I certainly did in my early years, to emphasize the differences. I know I will never meld completely into these societies. I will always be "the American" no matter how often I become "sister," "aunt," or "neighbor" to various individuals. I know the power of blood and, in certain contexts, religion, ethnicity, and geography in cementing relations. Unfortunately we haven't yet found the overriding bonds of common humanity that would unite us all. I'll remain the outsider because I haven't fully mastered the automatic responses in social situations or the many-layered understandings that come naturally to local people. I know a gulf exists between us that, as much as I want it to happen, will never disappear.

I've learned enough, though, to slip comfortably and happily into enjoying "their" company when the opportunity arises. Indeed, from my home in the United States, I sometimes long for the cushioned comfort of their sitting rooms and want to submit to the spoiling that's the right of every guest in the Middle East. I want to hear the soft murmur of voices interspersed with the relaxed silences of women sitting together. I want to eat again the elaborate foods prepared at home for guests and smell the wonderful aromas of good Arabic coffee and the personal perfumes of my hostess. These sights and sounds bring a remembered comfort to me when American individualism becomes too cold and isolating.

My world has broadened from these years of experience so that the homesickness I once felt for my own country now extends to the people of the countries where I lived and worked—to the generous people of Bulaq, the welcoming villagers of Syria, the earnest school teachers of rural NWFP, and the diligent Pakistani and Afghan children who, under terrible conditions, persist in memorizing their lessons, still hoping to become the doctors and engineers all evidence suggests is impossible. I won't forget the Yemeni women who came to my party despite their government's opposition, or the committed Afghan educators struggling to improve schooling for their children despite cynical foreign governments, or the shaikhas in the palaces of the UAE who warmly welcomed me. I hate the inevitable compartmentalization of life into "here and there," "now and then," and "them and us." In retrospect, in my own mind they all blend into a kaleidoscope of memories that has no borders.

So where did my cultural journey take me and what lessons did I learn? The most obvious lesson was the importance of finding the right niches and people where it was possible to learn. Culture is everywhere but its most cogent examples exist in the everyday interactions of people—in the words they use to communicate; in the ways they treat the poor, the elderly, and the vulnerable; in the ways they raise and educate their children and use their positions. It is found in their priorities, their sense of morality, and the way they value others. It shapes institutions and bureaucratic structures, and appears in symbols like dress that convey important messages. And it's found in the way people cope with joy or adversity. This book describes these venues and actions in some detail, including some of the insights I discovered along the way. But a cultural journey should be more than people and places and a few insights. It should be about deepening the understandings that will make future journeys smoother. It means finding the meanings that resonate with members of the culture while still remaining alien and inexplicable to outsiders. It means suspending one's own notions of right and wrong long enough to ask, "Why does it make sense?" If the journey is one of discovery, we have to put aside our own "veils of culture" that obscure the way we see others.

I hesitate to reduce such complexity to a few overarching principles, knowing full well the variety that exists in these countries. But there seems no other way to do it. To make the job easier, I have looked for principles that define major differences between us. The most obvious is the overwhelming loyalty Middle Easterners feel toward their groups—families, tribes, and sects—loyalties not activated all at once but when the need arises. Membership in these groups comes automatically with birth through ties of kinship and religion. Not being easily abandoned, they give a sense of enduring connection to those involved. The loyalty I am talking about is far deeper than anything family-loving Americans profess. Americans are more likely to look at groups as jumping-off points in a bid for personal fulfillment. Life challenges, we feel, are faced more effectively through individual endeavor rather than by subordinating our interests to groups. There is little room in Middle Eastern society for the person who goes it alone, whereas American society expects individuals to be self-reliant and independent.

A corollary of this communalism is a sense of obligation. Middle Easterners locate themselves within circles of personal relationships where each circle is defined by the specific obligations members owe one another. In the immediate family, parents are owed respect and obedience while they in turn owe the young nurturing and protection. These obligations grow weaker as family connections grow more distant. Other circles encompass peoples of the same religious faith, work colleagues, friends, and schoolmates—each with its own sets of obligations. Even the most remote connections with foreigners call for duties of hospitality and generosity in return for support and goodwill. The "cocoon effect" I felt was just one example of this sense of duty. These obligations are not just hollow prescriptions; they carry with them the force of moral mandate— what it means to be a "good person." The implication for human interaction is more profound than one might think. Imagine two people meeting and looking for the obligations they owe one another rather than what the other owes him or her. Compare this sense of duty with, for example, American children worrying more about whether parents are treating them equally with other siblings rather than about any deference they might owe their parents.

The third related point is the importance of religious underpinnings to human relationships. From the majority Muslim perspective, personal obligations are divinely inspired through the Sharia codes (or "Islamic law," as it is often somewhat erroneously called), which lay out behavior appropriate for Muslims. The Sharia principles derive from the Koran while the details for applying them come from the *Sunna,* or examples in the words and actions of the Prophet Muhammad. By the mid-tenth century, religious scholars had categorized all human behavior into what was obligatory, prohibited, recommended, or forbidden under Islam. From these the Sunnis developed four schools of jurisprudence with slightly differing interpretations. The Shi'ites added their own interpretation, mainly differing in what they include in the obligatory category of behaviors and in details of inheritance and dowries. Until today these prescriptions are considered by the majority of Muslims to be the basis for human behavior. The force of law backs some, such as the personal status codes of marriage, divorce, custody, and inheritance. Christians and other minorities in the region have their own laws regarding these matters, but they have the same strong feeling about the moral underpinnings of personal relationships.

The sects of Islam may differ in detail, but they all prescribe correct behavior for Muslims, from the person in the street to rulers and presidents. No other religion is as detailed and all-inclusive in its requirements for the moral life of the faithful. Although much is found about the importance of treating others justly, there is comparatively little said about rights. Westerners invent rights, some Muslims say, to protect themselves from secular governments that are not restrained by religious principle as are Islamic governments. To focus mainly on rights, they feel, is self-indulgent and individualistic and ignores social morality. At the very least, it ignores the balance that obligations provide. Citizens' rights, for example, should at least be balanced by citizens' responsibilities.

These three "cultural principles" (if they can be called that) governing personal relations—the preference for communalism over individualism, for obligations over entitlements, and for religiously inspired morality over secularism—create a model that not only consistently supports the importance of groups but also reduces conflicts within them by detailing a clear blueprint for behavior. They should be seen here as ideational principles, since they are only intended as a way of framing a very complex issue. In one way or another, they shape most of the behavior one encounters in everyday life—and certainly most of what I have described in this book.

Anthropologists like to look for the ecological—human and environmental—basis of social models. By this test, too, the principles stand up. The regulation of behaviors both within and among groups made sense in an early environment where nomads and urban dwellers lived in symbiotic relation with one another in the Middle East and where mechanisms to strengthen groups served people well for purposes of protection, subsistence, and survival.

Cultural visions inevitably exist at the expense of other human desires, and it doesn't take long to discover the "limitations" of communalism, just as there are limitations for individualism. Being indelibly tied to a group offers security and support, but it also limits unfettered personal fulfillment and ambition. Individuals must always be concerned about how their behavior affects the opportunities of their groups. They must believe the best way to succeed is through the advancement of the group and its interests, and they must focus their energies behind this effort. The model is conservative in the sense that it rewards the person who complies with the expected behaviors and leaves little room for the one who opts out.

Another implication is what some anthropologists call "amoral familism"[1] where contributions to the group outweigh any damage that might occur to society as a whole. What we call "nepotism" or "corruption," for example, can be redefined as for "the greater good" of the group. The high value placed in group reputation also excuses certain evasions such as *ta'ruf* (white lies to smooth communication) and *taqiyya* (full-scale dissimulation to protect one's self, family or religion). And some groups justify honor killings in terms of the higher good in wiping a family's moral slate clean. For us the belief in meritocracy, the right to compete fairly, and the right not to die for behaviors we view as not so egregious makes us deplore these practices. Yet we also have our own views of what behaviors warrant execution.

Intense loyalty to group suggests other problems. It's difficult to establish strong central governments (assuming they are desirable) when societies are composed of cohesive groups unwilling to cede their autonomy. In Iraq and Afghanistan we have seen how difficult it is to find neutral leaders who can bridge gaps between factions. The solutions to factionalism in the Middle East have never been entirely satisfactory: coercive strong men (like Mubarak of Egypt and Sadaam Hussein of Iraq), leaders from minorities who mediate between larger factions (like the Assads of Syria), leaders from non-tribal religious groups (like the old Imamate of Yemen), or kings who claim moral authority (like the Saudi royal family). The Islamic values that revere accommodation, peace, and justice suggest that solutions could be found in federated systems where group boundaries can still be retained (similar to the UAE). The Prophet Muhammad saw the problem and tried to overcome it by calling on believers to form communities based on common religious belief rather than on indelible kin ties. Unfortunately the groups heeding his call today have largely been those with radical agendas. In important ways, authoritarian kin-based groups with members of all ages and experiences tend to be antithetical to these agendas. Strengthening them in the short term may neutralize the effects of radicalism.

---

1. Edward C. Banfield, *The Moral Basis of a Backward Society* (New York: Free Press, 1958).

Comparing these Middle Eastern difficulties with our own rule-driven, legalistic society, we see why our system needed to impose order on our individualistic tendencies to go our own ways.

Reinforcing personal obligation with moral injunctions has implications for gender issues. When societies define obligations so closely, it's difficult for people to step out of the roles society assigns to them. Men still feel the sole responsibility for supporting their families whether or not it is possible for them to do so, and women still feel their priority is in fulfilling wife and mother roles even when they also occupy public roles.

One aspect of these cultural differences that has been brought home to Americans is the difficulty in trying to impose a model of liberal democracy on the Middle East. Our form of democracy originated in certain Western cultural values: "one person one vote," individual rights, separation of church and state, and equality under the law. We should have foreseen that this model would have little appeal for a culture that prefers group loyalty and religious morality. "Equality under the law" similarly runs up against Sharia laws that are not equal. The constitutions of most Middle Eastern countries state that their citizens should be equal under the law, but most also state that if there are contradictions with Islam, the Islamic principles take precedence. The Sharia codes governing marriage, divorce, custody, and inheritance were never intended to be equal. They can, however, be defined as "equitable" or fair if considered in the light of the roles men and women play. Men, for example, are given double the inheritance of women because they are wholly responsible for supporting families.

This is not to say that Middle Easterners are averse to democratic principles— such as greater participation in decision making and less arbitrariness in judicial proceedings—rather that they alone must shape the kinds of governance that best fit their cultures.

The American cultural model similarly has its own difficulties. While on the one hand there may be enormous opportunity for personal fulfillment and achievement, on the other there can be enormous loneliness and isolation and lack of support for those in vulnerable positions. Neither culture has a monopoly on advantages or disadvantages.

Finally, what was it like being a woman in the Middle East? More to the point, what was it like being an Arab, Pakistani, or Afghan woman? Obviously, on balance, it was more good than bad for me. I experienced few of the negative encounters that Americans assume are the norm for women. On the contrary, I was treated almost invariably with respect. A critic might say, "Ah, but you are a foreigner, and therefore people treat you differently." And I would reply, "Perhaps, but do we treat foreigners so well?" It's a difference and like all differences calls for explanation.

Like other Americans during this period, I was affected by the ferment going on in the United States. When we arrived in the Middle East in the 1960s, American women were becoming aware of their restricted roles and opportunities. From a young age, I recognized the subtle and not so subtle forms of discrimination faced by women in the United States, and I welcomed the women's movement when it came. But on my visits home, it seemed that, although overt acts of discrimination against women were decreasing, other more covert forms were emerging that were harder to confront. My experiences at Harvard were just one example. Although we women worked harder and produced more, our efforts were disparaged—not explicitly because we were women but because men still made the decisions and modeled the behaviors that were valued and emulated. As the spouse of an American diplomat, I was consigned to "the woman's role" on pain of affecting my husband's career. When the rules changed, the uncertainties surrounding our new roles and the criticisms of roles we chose made me personally feel as if I were an unappreciated relic of times gone by. In truth, there are no easy solutions without changing the world's views of women to fit our own, and I'm not sure we've come upon the only right view yet.

I quickly realized Middle Eastern women weren't rushing to adopt our gender models or to change what we saw as their discriminatory practices. True, there were Arab feminists working to reform marriage, divorce, and custody laws so women had more rights in the home, but movements like those in Egypt in the 1930s to gain political rights had largely petered out by the time I arrived. Women were increasingly going to school, entering the labor force, and eventually able to vote in most countries of the region. Indeed, to my surprise I found I was growing comfortable living in places where gender differences were not glossed over with talk about equality. Middle Eastern women were free to be "feminine" and didn't have to conform to the masculine images of success. What comes "naturally to women"—their sympathy, nurturing, and "quality of life" activities within families—seemed genuinely appreciated in the region, so much so that men weren't afraid of showing "women-like" qualities for nurturing children and forming intimate relations with one another. Rima was an example of someone who didn't feel demeaned by the services she provided her family and friends while still maintaining a strong personality. Following her example, I began taking pleasures in the small things—good food taken in a leisurely and pleasant environment with congenial people, relaxed afternoons with the children, and friends dropping by. Even in my work, I felt respected for my expertise without suppressing my femininity or competing aggressively with men for professional recognition. I was learning to enjoy the mannered propriety of the people of the Middle East, both in my social and professional lives.

At first I believed that societies still clinging to older ideas about gender roles had not caught up with our more sophisticated understanding of what they should be. It took my Syrian landlord asking "why American women all want to be men" to make me realize how much Americans glorify "men's work" and disparage "women's work." Women's freedom was beginning to look more like "freedom to be like men." Had we Americans tipped the balance too much toward personal fulfillment through employment while pushing aside the activities women traditionally performed? Could a self-respecting American woman actually choose to be a wife or mother, or would that just be viewed as a path toward dead-end "servitude"? Why didn't Middle Eastern women realize they were taking the "wrong" option in choosing women's roles? The women I knew weren't "shrinking violets," so how could they find satisfaction in these wifely, motherly roles? Why weren't they seeking the professional roles we find fulfilling? Why didn't women rebel against the smothering dress codes or their unequal treatment under personal status laws? These matters perplexed me until I came to see them as part of a worldview that made its own kind of sense. To be sure, there were costs to this way of thinking just as there were to our views, but I no longer saw the benefits of one necessarily outweighing the other except in our own minds.

It took time to realize that Middle Easterners had other priorities than those of Americans, and that it wasn't simply a matter of finding the "inner American" in others. It makes sense to me now that our American risk-taking forebears established the individualist society we eventually became, and that American women would come to question why, if everyone should have the same right to achieve their full potential, there were so many obstacles in their way. The obvious comparison in our case was to men who, unfettered by household responsibilities, were free to achieve the American dream as rugged frontiersmen, politicians, and captains of industry. It also began to make sense that other societies might find greater comfort in close-knit families with their safety nets for members in trouble. Viewing our high divorce rates, broken families, and disturbed teenagers, why would Middle Easterners aspire to becoming an impersonal society like ours, or if they did would it bring them a better life than the one their family loyalties afforded them now? Would they want to break the emotional bonds and safety nets to become individuals like us? What would they lose in the process? I had no final answers, but I could see the questions were not trivial. And I could see that whether these changes were desirable or not, there were unmistakable signs they were happening anyway. It was becoming apparent in the letters seeking moral guidance from newspaper columnists like Abdul Wahhab and the religious shaikhs, as well as in families I knew where many in the younger generation were becoming economically independent of their elders through better technical skills and salaried jobs.

In the Middle East, the separation of the sexes gives males and females complementary and indispensable roles in family life. Our effort to reduce people to a common denominator, in certain respects, diminishes the different ways males and females contribute to their societies. The common denominator unfortunately often fails to produce equal effort in private and public life, and women continue to bear the main "burden" of their private roles. There is no word for "gender" in Arabic or in other languages of the region, probably because sex differences seem sufficiently obvious to explain differences that are both biological and social. These differences, whether we like them or not, force the recognition of the importance of the other sex and the indispensable need to include both men's and women's contributions in family life.

~~~

One American woman told me that the issue of Middle Eastern women boiled down to choices. American women have choices, she said, while Middle Eastern women have none—their choices are made for them. I don't know where she got this idea, but I've heard it said enough to know it is commonly believed by Americans. But is it true? Do we have unfettered choices while they have none? A Saudi woman who studied in an American university told me she was shocked by the amount of time American coeds spent worrying about their relationships with men. "It's so much simpler in my country, where we concentrate on our studies knowing our marriages will be arranged." She felt American society was a vast meat market for the display of women's bodies, where in the end, men still made the final decisions about whom they would marry. When physical appearance becomes the main way of judging women, she felt, it left them few other ways of distinguishing themselves. Perhaps her observations are extreme, but they suggest the social pressures that shape women's choices in the United States. In the Middle East, women's choices are shaped by the status and reputation of their families, and therefore it makes sense for them to invest in their family's standing, by being good students, or of good character, or by cultivating dignified, modest behavior. I wonder, in the larger scheme of things, if working for "group good" is any less satisfying than working toward individual recognition in an often cutthroat world. Certainly contributing to the family doesn't preclude work roles for Middle Eastern women.

American women probably involve fewer people when they make their choices, and they probably also have fewer options when their choices go wrong. A Middle Eastern woman will more likely consult those affected by her choices— her parents, siblings, or husband—who will help her carry out her decisions and provide safety nets if something goes wrong. In reality, Americans' choices about roles, dress, and behavior are as subject to social pressures as those of Middle Eastern women. They may differ in kind and outcome, but they are still affected by social norms.

For years I unquestioningly met State Department expectations about the kind of wife I should be as the spouse of a diplomat. Did I have choices? Of course, but the alternatives had consequences—such as getting my husband fired—that I wasn't prepared to accept. Middle Eastern women have options too, and they are similarly constrained by what might affect their loved ones. Choosing to veil or not to veil is one of these choices influenced by social norms and the impact it might have on the reputation of a woman's family. Women's reasons for choosing one alternative over another are complex, but we shouldn't assume they don't make decisions for themselves. Choices are not as easy as they may seem, no matter where they are made. Culture programs us to take certain paths, and once we make the first in a series of choices, each succeeding one is limited by those that came before. A modern Middle Eastern woman makes choices about career and family, but the difference between us is that her society also values motherly and wifely roles, and if she chooses to do both she is more likely to find others to help her. The American woman may appear to have a broader array of choices, but she may also only find herself taking on larger burdens as her multiple roles increase.

But what about illiterate women in Pakistan or Afghanistan or elsewhere in the region? Indeed, there is no question that their choices are limited, just as the choices of the poor and undereducated in our own society. But choices in these cases are restricted not so much by patriarchal authorities acting independently, as they are by the circumstances that affect the choices and actions of both males and females.

What about power? Do women have power in the Middle East, or does power rest mainly with men? It depends, of course, on the definition of power, and certainly in a society where family is the focus of everyone's attention, power in the private sphere must be important. If power is the ability to make decisions, to direct the actions of others, or to make a difference in what happens, then women in the Middle East possess considerable power. Western talk about "empowering women" is a difficult concept to get across in Arabic where the closest equivalent means "increasing her physical strength." Usually, when the language lacks a word, it means people don't feel a need to express the concept. When enhancing the group is seen as a priority, acts of accommodation may be more important than acts of coercion, although that certainly doesn't rule out authorities of both sexes focusing members' behavior on what is good for the group as a whole. The representation of families by men in the public arena also does not preclude a consensus arrived at through private argument and debate by all the members of the group. In the tribes of the Gulf, for example, women's power has largely been invisible, taking place behind the secrecy that hides personal family matters. Women, however, were and are strongly involved in power-related actions such as arranging marriages that linked households, in displaying family hospitality and generosity, and in gathering information that informed tribal politics and legal judgments. Their very invisibility increased their ability to operate in these ways and prevented enemies from knowing the full extent of the tribe's assets. In communal societies, individual power may be less important than group power.

Middle Eastern women are not the passive victims of a society that focuses on men. Indeed, there are probably as many dignified, competent, and capable women as men. From childhood, both sexes develop complex personalities by practicing being followers and leaders in their age-graded households. Depending upon the context, they can be commanding or differential, nurturing or nurtured, competent managers or dutiful participants—in a range of personal interactions that make for fully evolved human beings. The fabric of personal relations in their families is clearly strengthened and solidified by distinctions of old and young, male and female, maternal and paternal without reducing everyone to sameness. While people may not be equally treated at any given moment, the system treats people fairly over a lifetime when deference and authority behaviors manage to achieve a rough balance. Women and men are the apples and oranges of life in the Middle Eastern view, and as far as I could see over four decades in the region, neither sex feels any the less for being one or the other. There are abuses and consequences in any society, but it would be unfair to focus on the abuses in one and ignore them in another. Certainly at the present time, neither culture has a monopoly on behaviors that lead to the good life.

I have neglected the final question: "Which country do you like best?" Perhaps that answer is best left to the reader since I truly have no answer. Hopefully, the book will show how very different each country is from the other and how each has something significant to offer—in people, scenery, and the amenities and pleasures of life. Although I have tried to connect them with some common themes of culture, my final conclusion must be that each is unique in its own special way and that I have enjoyed them all—even the ones that put obstacles in my way of knowing them.

About the Author

Dr. Andrea Rugh has been a technical adviser for USAID development projects in the Middle East, South Asia, and Africa. She was research associate for the Harvard Institute of International Development from 1987 to 1994 and worked for Save the Children and UNICEF in Pakistan and Afghanistan from 1998 to 2002. She has written several books on Middle Eastern culture and society, including *Family in Contemporary Egypt; Within the Circle: Parents and Children in an Arab Village; Reveal and Conceal: Dress in Egypt;* and *Political Culture of Leadership in the United Arab Emirates.* She is currently an adjunct scholar at the Middle East Institute in Washington, D.C., and lives in Garrett Park, Maryland, and Woods Hole, Massachusetts. She attended Swarthmore College in Swarthmore, Pennsylvania; received her B.A. from Oberlin College in Oberlin, Ohio; and her Ph.D. in anthropology from American University in Washington, D.C.